Rugman Reviews
International Business

Alan M. Rugman

palgrave
macmillan

First published 2009 by
PALGRAVE MACMILLAN

Palgrave Macmillan in the UK is an imprint of Macmillan Publishers Limited, registered in England, company number 785998, of Houndmills, Basingstoke, Hampshire RG21 6XS.

Palgrave Macmillan in the US is a division of St Martin's Press LLC, 175 Fifth Avenue, New York, NY 10010.

Palgrave Macmillan is the global academic imprint of the above companies and has companies and representatives throughout the world.

Palgrave® and Macmillan® are registered trademarks in the United States, the United Kingdom, Europe and other countries.

ISBN-13: 978–0–230–22125–3
ISBN-10: 0–230–22125–4

This book is printed on paper suitable for recycling and made from fully managed and sustained forest sources. Logging, pulping and manufacturing processes are expected to conform to the environmental regulations of the country of origin.

A catalogue record for this book is available from the British Library.

A catalog record for this book is available from the Library of Congress.

10   9   8   7   6   5   4   3   2   1
18   17   16   15   14   13   12   11   10   09

Printed in China

Summary Contents

Contents

International Finance

Part III Globalization and Economic Integration

Part V Regulation of Multinationals: Civil Society and Development

List of Figures and Tables

Figures

Tables

Preface

It is an honour for me to dedicate this book to John H. Dunning, the founder of the field of international business. The following aspects of his life have inspired my writing.

First, John Dunning writes books: excellent, thoughtful, interactive and boundary spanning. In an era when many North American universities only recognize articles published in so-called 'A' journals as being relevant for tenure and promotion it is inspiring that the field's most cited scholar has been most influential through his books. I believe that a well-rounded scholar should move on from the narrow confines of articles to read books and publish career-based and book-length statements.

Second, John Dunning welcomes dialogue; he sees the field developing through interactive seminars, conference presentations, paper development and publication. He is a referee for journals, book proposals and grant applications. In all such activities he is a gentleman, respecting and encouraging differences of opinion and fostering the deeper understanding of the field. In a small way the book reviews here attempt to build on this process of thought development and the ongoing debate about ideas relevant to international business.

Third, John Dunning has provided leadership to the 'Reading School', in which both a written and oral tradition has been created in which ideas are freely discussed and tested. I was a visitor at the University of Reading in 1976–7 when internalization theory was developed and refined at weekly seminars and daily lunches by Mark Casson, Peter Buckley, Bob Pearce and others. John Dunning has always welcomed bright minds to the table including younger colleagues such as John Cantwell, Sarianna Lundan, Rajneesh Narula, and others. This has inspired publications with analytical insight and empirical strength which have moved along the field.

It is fitting that this book is being published as I became a Professor at the new Henley Business School of the University of Reading. In dedicating this book to John Dunning I pledge to build upon and continue the dialogue of international business in the spirit of the 'Reading School'.

ALAN M. RUGMAN

Introduction

This is a unique book. It brings together 100 book reviews prepared over the last 35 years and published mainly in refereed academic journals, but also in some more popular outlets. These are arranged in five Parts by topic. Each of the five Parts reports the book reviews in chronological order starting with a review from 1973 and concluding with a review in 2008. At the beginning of each of the five Parts there is a new essay which relates the book reviews in that Part to the literature in international business and its cognate fields. At the end of each of the five Parts' introductions a basic framework is developed, which synthesizes the key literature in that chapter. The overall book thus provides an original yet contemporary perspective on the development of the field of international business. The Academy of International Business is celebrating its 50th anniversary in 2008, and the premier journal in the field, the *Journal of International Business Studies* is celebrating its 40th anniversary in 2008. This book appears at a propitious time in the evolution of thinking about the field of international business.

What is the value of this book for a student of international business? This book provides an unusual yet interesting introduction to, and summary of, much of the literature in international business. Students will relate to the end-of-Part frameworks, which synthesise the literature. The student will find it valuable to observe the historical context in which books have been published. They will be fascinated by the development of the field and the improved use of theory, econometrics, and other metrics of analysis. Students will be pleased to know that even well-known scholars can fail to impress their peers, and that scholarship develops in a Socratic method through debates in the published literature. Students should feel encouraged that their own reading and potential contributions will be recognised somewhere and will help develop the field of international business.

The introductory essays to each of the five Parts serve to review and synthesise the relevant literature summarised in the book reviews in each chapter. In addition, key material that is relevant for students in international business and that does not appear in the book reviews is included in these introductory essays. The method to achieve this is through the presentation of a major analytical framework which serves to synthesise the major topics in each Part. The following frameworks are developed.

In Part I the firm and country framework is used to demonstrate the required balance between a firm-level theory of the multinational enterprise and the country factors that influence international business. This matrix can be used for both strategic management of the MNE and also to analyse issues of public policy and regulation.

In Part II we use the economic integration and national responsiveness matrix to illustrate the two major ways in which an MNE can develop strategic capabilities. We show that most of the literature in international finance and international economics (from the 1960s to the 1980s) was concerned with methods to improve firm-level efficiency through tools of economic integration. Government policy usually reinforced this objective. But in the 1990s international business scholars started to realise that firms could utilise their networks of foreign subsidiaries to develop benefits of national responsiveness. This is a pure managerial capability that requires knowledge of the internal organisational structures and knowledge transfer possibilities within the MNE.

In Part III we synthesise much of the literature on globalisation with an original modelling of the work of Thomas Friedman. We demonstrate that Friedman has reverted to a focus upon aspects of economic integration (such as offshoring and outsourcing) but has neglected the potential managerial capabilities of national responsiveness as outlined in the Part II matrix. We also show that the empirical evidence suggests that globalisation, in the sense of world-wide integration and commonality, does not exist. Instead, most of the world's largest 500 firms operate on an intra-regional basis, and there is no empirical evidence of a trend towards globalization. Students need to develop some sophistication in dealing with issues of global versus regional strategy. The readings in Part III help this process.

In Part IV the issue of international competitiveness is analysed using the single diamond framework of Michael Porter, which works well for large economies such as the United States and Japan, but for few other firms and countries. In contrast, we then proceed to the double diamond framework which I have developed jointly with colleagues in Canada. The double diamond works well for firms based in smaller economies. Related to the issue of international competitiveness is the institutional context where regional free trade agreements, such as NAFTA, have been adopted, possibly at the expense of further integration fostered through multilateral agreements at the World Trade Organisation. The logic is that the international competitiveness of firms largely depends on market access to other economies, and this access is now being achieved through regional trade agreements rather than multilateral ones. This latter points links to work in Part V on the impact of civil society on trade agreements.

In Part V we use the five partners-flagship framework to examine relational contracts between leading MNEs and their partner firms and institutions. The partners include key suppliers, key customers, joint venture partners, and institutions in the non-business infrastructure. This framework is useful in summarising some of the work dealing with regulation of MNEs and the contribution that MNEs can make to economic development. It also helps to analyse the roles of government sponsored institutions and the impact of civil society and non-governmental organisations. Overall, this is a somewhat messy area, which has not been the topic of serious analytical inquiry. Yet, even there it is useful for the student to step back from the ongoing debates and attempt to focus on the key issues being raised in the hope of bringing some theoretical clarity to the debate.

There are four distinctive features about this book. First, and fairly obviously, each book review is of a newly published book which I was invited to review. As the reviews were composed they reflected the state-of-art thinking of the time. In retrospect, many of these books became classics or made a significant contribution to the field of international business; some did not. I have published over 200 book reviews and I have selected 100 of the most relevant which have stood the test of time. The introductory essays offer commentary on the eventual success or failure of the books reviewed.

Second, this book reflects the somewhat idiosyncratic views of the author. Starting with the very first book review, the author believes that a good book review consists of two components. One, for the reader's benefit, there must be an accurate yet succinct summary of the contents of the book. Two, there needs to be an opinion extended about the value of the book and its contribution. On occasion, these opinions are critical. Together these two components of a good book review should answer the reader's question: is this book worth reading? Fortunately, for the vast majority of books reviewed here, there is a positive answer to this question.

Third, the author believes that international business is both a multi-disciplinary and interdisciplinary field. Useful insights into the nature, performance, strategy and organization of multinational firms, business networks, joint ventures, and other forms of international business can come from a variety of disciplines. The author's main training is in economics, so there are chapters dealing with books published in international economics and international finance. Other scholars might come to international business with a background in sociology, psychology, political science, or other disciplines. In this volume, reviews have been included of books in the mainstream areas of economics, but on such occasions their relevance for international business is discussed, either in the book review itself or in the introduction to that chapter.

Fourth, the field of international business is a living field with tremendous implications for public policy and firm strategy. The author has been at the forefront of public policy and international business while working at universities in Canada. Over the 1986–1988 period he was the chief academic advisor for the Government of Canada as it negotiated the Canada-US Free Trade Agreement. He served on the government's International Trade Advisory Committee where he wrote the business agenda for the free trade negotiations and the business sector's proposal for rules on international investment. Subsequently, he served on the Forest Products Sectoral Advisory Group on International Trade as the negotiations for NAFTA took place between 1990 and 1993. The author was also active in public commentary on the issues of free trade and international competitiveness, engaging in extensive media appearances. Therefore, chapters in this book deal with book reviews dealing with issues of free trade, NAFTA, international competitiveness, and globalization. Indeed, globalization became a new word for the public policy aspects of international business which have their origins in the 1960s and 1970s. At that time the key debate concerned the power of multinational enterprises versus the nation state. This remains a central issue of globalization today, with the complexities brought to this debate by the growth of civil society and non-governmental organizations. The final section of the book reviews books dealing with globalization, civil society, and development.

One final historical note is relevant. As many of these reviews were written at an early stage of the author's career, the reader should be aware that the author did not know many of the authors of these books at the time that the book reviews were composed. Subsequently, the author has met such illustrious colleagues as John Dunning, Ray Vernon, Charlie Kindleberger, and others whose early writings are reviewed here. In retrospective, the author does not necessarily recommend this strategy to other junior faculty. It is highly unusual for a junior scholar to review in print the works of senior scholars. Today, the profession is often designed to mentor junior colleagues and to shoehorn junior faculty into comfortable pockets of scholarship. Yet, when these first reviews were written by an untenured faculty member at the University of Winnipeg, it was broadly accepted that any faculty member, even a junior colleagues, would be able to both summarize books and offer informed commentary on them. Only if the commentary is honest, rather than obsequious, can the field develop. In general, the reaction of senior colleagues at conferences and other events has been positive, indeed, appreciative of the attention paid to their work. Yet, there are some incisive yet critical comments in these book reviews which many junior scholars today would be unwise to imitate. It is to be hoped that senior colleagues will react in the same positive and supportive manner in the future as their own books are reviewed by new members of the profession.

Part I

Theory of the Multinational Enterprise

Introduction to Part I

The 24 book reviews reproduced in Part I were written between 1973 and 2003. In retrospect, it is remarkable that two themes emerge in determining the currently recognised theory of the multinational enterprise (MNE). The first is the emerging consensus that the core theory of the field is internalisation theory. This builds upon the brilliant conceptual insights of Stephen Hymer. He first identified the market imperfections that existed in international product markets and presented a microeconomic, industrial organisation approach to explain the international firm. As described below many of the books reviewed in this section build upon Hymer, and his influence is especially important in the work of John Dunning and Ray Vernon, the two founders of the field of international business.

The second theme is the attention paid to the power relationships between MNEs and nation states. While internalisation theory is best identified as an examination of the efficiency aspects of MNEs (in a world of market imperfections) it is clear that the resulting firm-specific advantages (FSAs) of MNEs can potentially generate monopoly profits. This power situation of the MNE is amplified when the firms often operate in oligopolistic markets. Many of the books in this section contain detailed empirical studies of the profits and performance of MNEs and their relationships with the governments of nation states. This second theme, therefore, deals with distributional issues rather than efficiency ones. However, the twin themes of efficiency and distribution run through the literature of international business. They reflect the two sides of the coin which is the MNE. I now turn to a brief discussion of each of the reviews. My aim here is to alert readers to the key contribution of each book to the development of today's accepted theory of the MNE.

Review 1 analyses a symposium organised by John Dunning in 1970 at the University of Reading. Even at this early stage in the development of the field of international business it can be noted that the leading scholars of the day were debating the key aspects of the theory, although there is little understanding of what would become known as internalisation theory. Instead, the major theoretical paper is by Bob Aliber advancing his financial currency market interpretation of MNE activity. In this book there is no discussion of Hymer's work on market imperfections. Instead, there are reports of long debates about the conflicts between MNEs and nation states. This latter theme seems to reflect the concerns of the majority of scholars at that time. The book therefore serves as a necessary reminder that in 1970 there was no widely accepted 'hard core' theory of the MNE. Instead, the field was floundering as an applied public policy branch of economics and political science. Much work remained to be undertaken by Dunning and Vernon as they established the school of thought which would integrate both theoretical and public policy insights into the role of the MNE in the world economy.

Review 2 is of Knickerbocker's research on the oligopolistic nature of MNEs. It is a high quality empirical study which used the databank on the largest 187 US MNEs compiled by Ray Vernon at Harvard Business School. In this book, based on his doctoral dissertation, Knickerbocker essentially tests Vernon's product life cycle. He tests how US MNEs develop their subsidiaries abroad through the use of an entry concentration index. Knickerbocker confirms Vernon's approach finding that US MNEs go abroad in waves to wealthy Western economies.

Review 3 is of the classic book by Stopford and Wells which examines the managerial structure and strategies of MNEs over time. Again, these two doctoral students of Ray Vernon used the Harvard databank to analyse the types of product lines and the number of subsidiaries of the 187 large US MNEs. In this book Stopford and Wells developed their famous evolutionary model of the organisational structures of MNEs. They argue that the US MNEs of the time (i.e. the 1960s) moved on from international divisions to either an area division structure or a world-wide product division structure. A few MNEs eventually transformed into a global matrix structure. However, the typical US MNE of the 1960s tended to be centralised and hierarchical with an 'M' form product structure. In many ways the Stopford and Wells book was ahead of its time. They are looking into the internal organisational structures of MNEs but using mainly the objective data from annual reports in the Harvard database. It was only two decades later that better data emerged from detailed in-house case research and interviews with managers in subsidiaries. It is perhaps not surprising that this book review was never published as the dominant journals of the time were in economics, and they did not then realise the value of this type of international management research.

Review 4 deals with the classic issue of transfer pricing in MNEs. As MNEs operate across national borders their subsidiaries need to report profits according to the tax laws of both the host country and their home country. As there is no world-wide tax system it has always been possible for MNEs to shift profits. Indeed, until a uniform tax system is adopted on a world-wide basis the imperfections in tax policies will lead to transfer pricing policy by MNEs. At the time of this book, by Nieckels, internalisation theory was not understood. Once it is, an argument can be developed that the internal transfer prices of the MNE are the efficient prices for its internal market. As the MNE itself is a substitute for missing external markets (the Coase-Williamson theory) an extreme version of this argument is that transfer prices are efficient. This point of view was examined and tested in Rugman (1981), Rugman and Eden (1983), and elsewhere. It would only be fair to report that this extreme view of internalisation theory has only been accepted within a small segment of the academic field. It has never been accepted by policy makers and tax authorities. They continue to believe that MNEs use monopoly power to extract excess profits and that they manipulate transfer prices to shift profits from high tax regimes to low ones. Much of the literature reports on ad hoc empirical studies which are, at best, neutral in demonstrating that transfer pricing increases the profits of MNEs over time.

Review 5 is an elegant summary of the theory of internalisation developed by Buckley and Casson. This review was written while I was a visiting professor at the University of Reading from 1976 to 1977. Internalisation theory states that the MNE exists as a response to imperfect markets, especially for knowledge. Since knowledge is a public good it will be underproduced unless property rights are established in an institution such as an MNE. In this sense the MNE is an efficient response to external market and imperfections. Chapter 2 of the Buckley and Casson book offers an elegant and still highly relevant modelling of internalisation theory. In my view Buckley and Casson answered the big question in international business: they invented the theory of the MNE. The value of this thinking was demonstrated when the *Journal of International Business Studies* published a special issue in 2003 which analysed the lasting value of internalisation theory as a basic driver for modern day research on MNEs, joint ventures, exporting, and other modes of foreign entry.

Reviews 6, 7, and 8 are shorter book notes commissioned by the *Economic Journal*. In these book notes, which have a limit of 500 words, only a sketch of the book can be reported. Yet, Review 6 by Teece signals his early and continuing work on the origins of the work of the resource based view of the firm. Teece is concerned with technology transfer and the modelling of tacit knowhow within companies. In Review 7 Michael Brooke and colleagues produced a bibliography of IB. It showed that theoretical contributions to the field were thin on the ground. Most of the bibliographies consisted of applied public policy aspects of people trained in the key cognate disciplines of economics, political science, and sociology. Review 8, by Thunell deals with aspects of political risk. He shows some linkage to the emerging theory of the MNE, but his work shows few of the insights of the real experts in this field, such as Steve Kobrin. Thunell's book, published in 1977, can be usefully contrasted with the last one reviewed in this section by Wit Henisz. Back in 1977 there was little awareness of MNE theory, whereas Henisz (as a student of Williamson) combines careful theory in modelling with extremely detailed empirical work.

Review 9 is not of Vernon's most famous book, his 1970, *Sovereignty at Bay*. This review is of the second major book he wrote based on the many publications from his Harvard Business School project. This book, *Storm over the Multinationals*, is a brilliant and clear statement of the contributions made by MNEs to society. Vernon debunks proponents of the market power view and shows that MNEs contribute in terms of a positive net social benefit to both advanced and developing economies. Vernon offers insights into the benefits of technology transfer and of the normal internal routines of MNEs, such as transfer pricing.

Review 10 is an influential review of Hymer published in *JIBS*. In this review I helped further popularise Hymer's market imperfections viewpoint. I cite the references in which he discusses imperfect markets in both product markets and intermediate markets, such as knowledge. I discuss his concept of firm-specific advantages. I also suggest that Hymer understood the concept of real asset diversification which was the focus of my own doctoral dissertation on international diversification by MNEs. In short, it's all in Hymer. This is something which younger scholars neglect at their peril. Even today, many scholars fail to recognise that the concept of liability of foreignness (host country risk) is elegantly examined in Hymer; it was not invented by Sri Zaheer. Indeed, Zaheer was a beneficiary of the MIT oral tradition which continued to propagate Hymer's views to MIT doctoral students long after his untimely death.

Review 13 is a collection of papers written by Stephen Hymer. These were collected after his premature death by a set of his friends and colleagues. In these papers Hymer wrote about the distributional conflicts between MNEs and nation states. At its most basic level Hymer's approach is strictly Marxist, i.e. concerned exclusively with distributional issues. Therefore this book stands in contrast to the more important and influential dissertation analysed above as Review 10. In his dissertation Hymer dealt with the efficiency aspects of MNEs, and he introduced the vital concept of firm-specific advantages (FSAs). We shall use the FSA concept in the concluding section of this introduction.

Reviews 11, 12, 14, and 15 are again short book notes. The first deals with research and development of seven large US MNEs. Not surprisingly, R&D was highly centralised in the early 1970s, confirming the work of Stopford and Wells. Review 12 is a collection of papers by European scholars. It reveals, even at this early stage, that European scholars have a strong focus upon theory rather than the typical detailed empirical work of North American scholars. Review 14 analyses licensing by MNEs. It can be usefully related to the more comprehensive work by Contractor in Review 22. Review 15 is a directory of the world's largest 430 MNEs. This was used by John Dunning's group at the University of Reading to produce some of the first studies of the performance of MNEs.

Review 16 by Lall, along with the later Review 21 by Wells, deals with MNEs in developing countries. Both of these writers focus upon the public policy issues of MNEs versus host national governments. If anything, Lall is somewhat more sympathetic to the social benefits provided by MNEs. In particular Lall finds that MNEs do not exploit less developed countries as their profits are not significantly different from advanced economies. However, Lall does criticise MNEs for the use of transfer pricing, and in this review I take him to task for this mistake.

In Review 21, Wells reports on the basic concepts of internalisation theory and FSAs and then attempts to apply them to third world MNEs. In this he is reasonably successful but the main contribution by Wells is his vast experience in dealing with MNEs in host nations. This comes through when he discusses actual cases of MNEs in developing countries. Both of these books are important to the literature on multinationals and development, but neither has been particularly influential with those working on developing countries. Partly to redress this continuing antipathy to the role of MNE, I have recently published a book with Jonathan Doh on this topic, see Rugman and Doh (2008).

Review 17 is of an advanced textbook by David Rutenberg. This book presents cases and highly relevant analysis across the three areas of international finance, international management, and international marketing. I used this book for about ten years with my advanced MBA students, due to its neat blending of theory and case examples. Rutenberg is one of those rare scholars who has written on the international aspects of finance, production, and marketing by first building a deep and detailed knowledge of these fields. I like the book due to its theoretical depth and understanding, and I regard the book as a useful advance in the field of international business due to the high standards it set for future textbook writers.

Reviews 18 and 20 are of books by Charles Kindleberger of MIT. Review 18 is of a conference organised by Charles Kindleberger at Middlebury College in 1981. There are excellent papers by the new generation of MIT doctoral scholars such as Bruce Kogut, Paul Krugman, and others. There is good discussion of internalisation theory and other approaches to foreign direct investment. The theory now percolates through the more applied papers although I criticise some writers, such as Eric Kierans, a former Canadian Minister of Trade, for their lack of theoretical knowledge and understanding of the MNE. Review 20 summarises many of Kindleberger's own writings and suggests that, somewhat like this book, his book reviews, as well as his articles, are worth reading.

Review 19 is an assessment of the path-breaking advanced textbook on MNEs prepared by Richard Caves in the early 1980s. This book has been extremely influential as it was the first mainstream textbook to build its analysis around the concept of internalisation theory. Caves himself contributed to the development of aspects of internalisation theory with his work on horizontally integrated MNEs. In the 1970s and 1980s Richard Caves was perhaps the most influential economist across the fields of industrial organisation and international economics. He mentored several generations of economists and doctoral students from the Harvard Business School including Michael Porter and Nobel Prize winner, Michael Spence. The adoption by Caves of internalisation theory in this textbook signalled the coming of age of rigorous theorising about the economic aspects of MNEs. Caves analyses interactions between MNEs and government. He presents a fairly standard economist viewpoint about the need for government regulation to offset potential excess profits earned by MNEs. He also advocates appropriate tax and subsidy policies, for example, the facilitation of technology spillovers through MNE activity in home and host countries.

Review 22 examines Farok Contractor's work on licensing as an alternative to the MNE. He shows, correctly, that much international business activity does not take place within the MNE, but is in the alternative form of non-equity foreign direct investment (FDI), especially licensing agreements. His book is a useful balance to my focus on the MNE. Yet, as stated in the review, I believe that internalisation theory (as a general theory of FDI) also explains licensing, joint ventures, exporting and any other modes of foreign entry. The relative costs and benefits of each mode need to be considered, such that licensing is chosen when it is a more efficient mode for the firm than is a set of wholly-owned subsidiaries.

Review 23 is an in-depth analysis of John Dunning's eclectic theory. It summarises his OLI model where 'O' stands for ownership, 'L' for location, and 'I' for internalisation. I report on Dunning's professional writing style, which is to read and synthesise the contributions of virtually everyone in the field over the last 40 plus years. My only mild criticism is that Dunning's OLI paradigm can be collapsed into a simple matrix for firm and country factors. Dunning's 'L' accurately reflects an axis of country effects where as the O and I can be usefully discussed as firm effects. In Rugman (1981) and subsequently, I have developed this model of country effects (CSAs) and firm effects (FSAs). In general Dunning and I would agree on 95 per cent of matters and the other 5 per cent is not significant.

Finally, Review 24 reports on the excellent work on political risk by Henisz. The strength of this scholarship lies in his carefully formulated and detailed empirical work. He has developed his own databank dealing with factors relevant to political and country risk. He has further developed Williamson type political hazard models and applied them to developing economies. This work obviously builds upon the pioneering efforts of earlier scholars, many of which have been reviewed earlier in this book.

Summary Learning Framework

Based on the literature summarised in Part 1 perhaps the most useful learning feature available is the framework which links firm and country effects. The firm effect was introduced into the literature with Hymer's (Review 10) focus upon firm-specific advantages (FSAs). The method by which FSAs can be internalised and used as a proprietary and unique advantage was first modelled by Buckley and Casson (Review 5). Many of the other reviews deal with aspects of FSAs; for example, the work on R&D and technology (Reviews 6, 11, 14, and 22). The ways in which FSAs can be developed and spread abroad by the use of subsidiaries is studied in Reviews 1, 2, 16, 17, 18, 20, 21, and 24. The ways in which FSAs can be utilised by MNEs and the nature of their organisational structures is studied in Reviews 3 and 23.

Long before the MNE was identified as the key actor on the stage of international business the field of international business largely concerned itself with country effects. International trade and international capital flows were explained according to international economics and finance as due to relative factor cost differentials across countries. Basically, the economist's law of comparative advantage explains country differences across goods and factor markets. (Note that this ignores the role of intermediate products which is the basic rationale for internalisation theory). In short, we need a theory of country specific advantages (CSAs). In a more sophisticated manner the CSAs may be nudged by government regulations. There may be a form of created comparative advantage. Much of the work of John Dunning explores the role of government and its interaction with MNEs. Here Reviews 1, 8, 9, 12, 18, 19, 20, 21, 24, and 25 explore the nature and relevance of CSAs and their interaction with MNEs.

Based on the thinking which has emphasised firm and country effects the following matrix (Figure 1) offers a synthesis of the literature in Part 1. On the vertical axis we place CSAs either low or high. On the

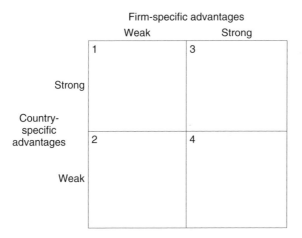

Figure 1   **The FSA-CSA Framework**
Sources: Adapted from Chapter 8 in A.M. Rugman, *Inside the Multinationals*, New York: Columbia University Press, 1981; 25th anniversary edn, Basingstoke, UK and New York: Palgrave Macmillan, 2006.

horizontal axis we place FSAs either low or high. This leads to four cells for analysis.

Cell 1 represents a situation in which only CSAs are important. This cell can be explained through the literature on international economics and international finance. Comparative advantage explains movements of goods and factors across nations. Financial capital depends upon interest rate differentials between countries. There will be MNEs in cell 1 and their competitiveness will depend upon natural endowments of minerals, oil wells, forest products, hydro-electric power and other natural resources in their home country. MNEs will also have CSAs based upon cheap labour (for example, manufacturing in China), or cheap skilled labour (information technology in India). Finally there may be state owned MNEs which have been created by government policy, as in Singapore and some of the oil rich Persian Gulf countries.

In contrast to the economics driven cell 1, we see in cell 4 a pure management explanation for the success of MNEs. In cell 4 only FSAs matter. The FSAs stand alone and are not influenced by CSAs. This is a cell reflecting the resource based view of strategic management. The firm has strong FSAs which are unique and proprietary to itself. There are isolating mechanisms (entry barriers) which prevent rival firms from acquiring the FSA. These isolating mechanisms may be entirely due to aspects of the organisational structure and nature of the top management team, a type of Penrose effect. When the resource based view is applied to MNEs it is necessary to examine the internal network of the firms. There will be codification of internal knowledge FSAs and routines for its use within the internal network of the firm. In general, the resource based view, when applied to the MNE, is fully compatible with internalisation theory as demonstrated by Rugman and Verbeke (2005).

Cell 3 is a special cell only available for students of international management. In cell 3 both FSAs and CSAs matter. The FSAs of the firm are enhanced and facilitated through home country CSAs. (The matrix can be reworked using host country CSAs, available to the foreign subsidiaries of MNEs, if necessary). In general, there may be internal managerial tensions in reconciling CSAs and FSAs. The better managed MNEs successfully combine FSAs and CSAs. We explore aspects of this further in future parts.

In cell 2 neither CSAs nor FSAs are important. Firms in this cell need to move to either cell 1 (building upon CSAs) or to Cell 4 (by developing FSAs).

The matrix in Figure 1 has its logical basis in Chapter 8 of Rugman (1981). However the matrix itself was not developed until the Japanese edition of my 1985 textbook. Since then, the FSA/CSA matrix has become a basic component of textbooks in international business, such as Rugman and Collinson (2006), and it is still the most useful starting point in bringing together analysis of firm and country effects.

References

Rugman, Alan M. (1981). *Inside the Multinationals*. New York, NY: Columbia University Press. (25th anniversary edition, Basingstoke, UK and New York, NY: Palgrave Macmillan, 2006).

Rugman, Alan M. and Collinson, Simon (2006). *International Business: 4th Edition*. London, UK: Pearson/Prentice Hall.

Rugman, Alan M. and Doh, Jonathan (2008). *Multinationals and Development*. New Haven, CT: Yale University Press.

Rugman, Alan M. and Eden, Lorraine (1985). *Multinationals and Transfer Pricing*. London, UK: Routledge.

Rugman, Alan M. and Verbeke, Alain (2005). *Analysis of Multinational Strategic Management, The Selected Scientific Papers of Alan M. Rugman and Alain Verbeke*. Cheltenham, UK: Elgar.

The Multinational Enterprise

John H. Dunning (ed.)
*New York: Praeger, 1972, 368 pp.**

This book is a collection of papers and comments delivered to a conference at Reading, England in 1970. The conference was 'concerned with the general repercussions of the growth of multinational enterprises in the world economy.' The major questions posed in the book concern the effect of the MNE on national sovereignty, on industrial relations, and on balance of payments and domestic stabilization policies.

The book is arranged in seven sections. Firstly there is a theoretical section consisting of a background review by Dunning and essays by Aliber and Pavitt on the MNE as the agent of transfer of factor inputs (capital and technology) across national barriers. One of the better papers is by Aliber whose model extends the one he published previously in the Kindleberger symposium. He considers the monetary aspects of foreign investment and shows that the large international firm with operations in many countries has an information advantage in gaining access to the cheapest possible capital market. Host country firms, on the other hand, have to pay more when borrowing. Furthermore, there are different exchange rate risks associated with each currency and it is possible for the international firm to manipulate its overall portfolio in order to minimize expected changes in foreign exchange rates.

In Part 2 some neglected areas of the MNE issue are discussed in contributions on the labor market. Steuer and Gennard report on an empirical study on industrial relations of foreign owned firms in Britain. They reveal that these firms were the first to introduce productivity agreements which have subsequently been adopted elsewhere in Britain. This paper (and the next on trade union interests) is mainly concerned with Britain and will probably be of minor interest to North American readers. In Part 3, Robertson uses standard trade theory to good effect

Southern Economic Journal 40(1) (July 1973): 156–157.

in his paper which considers the impact of the MNE on trade flows and trade policy. There is also a case study of the chemical industry considered from the firm's point of view. In Part 4 the impact of direct investment on the less developed countries is discussed separately by Edith Penrose and Paul Streeten. Penrose emphasizes the strength of nationalism in newly emergent countries and feels that they have an incentive to restrict foreign investment in order to retain their independence.

Kindleberger's statement that 'the nation state is just about through as an economic unit' is contested by most of the participants at the conference, and is specifically considered in Part 5. Murray agrees with Penrose that the nation state is not through because the MNE is opposed by an increasing nationalism in many less developed countries, and indeed in some wealthy nations such as Canada. Behrman argues that the nation state has the power to regulate the MNE but does not necessarily have the will to do so. Governments in general fail to adopt the more radical policies of (a) rejecting the MNE, (b) subsidizing competitive home industry, or (c) meeting to set new international rules to regulate MNEs. Behrman suggests that the governments take a more positive role to counter the MNE because the latter has no legitimate claim to power and decision making in a country as it is not publicly accountable. In Part 6, there is another case study, and there are finally two more summaries.

Did a general theory of foreign investment emerge from the conference? Unfortunately not. Many of the contributors talk about several variables in turn and naturally place different emphasis on them. Two separate types of theoretical explanation of foreign investment are considered. The traditional approach is that variations in real rates of return explain international capital movements, and that this monetary theory may be adapted to explain direct investment. An alternative approach is associated with Hymer and concentrates more on the real aspects of direct investment as a transfer of funds between the subsidiaries of a large firm which enjoys a monopolistic advantage in the ownership of knowledge or research activity. To achieve economies of scale an MNE extends into the host country either to gain access to a larger market or to avoid the tariff. Neither approach is clearly explained (although Dunning come closest on pages 57–60) and in this respect the volume lacks a contribution to match that of Harry Johnson in *The International*

Corporation edited by Kindleberger in 1970 in which Johnson considered the welfare implications of foreign investment by monopolistic firms.

Possibly the MNE cannot be readily modeled by economists as many non-economic factors are involved. Some of the papers in this volume are of a speculative nature, partly because of a scarcity of good empirical research. There are hopeful signs that this is being remedied and future writers on the MNE will benefit from recently published work such as that of the Harvard team under Professor Vernon. Another empirical avenue previously unexplored is that the MNE's have a large proportion of foreign operations in the form of exports and/or subsidiary sales. This international diversification may increase their utility as their profits appear to exhibit greater stability when compared with large firms operating in the domestic economy.

2 Oligopolistic Reaction and Multinational Enterprise

Frederick T. Knickerbocker
*Boston: Division of Research, Graduate School of Business Administration, Harvard University, 1973, xiii, 236 pp.**

This book is based on work which won a prize as the best doctoral dissertation of 1971–1972 at the Harvard Business School. It is of the same high quality as other published studies in the Harvard Multinational Enterprise Project under the supervision of Professor Raymond Vernon. The theoretical basis of these studies is Vernon's famous product cycle theory, while the empirical basis is a data bank of the foreign subsidiaries of 187 large American manufacturing corporations.

The main theme of Knickerbocker's book is that the expansion of American enterprises abroad has been determined by micro-level decisions in which foreign subsidiaries are established in response to initial direct investment by rival firms. It is assumed that the relevant market structure is characterized by oligopoly rather than a situation of perfect competition, leading to the implication that direct investment has to be explained by market imperfections rather than by differences in real or monetary rates of return. Coupled with the assumption of oligopoly is the hypothesis that American exports follow a product cycle in which product-pioneering American firms generate successive advantages in production of goods by innovations in manufacturing, marketing, management and technology. These market advantages are specific to the firm, and it is clearly in the firm's own interests to exploit its innovation not only in the domestic market, but also by extending sales abroad through exports and/or foreign subsidiaries.

Such an argument has been advanced previously by Kindleberger, Hymer and others. Knickerbocker extends the argument with his emphasis on oligopolistic reaction. Once a firm in an oligopolistic market situation has engaged in direct investment, there is an incentive for

---

Eastern Economic Journal, 1(1) (January 1974): 86–87.

rival firms to respond in order to defend their market share. Thus, in Knickerbocker's view, most direct investment is defensive in nature, and is governed by the interdependence of firms in such a market structure.

The concept of oligopolistic reaction is tested with the help of an 'entry concentration index' (ECI), derived from information on the foreign subsidiaries of the 187 American corporations in the Harvard multinational data bank. The ECI for each industry indicated how closely foreign subsidiaries are bunched together in their establishment, and is a proxy for oligopolistic reaction. A major finding is that almost half of the 2,000 foreign subsidiaries founded in the period from 1948 to 1967 were started up within three year peak clusters, and about three quarters were started within seven year peak clusters. This evidence is used to support the concept of defensive foreign direct investment. Such a follow-the-leader strategy of direct investment is measured by the ECIs, and very detailed testing is undertaken to find the relationship between ECIs and firm, industry and country characteristics.

Most of the book reports on conjectures and statistical tests of the relationship between ECIs and several independent variables. A review cannot do justice to the many nuances of the oligopolistic reaction theory examined by Knickerbocker but this summary many give a flavor. It is postulated that high ECIs are related in the following manner; positively to degree of concentration in the industry (Chapter 3); negatively to stability of industry structure, such that when there are few new entrants there is little direct investment abroad (Chapter 4); negatively to product diversification (Chapter 5); negatively to technical innovation or R and D in the industry, as scale considerations tend to discourage the establishment of foreign subsidiaries (Chapter 6); positively to profits on foreign operations (Chapter 7); and positively to the rate of growth of the host economy (Chapter 8).

The author has gone to a great deal of trouble in testing these hypotheses but his efforts are characterized more by technical competence than theoretical insight. For example, it seems that stepwise regressions are used as a last resort after finding that in the specified model for entry concentration by country 'few of the regression coefficients approached levels of acceptable statistical significance' (p. 181). More caution should be shown in the interpretation of equivocal regression results (for example on pp. 61 and 81), and some doubt must be cast on the procedure of averaging ECIs in Chapter 3. The choice of a second order polynomial equation as the appropriate functional form for regressions testing the relationship between ECIs and industry concentration rations (see p. 74) is not defended on *a priori* grounds, as it should be. The use of the ECI itself is open to question, since it ignores the great variety of oligopolistic market situations, whose existence makes it difficult to believe in a general index.

It might also be noted that Knickerbocker does not attempt to test the motivation of a firm's initial foreign investment (which he terms aggressive) to which oligopolistic rivals react as part of a defensive strategy. Instead he relies on the notion of the product cycle theory, and considers it to be a sufficient reason for aggressive foreign expansion. Work on the motivation of initial direct investment decisions remains to be done and may perhaps be advanced by the application of portfolio theory and capital asset pricing models in an international context. These models can be used to show that a firm may benefit from international diversification of sales as it will enjoy a more stable stream of profits over time. While this book is not concerned with such an analysis of uncertainty, there is at least the recognition of some risk elements facing the firm, as market shares are affected by the worldwide interdependence of oligopolistic decision making. This is a useful contribution to the literature on the motivation of multinational enterprises, and should stimulate further work. The book has also helped to improve the quality of empirical studies in this field.

3 Managing the Multinational Enterprise

John M. Stopford and Louis T. Wells, Jr.
New York: Basic Books; London: Longman, 1972, xvi, 223 pp.

This is one of the volumes produced by the Harvard Business School multinational enterprise project headed by Professor Raymond Vernon. It is an empirical study of the development of management strategy at the international level, especially as it affects the operations of the multinational enterprise (MNE). The study makes use of the data bank for the 187 American MNEs studied in the Harvard project.

Some of the main findings of the book are that international business strategies keep changing over time, leading to an evolutionary pattern of management organization. It is also found that MNEs prefer one hundred per cent ownership of their foreign subsidiaries in order to control their operations. Some firms were willing to undertake joint ventures with host country firms, especially in the areas of production and marketing. In addition, governments in several countries have involved MNEs as partners in local participation, but such activities are still on a small scale. The most important problem between MNEs and their partners in joint ventures is dividend policy, as the former wish to use the operations of a subsidiary to maximize profits of the whole operation.

The book focuses on two major issues. First, the structure of the MNE is examined in terms of management and organization. Secondly, the issue of control is examined and it is found that the willingness to engage in joint ventures depends on the stage of development of the MNE. Initial direct investment is often defensive in nature, that is, it is made in response to the establishment of a foreign subsidiary by a rival firm. This analysis assumes that the market structure is characterized by oligopoly and that the rival firms wish to retain their share of the market. The first firm setting up a subsidiary often does so as a gamble,

---

*Unpublished review, 1973.

but the rival firms react in order to defend their market share. There are higher costs involved in the setting up of such foreign subsidiaries, due to the lack of information and experience in the organization of foreign branches. To overcome such information costs it may be rational for the MNE to engage in a joint venture. In general all MNEs have a preference for wholly owned subsidiaries. This allows them to retain control over their foreign operations.

It is possible to summarize the main theme of a book in this manner. The management structure of the MNE is governed by the firm's desire to maximize profits. To do so control of foreign subsidiaries is essential, as this allows the firm to protect any monopoly advantage it may possess in the areas of knowledge, management or technology. Such advantages are specific to the firm, and their exploitation in foreign markets extends the area of the monopoly advantage. In order to achieve the maximum monopoly rent it is necessary to avoid local partners for such partners would dissipate the unique advantage of the MNE. The organizational structure of the MNE is arranged to prevent local autonomy and to retain the foreign subsidiary as part of the total operation.

Other variables probably influence direct investment, such as the tariff, size of the host country market, desire for vertical or horizontal integration, etc. These are summarized quite well in Chapter I, in which an additional point is made. It is argued that there is a close connection between management strategy and organizational structure of an MNE. In fact the development of an MNE is determined by its organizational structure. The stages of the organization of an MNE are defined, and related to several important variables. These relationships are tested by use of regression analysis.

Indicators of management strategy are related to the following variables. There will be a decline in the importance of joint ventures if there is an increase in the following: the ratio of advertising to sales, the ratio of research and development to sales, the sales subsidiary ratio, and the type of organizational structure. On the other hand there will be an increase in the importance of joint ventures, the smaller is the impact of the following variables: industry diversification, extractive nature of the industry acquisition ratio, and relative size. There is multicollinearity between these variables. For example, the variable for organization is related to both advertising and the sales subsidiary ratio.

There are three major conclusions to the regression analysis. First, firms which are market oriented have joint partners in large markets. There is then a common market strategy. In smaller markets firms use imported strategies, rather than developing their own. Second, recent takeovers are explained by the desire for international diversification. This is achieved through the control of foreign subsidiaries. Third, the MNE probably manages to retain control over the critical decisions made in a joint venture. In conclusion when the management aspects of international investment are considered it is clear that the preferred structure of organization is one which permits the MNE to retain control over all of its operations, both domestic and foreign.

Transfer Pricing in Multinational Firms: A Heuristic Programming Approach and a Case Study

Lars Nieckels

Stockholm: Almqvist and Wiksell; New York: John Wiley, 1976, xii, 190 pp.[*]

It is a considerable achievement to take the theory of intracorporate transfer pricing in a domestic economy (as developed by Hirschleifer, Shulman, Gould, and others) and extend it in an international direction by modeling the optimal transfer pricing strategy for a multinational enterprise (MNE). This Nieckels has done in a benchmark study which demonstrates the theoretical case for transfer pricing by an MNE. It is found that, given the assumptions and qualifications of the model, an MNE can increase its overall profit rate by using transfer prices which are not necessarily the world market (or arm's length) prices.

The book is an unrevised version of a recent doctoral dissertation and suffers from many of the faults of that format, being very repetitive and pedantic in its writing. Chapter one is an introduction; chapter two a literature review; chapter three presents a proposed model of transfer pricing for an MNE; chapter four has a case study and the final chapter a summary and policy applications. There is both an author and subject index. The book addresses a broad question – the role of transfer pricing by an MNE – but in practice deals with a narrow application of optimizing theory. Most of the points made by Nieckels would have more impact in a short article.

The main contribution of the book is a proof that the MNE can increase its profits by the use of transfer pricing. A deterministic model is produced by using mathematical programming techniques in an imaginative manner. Nieckels' basic model of international transfer pricing has a hypothetical MNE with two divisions – one in manufacturing and the other in marketing. Transfer prices are charged between these subsidiaries of the MNE on all intra-firm flows of goods and services, with the quantities of the latter being determined by standard profit

---

[*]*Journal of International Economics* 7(2) (May 1977): 217–219.

maximization subject to cost constraints. In some versions of the model the transfer prices are set within upper and lower bounds. In addition to this restriction, and the assumption of constant returns to scale and fixed coefficients involved in the linear programming technique itself, it is necessary to make addition assumptions, such as: centralized decision-making, profit maximization by the MNE rather than by subsidiaries, a short-run time horizon of under one year, and so on.

Given these assumptions it is possible to solve a deterministic model in which transfer prices are treated as explicit decision variables. In fact, three such models are formulated and described in turn. The most noteworthy point is that exact solution procedures cannot be found for the general model since transfer prices are included in both the objective function and the constraints. The author says that a quadratic programming method can be used to overcome this problem, but such an approach is rejected since it involves the assumption of linear constraints and a concave objective function, whereas Nieckels prefers to have transfer prices as nonlinear constraints in this model. Therefore another technique is used – that of heuristic programming. In this the original model is reformulated into a sequence of mini-models which have solutions. This iterative procedure leads, eventually, to a local optimum for the whole model, but not to a global optimum. Nieckels makes a further argument that it is more useful to have a model which demonstrates the increase in performance of the firm when it uses transfer prices than to worry about a global optimum for the model (it being implied that the local optimum is not too different from the global one). This, indeed, does seem to be a valid approach in his model since the resource allocation problem of the MNE is solved by adjustment of its transfer prices, which are the variables of primary importance in this study.

The model of the MNE can be generalized to include n sets of divisions, various hierarchical levels of decision-making, and many sets of transfer prices. It is also possible to incorporate taxes, custom duties, variable profit rates and other refinements; all of which still permit a heuristic solution procedure in which transfer prices are included as explicit decision variables. One weakness of the model is that it excludes analysis of financial variables and currency aspects. Thus interesting questions not considered are the effects of foreign exchange rate risk, inflation and other macro-level variables. Perhaps this work can be attempted by other writers using the basic models advanced here by Nieckels, and elsewhere by Rutenberg.

An interesting case study is presented in chapter four; one which uses actual data on transfer prices of an MNE active in the textile industry. Upper and lower bounds of twenty percent from the world price are set on these transfer prices to generate model solutions. There is a painstaking description of the computer techniques and costs required to solve versions of the model, and it is suggested that most managers of an MNE could use the model without too much difficulty. The most striking result of the case study is that under the conditions of the programming model, the MNE can increase total net profits after taxes by thirty-nine percent. This is a considerable gain from transfer pricing, but is not nearly as great as that found by Vaitsos and Lall in their studies of MNEs active in Colombia and other countries in the Andean group. Given these conflicting results it is to be hoped that more empirical work on transfer pricing will be undertaken in the near future. While the theoretical case for transfer pricing has now been established, the actual use and effects of this device by MNEs still remain a subject for speculation.

5. The Future of the Multinational Enterprise

Peter J. Buckley and Mark Casson

London: Macmillan; Teaneck, NJ: Holmes and Meier, 1976, xi, 116 pp.*

The provocative claim of Buckley and Casson is that they have developed a 'general theory' of the multinational enterprise (MNE), within which the alternative theories of Hymer, Kindleberger, Vernon, Caves and Harry Johnson, amongst others, can be incorporated as special cases. This claim (made on page 66) is not entirely unjustified and their book may well come to be accepted as the definitive synthesis on the motives for foreign direct investment (FDI).

The book has five chapters; the first with background tables and charts on the important role of the MNE in the world economy; the second with an original synthesis of the theory of the MNE; the third on alternative theories of the MNE; the fourth reporting empirical research on the relationship between multinationality, and R and D; and finally a concluding chapter on policy implications for the MNE. There is a consistent theme underlying these chapters, namely that the MNE is efficient and can be explained by conventional economic theory.

The crux of the book is Chapter two which develops the concept of internalization as an explanation for international production by MNEs. The emphasis upon imperfect markets for knowledge, research, marketing and management has been made by previous writers but, for the first time, Buckley and Casson offer a consistent and well rounded international application of the Coase theorem. It is assumed that market imperfections are initially exogenous to the MNE, and that to overcome these it creates an alternative internal market to replace the missing external one. The organizational structure of an MNE can be used to proxy market signals in at least five areas of market imperfections and, in particular, the MNE

**Southern Economic Journal* 44(2) (October 1977): 410–411.

can treat knowledge as an intermediate product in its transfers between home and foreign subsidiaries. This permits the MNE to market products on a world-wide scale and recoup costs that cannot be covered by sales in the missing external market for knowledge.

One problem with this theory is the crucial assumption that the market imperfection is exogenous to the MNE. If the MNE is clever enough to respond to an imperfection in the market for knowledge then it is efficient. However, much of the current criticism of MNEs stems from a view that they exert market power, i.e. that they create endogenous market imperfections. It is often argued that the MNEs erect barriers to entry, use patents and exploit, in foreign markets an advantage secured by monopolistic action in the home market. In this case MNEs are inefficient. The extent to which market imperfections are exogenous or endogenous will probably never be discovered since both factors operate simultaneously, but at least Buckley and Casson throw some light on the fundamental issue of internalization.

In the empirical sections of Chapters one and four there is close attention to detail. For example on page 12 MNEs are ranked by value added, not just by sales, and correlations are found between industry characteristics of MNEs. In the regressions dependent variables for degree of multinationality, growth and profitability are explained by independent variables such as R and D and by dummies for country, industry and firm-specific factors. The authors are careful to stress the problems and limitations of econometric work in this area, but are pleased with their own results.

I have two final criticisms of material which is not central to the main theme of internalization. First, on page 27 a secondary source is used to justify the conclusion that 'MNEs are more profitable than other firms in the same industry.' This may be correct for U.S. subsidiaries in Britain (as shown by Dunning in this source) but it is not true for U.S. MNEs in general. Data from the 'Survey of Current Business' show that the rate of return on foreign and domestic investment by U.S. manufacturing corporations is about the same, at 12 per cent, for industry groups, and my own research confirms this for individual firms. Where I have found a significant difference is in variability of profits rather than in average level of profits; more specifically MNEs exhibit greater risk in their profits (and share earnings) than do non MNEs of similar size.

A second error occurs on pages 82/4, where it is argued that the principles of international diversification cannot be applied to MNEs. In fact there are barriers to individual portfolio diversification on a world scale, so purchase of the shares of MNEs offers an indirect vehicle for international diversification. A controlling interest is not required since shares can be bought, and these will reflect the advantages of multinational operations.

6 The Multinational Corporation and the Resource Cost of International Technology Transfer

D.J. Teece

Cambridge, MA: Ballinger, 1977. Distributed by J. Wiley & Sons, xv, 129 pp.

The main theme of this monograph is that the transfer of technology is not costless. Dr. Teece offers empirical support for this proposition and uses it to criticize the traditional assumption that knowledge is a public good with a zero price. In the empirical work a wide definition of technology transfer costs is used; one which included not only the transmission of knowledge but also the absorption of it at plant level. Four stages of technology transfer are defined: A, the transfer of research and design; B, engineering, design and production planning; C, construction, tooling, and installation; D, manufacturing startup. Using data costs for twenty-nine transfer projects by multinational firms Teece finds that the mean percentages of total transfer costs are: 1 for stages A; 9 for B; 75 for C, and 14 for D. To this reader these figures reveal the trivial nature of actual knowledge transfer costs in stage A, and the overwhelming influence of what are really production costs in the latter stages of the project. However, in another section Teece finds that royalty payments for the rights to use intellectual property are about 10% of total project costs, but with considerable variation by project. He also finds that the costs of transfer decline with each application, and with the extent of diffusion; and that the experience, and size and ration of R and D to sales are significant variables determining the transfer costs of multinational technology. These results are based frequently upon subjective data generated in interviews with executives of 16 chemical, 3 petroleum, and 10 other manufacturing firms with experience of project-level technology transfer. Despite the poor data base and sometimes sloppy econometric work (in which problems of multicollinearity abound), this is an interesting attempt to add empirical content to the debate on technology transfer by multinationals.

---

* *The Economic Journal* 87(347) (September 1977): 666.

7 A Bibliography of International Business

Michael Z. Brooke, Mary Black, and Paul Neville
*London: Macmillan, 1977, xv, 480 pp.**

Over the last decade study of multinational enterprise has led to the development of a new field of academic research, that of international business. The high degree of activity in this field is confirmed with the birth of this bibliography, since it lists over three thousand references, consisting of articles published in the last five years, books of the last twenty years (where still relevant), and a fairly large number of recent unpublished research reports and conference papers. The champions of the new field of international business, at least in terms of quantity of output, with over twenty entries each, are (in descending order): Behrman, Vernon, Litvak and Maule, Dunning, Stobaugh and Franko. As the reader looks through the listings, many of which are annotated, it becomes clear that while many of the articles have been published in established field journals in the disciplines of economics, finance, management, marketing and operations research, there is a growing tendency to publish in journals specific to the field. For example, of the nine entries for Harry Johnson three are published in the *Journal of World Trade Law* and another three in the *Columbia Journal of World Business*. Another popular outlet is the *Journal of International Business Studies*, sponsored by the Academy of International Business, the senior academic body in the profession. The authors of the bibliography, from the International Business Unit of the Manchester Institute of Science and Technology, have been reasonably discriminating in their choice of literature. Future editions of the book will no doubt provide any aggrieved authors with the opportunity to contact the Manchester team to supply information on new and missing publications, and to provide any corrections.

The Economic Journal 87(348) (December 1977): 832.

Political Risks in International Business: Investment Behavior of Multinational Corporations*

Lars H. Thunell

New York: Praeger, 1977. Distributed by Martin Robertson, xi, 133 pp.

Dr. Thunell endeavors to show that 'to the traditional economic theories of foreign direct investment (DFI) one has to add a political theory describing the importance of political events and especially of government events.' It appears that the market imperfections approach has already become accepted as the 'traditional' explanation of DFI, but Thunell believes that this recent approach still ignores political factors which may influence the investment decisions of multinational corporations (MNCs). He suggests, correctly, that MNCs prefer a stable political climate for DFI and that they like to work with the governments of host nationals to find out the rules of the game. The foreign investment decision of an MNC is found to depend on economic criteria but political instability may lead to its cancellation or diversion. Thus political considerations enter into the decision-making on DFI as essentially negative factors; instability can deter an investment but a stable political environment does not encourage DFI. The empirical work which supports this proposition, and also tests several related hypotheses, uses qualitative data on political variables such as riots, strikes, demonstrations, assassinations, changes in executive tenure, etc. These variables are used to explain DFI by manufacturing (not resource) MNCs and are not found to perform very well in stepwise regressions, nor in factor analysis. Perhaps this is due to problems of multicollinearity or the unsatisfactory manner in which the author deals with the time trend. Indeed, the econometric work raises more questions than it answers – a situation which is only partly due to the difficulty of modeling these non-economic variables. Given the

* *The Economic Journal* 88(349) (March 1978): 200.

interesting issues raised in this book it would seem that future work on DFI should attempt to incorporate both economic and political variables in a new model. Until both sets of variables are tested simultaneously we do not know which set dominates the other, or if either is significant and independent.

9 Storm over the Multinationals: The Real Issues

Raymond Vernon
London: Macmillan, 1977, vii, 260 pp.*

Professor Vernon has done the economics profession a valuable service in writing a readable book on the multinational enterprise (MNE). His intelligent synthesis of recent academic research on the MNE can be placed in the hands of motivated students lacking formal training in economic theory. In the past such readers may have stumbled upon misconceived works such as that by Barnet and Muller but now an orthodox explanation of the MNE and associated policy issues has been produced by Vernon. The first half of the book examines the typical organizational structure of an MNE. The large size, geographical diversity, centralized management control and oligopolistic nature of the MNE are all aspects of its desire for stable earnings. The potential market power of the MNE is held in check by the specter of entropy, a process which constrains the MNE to search constantly for new product lines and markets. The innovations made by the MNE generally require large quantities of capital and organizational skills. These are available in the home nation at low relative cost and explain why most research is done by the parent firm rather than by its overseas subsidiaries. The remainder of the book reviews the current policy conflicts between the MNE and governments of advanced and developing nations. In these chapters Vernon presents new insights into the process of technology transfer and the appropriate pricing policy for a MNE. He is critical of the study by Vaitsos with its 'exotic estimates' of transfer pricing. There is no hard evidence of excessive profits being earned by MNEs. Since governments of host nations have the power to impose their own tax policy on the MNE ultimate power resides with the nation state. This study deserves a wide readership.

---

* *The Economic Journal* 88(350) (June 1978): 404.

The International Operations of National Firms: A Study of Direct Foreign Investment

By Stephen H. Hymer
Cambridge, MA: MIT Press, 1976, xxiii, 253 pp.

The story about the delayed publication of this seminal work is by now probably familiar to most specialists in international business. As reported in his laudatory introduction Professor Kindleberger recommended Hymer's doctoral dissertation for publication by the M.I.T. Press in 1960. The publication committee of the Department of Economics at M.I.T. rejected publication of the thesis, one of the reasons being that 'the argument was too simple and straightforward.' Hymer apparently did not bother to have the thesis chapters submitted for journal publication, and so it was left to Kindleberger to advertise the thesis in his textbook on international economics. Professor Kindleberger is also too modest to mention that his own first rate book on *American Business Abroad* is a brilliant summary and extension of Hymer's theoretical work. In any case the 1960 Hymer thesis became a basic reference in all subsequent work on the multinational corporation (MNC), but one which many readers found hard to acquire. Its recent publication is to be welcomed, and is a belated recognition by M.I.T. of the brilliance of Hymer's thesis.

The seminal nature of the book lies in its now classic statement of the theory of direct foreign investment (DFI). The modern theory of DFI with its emphasis upon market imperfections and the concept of internalization is clearly stated by Hymer. In Chapter Two he explains that the MNC uses its international operations either to remove competition, or to exploit some advantage due to an imperfect market – a situation which is preferable to licensing from the viewpoint of the MNC. He states that the MNC 'is a practical institutional device which substitutes for the market. The firm internalizes or supersedes the market' (p. 48). It is the imperfect market 'which leads the possessor of the advantage to choose to

Journal of International Business Studies, 9(2) (Fall 1978): 103–104.

supersede the market for his advantage' (p. 49). Hymer believes that the MNC is an organization which allows for 'centralized decision making' and that 'whether or not this will occur depends mainly on whether the markets are perfect' (p. 37). Again in Chapter Three Hymer emphasizes that the basis for the theory of international operations by the MNC is its 'motivation to separate markets and prevent competition between units' (p. 67). He repeats 'that many of the reasons for choosing not to license arose from the imperfect nature of the market for the advantage. These imperfections prevented the appropriation of all the returns to the advantage' (p. 87). The importance of these quotations cannot be overemphasized. They have led to the subsequent theoretical expositions of DFI by Caves, Kindleberger, Johnson, Buckley and Casson, Magee, and many others.

In another area Hymer provides the genesis of the concept of international diversification. He suggests 'that profits in one country may be negatively correlated with profits of another country' (p. 94), and that 'an investor may be able to achieve greater stability in his profits by diversifying his portfolio and investing part in each country. This investment may be undertaken by shareholders of the firm, and not the firm itself' (p. 95). Hymer does not go on to make the point that the degree of segmentation of world capital markets and the existence of barriers to international portfolio diversification are crucial problems facing an individual investor and that these barriers can be overcome by investing in the MNC. Neither does he attempt any empirical work to support the concept of portfolio diversification. In fact, he does not seem to grasp the vital distinction between international diversification and the product diversification he has discussed earlier on page forty. Further, his discussion of cross investments in Chapter Four is in error since he does not discuss risk. I have the impression that Hymer did not really understand the full implications of his statement on portfolio diversification, and indeed these have only become clear with the subsequent development of modern finance theory.

Hymer was the first economist to apply the theory of industrial organization to the international sector and DFI. The market advantages of the MNC result from four possible factors: first, lower cost in acquiring factors of production; second, control or special knowledge of the process of production; third, better marketing and distributional facilities; fourth, a differentiated product. It is also made clear in Chapter Five that an additional market advantage accrues to the MNC in the money markets, since it is better able to finance itself and may be a better credit risk than rival, domestic firms. Hymer thinks that nearly half of the capital for DFI is raised in the host nations when subsidiaries of the MNC are given loans or make equity issues. This phenomenon has been especially irritating to Canadians concerned about the almost total foreign control of their resources and manufacturing industries. It has led nationalists in many countries to complain that the process of DFI involves the host nation in financing its own sell out. Hymer attempts some very rough calculations of the net benefits of DFI and concludes that 'international operations from 1946 to 1958 have provided a net gain of foreign exchange for the United States' (p. 205). However, he does not stray into the area of political economy by attempting to evaluate social and political factors – an omission which he corrected in his later academic career.

The weakest parts of the book are the empirical sections. Chapter Four relies almost entirely on secondary sources and presents very elementary tables. No econometric work of any sort is attempted. Hymer relies very heavily on work done by Professor John Dunning. In fact, Dunning is quoted so often, both in the theoretical and empirical sections, that one wonders how far Hymer would have gone had Dunning's 1958 work not been available. The other major sources used by Hymer are Brecher and Reisman on Canada, Phelps on Latin America, and Southard on Western Europe. Virtually all of the seventy pages of the 'empirical' Chapter Four reproduce tables and statistics from these sources. Yet the evidence chosen by Hymer supports his theoretical work very well and he did manage to 'put it all together' for the first time. Although the departmental committee at M.I.T. was probably correct in rejecting publication on the grounds of inferior empirical work, we now know, with the benefit of hindsight that some latitude should be allowed to pioneers. The brilliant theoretical conception of Hymer has become clearer with the passage of time.

11
Research and Development Abroad by U.S. Multinationals

Robert Ronstadt
New York; London: Praeger, 1977, xxi, 127 pp.

This book is the result of yet another doctorate supervised by members of the Harvard Business School. In it Professor Ronstadt, now of Babson College, examines the research and development (R&D) undertaken by the foreign subsidiaries of seven U.S. multinational firms. The seven multinationals selected for the study have an increasing amount of R and D performed by their foreign subsidiaries, this estimated percentage of foreign to total R&D. being shown in parentheses: Corning (9), Union Carbide, chemicals and plastic only (12), Exxon Chemical (23), Exxon, energy only (24), IBM (31), CPC International (39) and Otis Elevator (45). The author's approach is to first provide a description of the history and development of each of these seven case studies while secondly to attempt an 'aggregate analysis' of these firms, on the assumption that they are a representative group of multinationals with R&D abroad. Most of his findings under the latter category can be interpreted as evidence that these multinationals are efficient in their use of R&D. For example, the author finds that 'the seven parent organizations created R&D units abroad for reasons directly related to performance of the R&D function' (p. 61) and that, of the reasons for creation abroad, 'the most frequent purpose was to help in the transfer of technology from the U.S. parent to foreign subsidiaries' (p. 76). These conclusions are based on a somewhat limited data base of fifty-five R&D units owned by the seven multinationals interviewed by the author in 1974. Perhaps he is pushing the data a little too far when attempts are made to use models from the theory of management science to evaluate the structure, organization and performance of this small sample of foreign subsidiaries active in R&D.

The Economic Journal 88(351) (September 1978): 640.

European Research in International Business

Michel Ghertman and James Leontiades
*Amsterdam: North Holland Publishing Co., 1978, ix, 368 pp.**

This is a useful collection of seventeen papers selected from over sixty delivered to four conferences of European professors of International Business during the period, 1973–1976. It would have been even more useful if publication of this rounded selection of papers had been possible two years ago. Since then several of them have been developed into books or have been published in journals. These include the excellent theoretical essay by Buckley and Casson; the well-known 'mother-daughter' organizational structure of multinationals applied to Europe by Franko; the related paper on ownership and control of foreign operations by Stopford and Haberich; the empirical paper on multinational investment behavior by Hawkins, and the provocative testing of the risk and interrelationships of stock markets by Solnik and Jacquillat. The last paper is a particularly good example of the imaginative application of econometric analysis to a vital empirical issue – the degree of integration of world stock markets, with its implications for or against international diversification. Other papers of interest are: Schöllhammer on the evaluation of political risk; Leroy on technology transfer; Ghertman on strategic decision-making processes; and Hochmuth with a criticism of the term 'transnational' by the United Nations, instead of the more acceptable 'multinational.' The final group of papers focuses upon international marketing and management. In one of these, Leontiades argues that multinational companies gear their marketing towards local market patterns. And in another Will Straver examines the attitudes of executives working for multinationals. In these and other papers, it emerges that there are some differences between European and American multinational firms. We can look forward to further research on the special characteristics of European multinationals using this collection of papers as a valuable starting point.

---

* *The Economic Journal* 89(353) (March 1979): 219–220.

The Multinational Corporation: A Radical Approach

Stephen H. Hymer. Robert B. Cohen et al. (eds)
Cambridge: Cambridge University Press, 1979, xii, 323 pp.*

The preparation of this memorial volume by the Stephen Hymer Papers Collective began in 1974. After five years of labour they have produced a representative collection of Hymer's papers on the Multinational Corporation (MNC). Of the eleven papers selected, all but two were originally published in the 1970–1972 period. Thus they reflect that period of Hymer's brief academic career when, as a self-proclaimed Marxist, he attempted to advance a radical critique of the MNC. These papers stand in sharp contrast to his 1960 doctoral dissertation, when, still a liberal economist, he developed a brilliant original analysis of the MNC based upon the market imperfections approach. While his dissertation has been very influential in subsequent work on the theory of the MNC it is not clear that this volume does anything more than preach to the converted. These include Levitt, O'Connor, and Rowthorn, who introduce the three departments of the book, and the editors who add a rather rose-tinted perspective including irrelevant details of Hymer's personal life. Indeed, about 20% of the book consists of editorial comment or biography, space that could have been used more effectively (if not equitably) by inclusion of more of Hymer's own work. His papers anticipate many of our current policy problems as nation states, especially in developing countries, attempt to confront the perceived economic power of the MNC. Such perceptions are reinforced by Hymer's emphasis upon the internationalization of capital and his argument that the MNC hinders economic development. Readers who are more concerned with efficiency than the Marxist emphasis upon distribution will not accept much of this analysis. In their view regulation of the MNC is somewhat myopic, since it involves foregone economic opportunities. Yet Hymer has raised relevant questions of political economy which need to be debated by all students of the MNC.

---

* *The Economic Journal* 90(360) (December 1980): 985.

14 Technology Licensing and Multinational Enterprises

Piero Telesio
*New York: Praeger, 1979, xiv, 132 pp.**

This is one of a growing number of studies which consider licensing as an alternative to subsidiary production by the multinational enterprise (MNE) as a method of servicing foreign markets. Based on a Harvard Business School Dissertation supervised by Professor Stobaugh this book is one of the first attempts to add an empirical aspect to the theoretical work on alternatives to the MNE. Motives for licensing are twofold: first, to substitute for foreign direct investment when there are restrictions on entry of the MNE or net costs are too high and, second, for reciprocal exchanges of licenses. The latter occurs especially in such areas as semiconductor and pharmaceutical technologies where interlocking patents occur frequently. The author finds that there is a gain from trade in licensing. The MNE gains access to valuable assets of the licensee, namely familiarity with the local market and culture, not to mention the avoidance of political risk and regulations restricting subsidiary production. In exchange, the MNE surrenders its proprietary rights over certain firm-specific advantages such as knowledge. Thus, by licensing, there is always a risk of dissipation of the MNE's secret technology. Five variables are hypothesized to affect the evaluation of the net benefits of licensing to the MNE. These are: the firm's internal supply of proprietary knowledge (as proxied by R and D expenditures); its degree of product diversification; its size relative to other firms in its main industry; its experience of foreign markets; and the degree of competition in technology. A sample of 66 MNEs (mainly US based) is used and data on royalties, product lines of licensees, and so on were obtained by questionnaires and interviews. These data permit the construction of those indexes (sales, royalties, and licensees) which are alternative measurements of the degree

* *The Economic Journal* 90(360) (December 1980): 986-987.

of each firm's licensing activity. The author assumes average royalty rates of 3% of licensee sales to generate the licensee sales index (page 45). The empirical work is somewhat exploratory in nature and it does not serve to resolve the many questions raised by this innovative study of licensing.

The World Directory of Multinational Enterprises

John M. Stopford, John H. Dunning and Klaus O. Haberich (eds)
London: Macmillan, 1980, 2 vols xli, 1186 pp.*

The two volumes of this pioneering directory of multinational enterprises (MNEs) are a godsend to researchers in the fields of international business and industrial organization. Detailed information is provided, in a consistent format, on the largest 430 MNEs which account for over 80% of the total foreign direct investment in the world. Two features of the format are of particular interest. First, the financial data is broken down by major countries and regions. This permits the ratio of foreign to total sales (or assets, or profits, etc.) to be computed, and, when combined with the listings of country location of subsidiaries, provides insights into the degree of multinationality and potential political risk facing the MNE. Second, data on R&D expenditures, at home and abroad, is provided (the latter on a limited basis). Such data are hard to come by and represent a valuable addition to the literature. The firm listings also include a breakdown of product sales by major line of business and a background history of each MNE. Also fascinating are lengthy introductory essays, tables, and appendices which analyze the pattern, growth, structure, and other important attributes of the MNEs. There are, of course, other sources of corporate data available, but these are not as convenient; for example, the cost of acquisition and storage of annual reports from which most of the data are drawn is often prohibitively high for most individual scholars and, indeed, for many libraries. This is particularly true when analysis needs to be done of profit rates and other performance measures over a time period of, say, ten years. The new directory contains information for the five year period, 1974–1978, and updates are promised. Several other good directories are available, but their coverage is not confined to the MNEs. For example, *Informations Internationales* is particularly strong on European firms and

**The Economic Journal* 91(364) (December 1981): 1112–1113.

its overall coverage is about 1,000 major companies, listed by industry groupings, in a score of nations. The new *Moody's International Manual* covers several thousand companies, including many non-US firms. Both of these directories carry comparable financial information and have data both on foreign to domestic sales and on the location of foreign subsidiaries, so that MNEs can be identified, if required. Yet it will probably be quicker to send students and researchers directly to Dunning, Stopford and Haberich, since they have already defined their work to include only MNEs. Overall, this is an excellent and convenient source of relevant information, which should help to improve our knowledge of multinationals.

16 The Multinational Corporation

Sanjaya Lall
London: Macmillan, 1980, xii, 264 pp.[*]

Sanjaya Lall has done more than most in adding analytical precision to the study of the multinational enterprise (MNE). This is a collection of nine of his recent articles and it is rich in the imaginative application of economic theory and statistical technique to the MNE. There are three papers on the pharmaceutical industry in less developed countries; three on intra-firm trade and transfer pricing, and three on foreign involvement and structure. Much of the work was done by Lall while at the Oxford Institute of Economics and Statistics, with some papers being commissioned by the United Nations, UNCTAD, and other international agencies. As there is no attempt to synthesize the work, I shall discuss three recurring themes in the book with which I found myself in some disagreement. Other readers may find different attributes of Lall's work of greater importance, and I encourage those interested in the MNE to pursue the many other issues addressed in the book upon which I cannot comment in this brief review.

The first theme in these papers which is of concern to me is the discussion of performance of the MNE. For example, in a paper first published in 1974 Lall refers to the multinational pharmaceutical industry as being 'exceptionally profitable relative to other industries', an observation dependent upon data for only one year. Yet Lall should analyze the mean and standard deviation of profits over a ten or twenty year period for MNEs in this industry and conduct statistical tests to demonstrate if a significant difference persists against the all-industry average over time. In such work I do not find any evidence of excess profits for MNEs. I do not find it surprising, therefore, that in another paper, published in 1978 and preprinted here as Chapter 2, Lall reports that in most studies in the

[*] *The Economic Journal* 92(365) (March 1982): 196–198.

literature 'the declared profits of TNCs and others do not differ significantly from each other.' The conflicting evidence on profits in these two sections of the book is not explained. Lall then goes on to suggest that, since these studies (of normal profits for MNEs) 'are at variance with *a priori* expectations about MNE performance and with many of the findings for developed countries,' it is necessary to explain them away by data problems, small sample size, transfer pricing, or government policies.

Perhaps Lall is missing the point here. If there is indeed no evidence of excessive profitability in MNEs then it is time to revise the *a priori* expectations, since they are clearly in error. My own explanation of the lack of excess profits earned by MNEs over time is that the high costs of running their internal markets offset the potential rents available from exploitation of their monopolistic advantages in proprietary information or other firm-specific advantages. In a similar vein, in his discussion of risk (described as a 'bogey') Lall shows little understanding of modern capital market theory. He does not present any data on risk measures, such as standard deviation of profits or beta coefficients, nor does he acknowledge that high risk must be compensated by high return. Indeed, Lall falls into the common trap of examining profit rates without reference to risk. Yet it has been shown elsewhere in the literature that, even though they do not make greater than normal profits, the MNEs benefit from more stable earnings than non-MNEs of similar size. It is this risk dimension of performance that requires more work by scholars now that the issue of 'excess profits' of MNEs has been found to be an empty box.

The second problem I found was in Lall's work on transfer pricing. His well known 1973 paper in the *Oxford Bulletin* is reprinted as Chapter 5, along with two other papers, one of which, on intra-firm trade, manages to avoid any reference to the pioneering work in this area by Grubel and Lloyd. Using the overworked example of the pharmaceutical industry in Colombia, Lall finds evidence of transfer pricing by MNEs. He, like Vaitsos, then generalizes this case study to argue for policy by host governments for 'monitoring intra-firm trade and enforcing reasonable transfer prices.' Yet it is not clear to me that such regulation of the MNEs is required, especially since the particular Colombian example of transfer pricing took place in an environment of market imperfections such as foreign exchange controls and effective tax rate differentials. These environmental imperfections are basically external to the MNE and naturally encourage it to use its internal market to by-pass such government-induced barriers to trade. Indeed, I have argued elsewhere that 'arm's length' prices simply do not exist for MNEs with firm-specific (monopoly) advantages and that transfer prices are merely the internal prices used by the MNE to clear its own internal market. As such, transfer prices are efficient. The perceived social welfare losses of transfer pricing can only be tested indirectly by examination of the performance of the whole MNE, but, as discussed earlier, there is no evidence of MNEs earning excessive profits over time. It appears that the transfer pricing issue is another empty box.

The third issue on which I disagree with Lall is his treatment of technology transfer to less developed countries and especially his analysis of linkages and spillovers resulting from the presence of the MNEs. This occurs mainly in the first three chapters of the book. It is not clear to me why the MNEs should be expected to contribute to the economic development of host nations; MNEs are businesses not development agencies. If the host nation desires to increase its stock of technology it can use an infant technology argument to justify a subsidy to its domestic producers. It is unfair to charge the MNEs with inappropriate or insufficient transfer when they do not exist to satisfy such social objectives of the nation state. Indeed, given the power of governments to change the rules of the game and erect new market imperfections, the MNEs continue to respond to such changes and operate their internal markets in a remarkably efficient manner.

The debate on the MNE continues. Lall's book is a controversial but welcome addition to the field of international business. It takes the debate to a higher analytical and empirical plane. There is still room for others to make similar valuable contributions before the issues touched on in this review can hope to be resolved.

17 Multinational Management

David Rutenberg
*Boston: Little, Brown and Company, 1982, 265 pp.**

The publication of David Rutenberg's textbook will be welcomed as it introduces a distinctive new product line into the rapidly expanding market of international business studies. The focus of the book is the decision making of the multinational enterprise (MNE). It is one of the first books in the field to explore fully the implications of recent literature on the MNE, and it offers an interesting (if individualistic) new synthesis of international business management. It is really three books in one as the author offers pretty well self-contained sections in three core areas of the field: international finance, multinational management and multinational marketing. Rutenberg can be used as a supplement for a course in any of these areas, but it is most suitable for an advanced course in international business policy. The structure of the book is extremely appropriate for a policy course; each chapter starts with a pertinent case, leading the class into a case analysis followed by lectures or discussions of good textual materials which go to considerable depth in applying models and concepts relevant to the theme of the chapter. The textual material builds upon Rutenberg's earlier published papers but simplifies his mathematical models so that they are understandable for M.B.A. students.

In Chapter 1 the organizational structure of a business is discussed, the major focus being upon the extent to which critical management functions can be centralized or decentralized. The Citibank (A) and (B) cases are used. In the text Rutenberg describes the matrix form of organization appropriate for many geocentric firms. He also uses this chapter to introduce key concepts such as the importance of the experience curve in ethnocentric product structured firms and the opportunities for risk spreading in polycentric geographically organized firms. Indeed, the cornerstone of the book is Perlmutter's three classifications

Journal of International Business Studies 14(2) (Fall 1983): 160–162.

of organizational attitude into ethnocentric (home oriented), polycentric (host-country oriented) and geocentric (global oriented). Rutenberg usually argues that polycentric firms are decentralized and that geocentric firms are centrally directed.

Chapter 2 examines the management of foreign exchange in an MNE. The case analyzes the exposure to foreign exchange risk of a U.S. corporation, Dozler, at the time of the 1976 depreciation of the British pound. The chapter introduces the concept of foreign exchange risk and exposure in the context of the internal decision making of the MNE, where the firm has the options of hedging, using forecasting services, and so on. The remaining two chapters of Part 1 deal with a medium-run problem of maneuvering liquid assets in Chapter 3 and a long-run problem of expansion to a new location in Chapter 4. The cases are Paisley of France and the Michelin Tire expansion to Nova Scotia, respectively. A favorite phrase of Rutenberg's is 'polycentric corporations become multinational by a process of creeping incrementalism,' where expansion abroad is viewed as risk pooling. In contrast, ethnocentric firms generally seek to avoid the perceived risk of foreign expansion, and product divisions are left to go abroad on their own initiative. The geocentric MNE analyzes the impact of foreign expansion on key 'stakeholders' in the host and other nations. There is an error in the equation on page 53.

Part 2 on multinational management has three chapters which deal with logistics (Chapter 5), production smoothing (Chapter 6) and plant location (Chapter 7) in a manner loosely related to product life cycle model. The cases are Ascendant Electric, Ford's European car and Bell's plastic cosmetic boxes respectively. The operations management decisions are interrelated so that the simultaneous solution of the logistics problem, subject to inventory smoothing and plant location decisions, will minimize total costs. An important consideration for plant location considerations is the trade-off between economies of scale in one plant versus the logistics cost of transportation, tariffs and quotas. Other trade-offs occur between the choice of inventory held against the danger of stockouts and the adoption of sub-assemblies in polycentric marketing organizations. I thought that this section of the book on multinational operations management was much stronger than the section on financial management which was rather idiosyncratic in its coverage.

Part 3 on international marketing is an excellent section, which breezes along on intuitively familiar territory. Chapter 8 looks at product launch and uses the Philip Morris cigarette case (in which Parliament cigarettes failed to penetrate the culturally dissimilar Quebec market) as an example of the need to decentralize marketing decisions and interpret market forecasts in a scientific manner. Chapter 9 deals with pricing strategy by firms assumed to be price setters or, at least, dominant competitors in an oligopolistic market framework. The Tyler Abrasives case is a fascinating example of the need for polycentric pricing when over 200,000 'product lines' are being manufactured. Chapter 10 is on product design and develops a new case in which Black and Decker, Canada, are able to secure a world product mandate to produce and distribute the orbital sander machine. Chapter 11 on international executive development is an excellent self-contained, concluding section. The case on 'The Road to Hell' draws out the perils of cultural difference and inadequate perceptions of racial prejudice in human resource management. The manner by which the MNE can avoid such problems is by skillful training of its executives, coupled with planned managerial rotation to achieve adequate experience of foreign nations and different aspects of the company business. The students who have persevered thus far in the book will find this chapter a fitting reward as they check off the guidelines developed for an optimal executive career path in the MNE.

By now it will have become clear how Rutenberg thinks and why the book has the structure of a matrix. Rutenberg likes to explore systematically and with equal depth every single cell of the matrix of his mind. Thus we have in each of the chapters a similar structure of case, theory, and application to the three attitudinal situations. Of these, the polycentric and ethnocentric cases are often straw men setting up, as hero, the geocentric attitude. Each of the 11 chapters ends with a set of 'questions from other viewpoints', ranging from the 'Corporate Rational Normative Global' viewpoint to 15 other combinations of viewpoints, all the way down to the 'Societal Emotional Descriptive Subsidiary' one. This matrix method of exposition is rather repetitive and becomes a little tiresome after the initial original insights wears off. It also leads the author into some redundancies. For example, the experience curve is defined and explained in nearly every chapter, an unfortunate example of this proposition not always being relevant.

Overall, this is a brilliant original work. It is designed to challenge the thinking of teachers and students of international business. Rutenberg's innovative method, fresh examples and careful use of relevant theory bring a sharper analysis to the subject of international business policy. Rutenberg's cases are so well chosen they take on the garnish of fables rather than merely illustrative stories. The book is also rich in anecdotes, metaphor and humor. This has made Rutenberg a popular and successful text with my students in both the U.S. and Canada. It is a strong competitor to related texts on multinational management by Robinson, Fayerweather, and others. In summary, this book raises the mean for textbooks in international business; naturally it also increases the variance. For students and instructors who have doubted the analytical foundations of international business, a reading of Rutenberg will be an eye opener; they are in for a rich feast at the table of a master chef.

18 The Multinational Corporation in the 1980s

Charles P. Kindleberger and David B. Audretsch (eds)
*Cambridge, MA; London: MIT Press, 1983, 376 pp.**

Charles P. Kindleberger's symposium volume on *The International Corporation*, published in 1970, has become a well-known text. The papers in this new book help to up-date the path-breaking works of the earlier symposium and offer an interesting perspective on the rapid development of the theory of foreign direct investment over the last twelve years. The strongest papers in the book are the theoretical ones by Stephen Magee, Paul R. Krugman and Bruce Kogut, while the strength of the modern theory of foreign direct investment is attested to by good empirical tests and policy applications of it in papers by such people as Daniel M. Shapiro, K. Celeste Gaspari, Howard Curtis Reed and Richard S. Newfarmer.

The fifteen essays in this book are of somewhat uneven quality. The book starts off well with an excellent political science paper by Joseph Nye, followed by three extremely clever theoretical papers. As examples of the variability of the papers, let me focus on two good ones and another.

First, there is a comprehensive and balanced survey of modern theories of foreign direct investment by David McClain. He finds that the market imperfections approach – that is, internalisation theory – broadly explains the experience with foreign direct investment of the United States.

Second is the provocative and thought-provoking paper by Robert Z. Aliber, entitled 'Money, Multinationals and Sovereigns,' which updates his well-known version of the theory of foreign direct investment by shifting the focus to Tobin q ratios (the ratios of the market value of an asset to its replacement cost). Professor Aliber's paper in the 1970 volume became something of a minor classic in the field. The model in the new paper draws heavily on the previous work, and as Professor

---

The World Economy (September 1983): 356.

Kindleberger himself said in commenting on the seminal paper, 'it may even be right.'

Third is the disappointing paper by Eric Kierans who does not seems to have read very much of the recent literature on the theory of foreign direct investment. This leads him into a series of nonsensical criticisms of the multinational enterprise in which notions of sovereignty, power and ownership are confused with (an inaccurate) analysis of the efficiency aspects of multinational enterprises. Yet perhaps this is the nub of the public policy debate over foreign direct investment. Multinational enterprises are clearly efficient vehicles for the international transmission of knowledge; frequently they arbitrage barriers to trade and investments. But the very success of multinational enterprises as efficient economic institutions draws the ire of countless political interest groups. So long as we have no effective methods of ordering the preferences of competing groups of stake-holders the criticisms of the multinational enterprise will continue.

19 Multinational Enterprises and Economic Analysis

Richard E. Caves

Cambridge and New York: Cambridge University Press, 1982, xi, 346 pp.[*]

As is to be expected from the pen of Professor Caves, his Cambridge survey of economic literature is an excellent synthesis of theoretical, empirical, and policy work on the multinational enterprise (MNE). The book is in the tradition of Caves's *Trade and Economic Structure*. In the intervening twenty-five years Caves has lost none of his skill in weaving together difficult and often lengthy technical articles into a rich synthesis, where the final product is inevitably greater than the sum of its parts. With his complete mastery of the twin fields of international trade and industrial organization, Caves is almost uniquely well equipped as a master builder to transform the recent disparate literature on the MNE into a significant edifice of its own. This Caves has done in a sensible and well-written book, which will become the standard introduction to this new subfield.

What then, is the modern theory of the MNE? In Chapter one Caves make clear that it is what some of us have identified as the theory of internalization, which Caves refers to here as 'the transactional approach.' In either usage, the message is the same; the multiplant MNE develops an internal market, in circumstances when there are lower net costs than using an arm's length market. This occurs, for example, in pricing intangible assets such as knowledge, which 'are subject to a daunting list of infirmities for being put to efficient use by conventional market' (4).

Horizontally integrated MNEs have a transactional advantage in using a hierarchical administrative structure to control their international production. Vertically integrated MNEs also use internal markets to overcome 'contracting costs and uncertainties that would mar the alternative state of arm's length transactions' (16). Usually each MNE has a special

[*]*Canadian Journal of Economics* 16(4) (November 1983): 742–744.

firm-specific advantage, in the form of either some intangible asset, or a more physical advantage, unique to the firm, in its production or distribution. The firm-specific advantage can be technological knowledge, management skills, marketing know-how, secure supplies and markets, perhaps even cheaper sources of capital. At times the firm-specific advantages can be patented; at other times MNEs attempt to differentiate products and services or introduce brand-name product lines to reduce buyer uncertainty.

In summary, transaction costs face both horizontally and vertically integrated MNEs and occur in both static and dynamic situations. Caves argues that the remaining types of multiplant MNEs are explained by the principles of international diversification. He finds that there is considerable empirical support for both the transactional and the diversification explanations of the MNE. Caves extends this model in Chapters two and three to analyse the choice between exporting, foreign direct investment, joint ventures, licensing and other non-equity arrangements for servicing foreign markets. Some general equilibrium concepts are used, but comparative statics is the main method of analysis.

The remainder of the book relies heavily upon the transactional model. Many examples are given of the ability of the MNE to use its internal market to evade the market imperfections that confront it. For example, both Chapter four on patterns of market competition and Chapter seven on technology transfer expand on the transactional model. They demonstrate convincingly that the appearance of the MNE in concentrated and R&D-intensive industries is predicted by the theory. Even Chapter six on the financial behavior of the MNE, is focused on the issue of the degree of segmentation of international capital markets and the extent to which this imperfection constrains the optimal financial management of the MNE. Incidentally, in this chapter Robert Aliber's model of exchange risk gets short shrift in comparison to the large literature on international diversification.

Other chapters in the book deal with wages, taxation, the role of MNEs in developing countries, and issues in public policy. In these more applied sections Caves dwells upon the efficiency aspects of MNEs rather than upon issues of political economy for their own sake. He is able to call upon a surprisingly large body of good analytical and empirical work, almost none of which finds MNEs to be the all-powerful devils of popular mythology. For example, Caves finds that host governments have demonstrated considerable bargaining skills in recent years in their efforts to extract the perceived 'rents' of MNEs by taxation or threats of expropriation.

The depth of Caves's scholarship is apparent throughout the book; where appropriate, he even guides the reader to the relevant chapter in a book rather than to the general reference itself. After some 300 pages of this comprehensive survey of complicated theoretical, empirical, and policy literature, Caves boils it all down into a short, five-page 'bibliographic essay,' where he selects 'the good stuff,' that is, the most useful references for the student or general reader. This no mean feat, since the bibliography, itself, runs to some thirty pages of small type. The care and insight with which Professor Caves has produced this book will make it invaluable for many years to come.

Multinational Excursions

Charles P. Kindleberger
Cambridge, MA; London: MIT Press, 1984, vii, 275 pp.*

This is a collection of Professor Kindleberger's writings on the multinational enterprise (MNE) over the last fifteen years. The majority of the score of chapters deal with conflicts between the MNE and nation states. Kindleberger is a wizard at painting both sides of the fence on these issues, and readers from all camps can expect to find a fair statement of their viewpoints. One only wishes that at times Professor Kindleberger would pay less attention to balanced coverage and rather more to knocking over obvious examples of economic illiteracy. On the one occasion where he does this, in his devastating review of Barnet and Müller's *Global Reach*, we see his brilliant insights and witty writing style at their best. Perhaps the key paper in the book is that on 'Size of Firm and Size of Nation,' where Professor Kindleberger reaches the important conclusion that 'the optimum economic area is larger than the nation state, the optimum cultural area smaller' (p.30). This is an important insight into the debate over efficiency of the MNE, since it suggests that the 'fundamental conflict between the economics and politics' of the MNE can never be resolved. Somewhat less satisfactory is the short chapter on the new literature on the theory of the MNE, where Professor Kindleberger seems keener on saying that 'it's all in Hymer' rather than on conducting a fully accurate review of the recent literature. Indeed, the book seems to tail off towards the end, where some Congressional testimony and proposals for harmonization of policies towards the MNE appear to be either out of date or unrealistic. Overall, this book is well worth reading for its rich mixture of analytical insights and generally sensible policy advice on the MNE.

**The Economic Journal* 95(379) (September 1985): 865.

Third World Multinationals: The Rise of Foreign Direct Investment from Developing Countries

Louis T. Wells, Jr

London: MIT Press, 1983, 206 pp.*

For many years developing countries have complained about the role of multinational enterprises (MNEs). These firms, involved in private foreign direct investment (FDI), are thought to engage in practices solely geared towards their own economic efficiency, neglecting wider issues of social justice, income redistribution, technology transfer and growth; all of which are of prime importance to developing nations. Whether this is true or not is a complex matter, but now the debate has a new element. In the last fifteen years several Third World nations have generated their own multinationals. Professor Wells, of the Harvard Business School, has completed a remarkable study of these new multinationals, based on many years of detailed field work and personal involvement in developing nations. His recent book needs to be read seriously by all those interested in development.

The theoretical framework used by Wells to analyse the Third World multinationals is interesting since he attempts to take on board part of the new concept of internalisation, namely the associated notion of firm-specific advantages. Following a rather cryptic review of the theory literature (Chapter 2) which leans toward product-cycle thinking, Wells then discusses several types of firm-specific advantages (he calls them competitive advantages) of Third World multinationals. These are: advantages due to small-scale manufacturing (Chapter 3); advantages due to local procurement and special products (Chapter 4); advantages due to access to markets (Chapter 5); and a miscellaneous group, including defence of export markets, low-cost production, ethnic ties, and diversification (Chapter 6). Here the focus on firm-specific advantages in marketing (in Chapter 5) is particularly welcome, since it serves to complement the traditional theoretical emphasis upon technological and

* *Third World Affairs* (1986): 444–445.

knowledge-generated advantages, which Wells deals with at length. Here the Third World multinationals tend to have advantages in labour-intensive adapted process technology, as well as in low-price, standardized products.

The remaining four chapters in the book discuss the issue of FDI or licensing (Chapter 7); non-manufacturing investment (Chapter 8); home and host government policies towards Third World FDI (Chapter 9); and, in conclusion, prospects for these firms (Chapter 10). Tariffs and non-tariff barriers are important reasons for shifting from exporting to FDI, while the desire to control proprietary knowledge often precludes licensing. The first chapter outlines the data and defines the parameters of the study. Since this chapter also contains many useful facts on Third World multinationals, plus several puzzling results, I shall pay particular attention to it in this review.

It is estimated by Wells that by 1980 the stock of FDI from Third World nations was between $5–10 billion. While this is only a small fraction of the total world stock of FDI (estimated by Stopford and Dunning to be about $600 billion for 1980) it is still an important and growing source of international activity. The basis for the gener-alisations about the nature of Third World FDI made by Wells is his 'data bank' consisting of 963 parent MNEs and their total of 1,964 over-seas subsidiaries in 125 host nations. Therefore it is apparent that most of these Third World 'multinationals' must be fairly small firms, and they are likely to 'have much more in common with the smaller firms from the advanced countries than they do with the big multinationals' (p. 48).

One of the most significant findings of Wells is that virtually all of the Third World FDI is into other Third World nations. This instance of South–South investment linkages is one of the few successful examples of such cooperation in a world where trade and investment flows are still mainly North–South. It many seem somewhat paradoxical to some readers that this South–South transfer of technology by the process of FDI is being undertaken by a group of capitalist-type institutions, the multinationals. It appears that MNEs are not necessarily the unmitigated villains of popular *dependencia* theory after all.

Further evidence of the attractiveness of Third World FDI is that 90 per cent of the 938 manufacturing subsidiaries indentified by Wells were of the joint venture variety, rather than wholly owned subsidiaries. In contrast, US-owned multinationals on a world basis, have about 40 per cent of their subsidiaries as joint ventures, according to Wells, although this figure is much higher than in estimates for British multi-nationals made by Buckley and Davies. In any case it would appear that Wells has identified an interesting set of Third World international investment activity, but most of which is not normally defined as multi-national activity, i.e. wholly owned subsidiaries engaged in international production.

A further source of unnecessary confusion is the failure by Wells to present anywhere in the book a table listing, by name, the world's largest Third World multinationals. Although some of the firms are identified in the text itself, given the unusual nature of his definition of multinationals, I found this to be a particularly annoying oversight. Of course, from the annual *Fortune* magazine listings of the world's largest international (non-US) corporations it is possible to complete such a table. This I have done, and, for 1979 it reveals that eight of the largest twenty-four Third World multinationals were petroleum firms, *viz*. Petróleos de Venezuela, Petrobrás of Brazil, Pemex of Mexico, YPF of Argentina, Kuwait National Petroleum, Indian Oil, Chinese Petroleum (Taiwan), and Korea Oil. Therefore, another fact emerges; most of the very largest Third World multinationals are state-owned. In fact, fourteen of the largest twenty-four are state owned, the seven from South Korea being privately held. Another four of the largest twenty-four are mining multinationals from Chile, Zambia, Zaire, and Brazil and most of the remainder are in metal refining or textiles.

The size of these multinationals (the largest three with 1979 sales of over $30 billion) would lead one to suspect that Wells has somewhat underestimated the amount of Third World FDI. His focus upon what appears to be the smaller Third World 'multinationals' raises questions about the relevance of his study. It is difficult to acquire a perspective on the potential policy issues arising from the growth of Third World multi-nationals, since it appears that some of the major actors are not on the cast list. The existence of large, state-owned multinationals from politically sensitive Third World nations raises many interesting challenges for the conduct of international relations, few of which are explored by Wells. What Wells has done (along with another recent book by Sanjaya Lall) is to point us towards an appreciation of the countervailing economic power of Third World nations, which now are developing their own multinationals. In the future we are likely to witness an even greater degree of global competitiveness as Third World multinationals move up to join the big leagues in international business.

Licensing in International Strategy: A Guide for Planning and Negotiations

Farok Contractor
Westport, CT: Quorum Books, 1985, xix, 254 pp.*

It is a pleasure to report that the topic of international technology transfer has at last generated a book characterized by the rigour of its theoretical and empirical analysis. Professor Contractor has made a major contribution to the theory of the field of international business in this work of careful scholarship. It will undoubtedly become established as a classic reference expounding the viability of licensing agreements as an alternative to organization by internal markets (when the third modality of servicing foreign markets, exporting, is not viable in a world of non-tariff barriers to trade). Licensing is preferred to foreign direct investment when the multinational enterprise has a proprietary knowledge advantage but faces host-national environmental constraints (including government regulations on investment) and/or low dissipation risks which render the benefits of internalization less than its costs.

Contractor offers convincing evidence of the nature, extent and importance of licensing arrangements in today's regulated world economy. He identifies the growth of joint venture agreements as a major trend in the conduct of international business activity. He implies that there is a corresponding decline in the extent of foreign direct investment and exporting activity to accommodate the growth of the licensing option. He paints this picture in two strong theoretical chapters (2 and 4); three empirical chapters (3, 6, and 7) built around new firm level data; a strategic management chapter (5); a negotiating chapter (8), in which all three modalities are involved in a single deal; and a final chapter on government regulation of technology transfer (9). There is also an interesting preface and introductory chapter. Access to the results is aided by 76 tables and diagrams, plus a workmanlike index and bibliography.

**Journal of International Business Studies*, 18(1) (Spring 1987): 99–101.

As background for his study Contractor uses U.S. Department of Commerce data to demonstrate that, in 1981, the gross royalties and fees received for licensing amounted to about $8.7 billion while the gross dividends from foreign direct investment by U.S. multinationals totaled 14.7 billion (the net figures were 7.3 and 9.5 respectively). Thus, on the gross figures, licensing is 60% of the size of foreign direct investment. It should be noted that Contractor's work is confined to U.S. data on the licensing of proprietary technology. It is not at all clear that his findings would apply to other nations in Europe, or especially to the vastly different situations in Japan and Canada, to name but two countries with competitive advantages that are based as much on marketing skills as on production technology. Contractor states that in the 1970s only four nations were net exporters of technology and that most of it came from the United States. However, times are changing and an exclusive focus on the U.S. experience is no longer warranted. Naturally, this offers scope for non-U.S. scholars to try out Contractor's ideas for other nations.

Contractor states that there are four key propositions made in his book. First is the argument that 'broader-based agreements are profitable where traditional licensing may not be' (page 9). Yet, while he keeps repeating this point the survey data of Chapter 6 suggest that this is not recognized as an important consideration by respondents engaged in licensing. It ranked eighth out of twelve variables (page 119). Second, Contractor states that 'control can be achieved without an equity position' (page 9), which seems to be related to the third proposition that 'in many nations licensing can be as profitable as direct investment' (page 10). I comment on the (somewhat ambiguous) tests of these propositions below. Finally, Contractor's fourth hypothesis is that 'the global business climate has become more stringent *vis-à-vis* equity investment' (page 11). This is correct, but it helps to explain why this second and third propositions can be taken out of context and perhaps misunderstood within the profession.

My major quibble with this study (perhaps addressed to those of my colleagues who will not read it rather than to Professor Contractor himself), is that unfortunate overemphasis on licensing *as an alternative* to internalization or exporting. The emergence of licensing agreements and joint ventures does not invalidate the premises of internalization theory or Dunning's eclectic model. These works have always stressed that the *choice* of entry modality depends upon an evaluation of the relative costs. Thus when Contractor observes an increase in licensing agreements and joint ventures, it simply reflects the increasing net costs of the other two modalities. Yet this is not surprising given the escalation of administered protection and related non-tariff barriers to trade (which reduce exporting) and the increased regulations affecting the multinational enterprise (which reduce the opportunities for foreign direct investment).

As evidence for my point let me discuss Contractor's own tests (in Chapter 6) of the importance of the twelve strategy variables theorized to determine licensing, first identified in Chapter 5. On the basis of having identified these twelve variables in Table 20, Contractor states that 'the theoretical generalization that multinational firms will prefer "internalization" via direct investment over the sale of technology via licensing is a proposition that needs to be examined with greater circumspection in the emerging climate of international business' (page 80). Yet in his own test of these twelve strategic factors influencing licensing, in Table 32, he finds that the most important one is 'environmental constraints on FDI or FDI income'. Indeed, Contractor concludes that 'the salient factor promoting licensing is that the country's regulations or political risk inhibit forming majority-owned subsidiaries' (page 113). No exponent of internalization theory and the eclectic model will have any difficulty living with this observation, but she or he might raise an eyebrow at the first.

There are a few more technical points which merit a note in passing. First, Figure 2 on page 79 is a bit of a puzzle since the relationship between the axes (discount rate; net present value) and shift parameters such as dissipation risk and political risk (which are alleged to shift respectively the licensing and investment curves) is poorly explained. Second, the regressions in Chapter 4 indicate that the dummy variable used for government intervention is insignificant, but this may be due to its poor specification in the equations, relative to other independent variables which seem to incorporate elements of 'government intervention'. For example, many host nations have government policies to promote indigenous R and D; so the significant R and D variables in the regressions are not truly separate variables. Contractor, indeed, appears to doubt his own results in this chapter when he concludes that 'clearly, government policy influences the choice of business methods' (page 59).

Any work at the frontiers of the field will exhibit such minor technical problems. Yet, as suggested in the opening paragraph, the great strength of Contractor's book is its unrelenting focus on licensing as one of the methods of servicing foreign markets. While the commitment to his own research sometimes leads Contractor to overemphasize the value added of this focus, it is clear that Contractor himself sees that the strategic choice of entry mode by the multinational enterprise is at the core of studies in the field of international business. In his own words, 'the results lend credence to the idea that the strategy choice of arm's length licensing versus direct investment made by U.S. multinational firms is influenced by both country factors as well as industry characteristics but in a complex way' (page 56). Amen to that.

Global Capitalism at Bay?

John H. Dunning
*London; New York: Routledge, 2001, 279 pp.**

John Dunning is the greatest living scholar in the field of international business. Each year fellow scholars cite his research in their new publications, to the tune of over 100 citations a year, far ahead of all other scholars in the field. In addition to the widespread influence of his scholarship, John Dunning, has helped advance the field of international business by serving as the leading academic advisor to the United Nations Centre on Transnational Corporations, at UNCTAD, and its predecessors for the past quarter century. His latest book lives up to the high standards that he sets for himself and others in the international business field.

Over the last 40 years, another leading academic in the field was Raymond Vernon. His most widely read book was *Sovereignty at Bay* (1971). Dunning pays tribute to Ray by paraphrasing the title of Vernon's book. For Dunning the entire 'contemporary capitalist system (of) ever closer economic interdependence...fuelled by...market friendly government policies...is at bay' (p. xi). I think that this is a good title and John Dunning can pay no higher compliment to Ray Vernon than to continue to set high analytical standards for research in international business, as all the essays in this book demonstrate.

The book offers a set of 11 essays, the majority published in academic journals and books over the 1997–2000 period. They are right up to date. In particular, the first seven papers were all published in the last three years and reflect Dunning's latest thinking. Two chapters contain rich empirical tables (Chapters 7 and 8) while the remainder is theoretical and/or public policy oriented. Several of the early theoretical chapters are masterpieces of synthesis and insight. They deserve to be read and used as professional building blocks for future theoretical and

* *Transnational Corporations* 11(2) (April 2002): 113–116.

empirical research by all serious scholars in the field of international business.

By far the best paper is Chapter 3 on 'The eclectic paradigm as an envelope for economic and business theories of MNE activity.' Somewhat unfortunately this was published in *International Business Review*, a well meaning and high quality journal, but one with somewhat limited circulation. This brilliant paper was in some danger of being neglected until being reproduced in this book. Basically, this is the best synthesis of theories of foreign direct investment ever written. It even surpasses Dunning's earlier excellent synthetic work on the eclectic paradigm in his earlier books. If busy students read nothing else of Dunning, they should read this chapter.

As is well known, Dunning first developed the eclectic paradigm in 1977 as an overarching explanation of foreign direct investment (FDI) or the equivalent term, international production (i.e. production financed by FDI), p. 106, footnote 2. Over the intervening period, Dunning has refined and extended the eclectic paradigm to make it include asset-seeking FDI (in addition to the market seeking, resource seeking and efficiency seeking types) and to fully incorporate dynamic elements. The eclectic paradigm also incorporates the resource-based view, the knowledge enhancing theories of e.g. Kogut and Zander and the public policy literature on FDI.

Dunning's singular contribution and key theoretical insight is to group all FDI literature into three sub paradigms. These are the well known (i) ownership-specific advantages – the O of the triumvirate (ii) location-specific factors – the L variable and (iii) internalization theory – the I variable.

Dunning makes a convincing case in demonstrating that the eclectic paradigm is an envelope of explanation of 'a number of different economic and business theories' (p. 85). Indeed, all published papers on FDI theory and performance are beautifully encompassed by the eclectic paradigm. The three tables summarizing all important contributions to the FDI literature over the last 35 years need to be fully understood by all researchers and students of international business. These are (i) theories explaining the O advantage (pp. 90–92) (ii) theories explaining the L advantage (pp. 95–97) and (iii) theories explaining the I advantage (pp. 102–103). Taken together, these three tables, along with the accompanying text offer the best synthesis of international business literature ever written.

Within the OLI paradigm, I have always found it useful to link together O and I as firm-specific advantage and the keep the L as a country-specific advantage. This leads to my FSA/CSA matrix. However, in doing so, it is very important for other researchers to recognize that my FSA/CSA approach is fully compatible, indeed identical with Dunning's eclectic paradigm. I agree 100 percent with Dunning, e.g. in footnote 9 on page 106 where he endorses the views of Buckley and Casson to the effect that our 'paradigmatic and model building theoretic structures to understanding international business activity are complementary rather than alternative scientific methodologies.' I also fully accept Dunning's view that the 'eclectic paradigm is a systemic framework which provides a lot of good assumptions and boundary criteria in which operationally testable theories, germane to FDI and MNE theory, can be comfortably accommodated' (p. 106).

Another strength of this particular book is its focus on geography – the L factor in the OLI eclectic paradigm. Of particular interest are Chapters 4 on 'Location and the MNE: a Neglected Factor?' (previously published in *JIBS* (1998) and the five chapters in Part III on 'regions and geography'. Within Part III, Chapter 8 deals with FDI in Asia and Chapter 9 with FDI in the E.U. What I like here is Dunning's ability, again, to synthesize, tying relevant literature from geography, economics and management into the core FDI literature itself. For example, he uses the 'knowledge as a resource asset' literature from strategic management to explain clusters and 'sticky' places. Dunning states that: 'clustering is...likely to be strongly activity specific; and to be most marked...in sharing, tacit knowledge' (p. 195).

I was always amazed as to how Dunning could manage to produce his masterly syntheses of other peoples work; no other single scholar has ever been able to do justice to the huge literature in FDI. I discovered the reason when I visited John Dunning's house. In his study were copies of hundreds of I.B. books and every article on FDI theory ever written. Authors send their manuscripts and off-prints to John; he reads JIBS, other key I.B. journals and books from the 'cognate' disciplines of economics, management, history and politics; he referees papers and book proposals. All this work is summarized, placed and synthesized within the literature of international business. For 40 years John Dunning has read and reinterpreted every single significant publication in the field – and this book, like his other, provides a state-of-the-art review and integration of the literature. If you are not cited by Dunning, you are not a relevant player in the field. And yet, Dunning has often been the first to recognize and integrate the work of younger scholars, leading to development and intellectual renewal of the field of international business. For a senior scholar Dunning is young at heart.

He is also a gentleman, as well as a scholar. How else does one explain Chapter 2 which is called 'The Christian Response to Global Capitalism.' This was prepared for a special session of the EIBA, 1998 Annual Meeting in Jerusalem at which 'similar talks were given by Jewish and Moslem scholars' (p. 75). This paper is a model of respect and attention to the viewpoints of others, complete with a deep belief that global market-based capitalism is a moral imperative for economic development, social justice and personal freedom. The 'kernel' of Dunning's argument is that democratic capitalism 'is dependent on its being grounded in a strong and generally acceptable moral foundation' (p. 58). John Dunning has done more than any other scholar to build the field of international business on similarly strong moral and theoretical foundations.

Politics and International Investment

Witold Henisz
Cheltenham: Edward Elgar, 2002, x, 195 pp.*

According to Oliver Williamson's foreword, this is a 'pathbreaking book'. It is certainly a challenging research monograph that will appeal to international business scholars in the area of transaction cost economics, (TCE), political risk, multinational enterprise/host country bargaining and international joint ventures. It offers both theoretical and empirical advances in this area. The basic theme of the book is that host country political risk can be analyzed by multinational enterprises (MNEs) in a scientific manner such that they can act strategically to mitigate such political hazards. One way is by 'partnering' with local organizations in a joint venture. Yet, it is not an easy book to read as Henisz uses TCE jargon, basing the book on a set of technical papers published in specialized academic journals in the area of modern political economy.

The stated objective of this book is 'to provide policymakers, managers and scholars alike with a new set of tools for assessing the extent of political and regulatory risk faced by a given investment project in a given country...' (p. 1). The set of tools is drawn from 'positive political theory to model the political system and identify the determinants of policy (in)stability' (p. 10). The model is to be exercised by 'senior management' (p. 11) as part of their 'cost effective corporate strategies' (p. 12). A favored strategy is that 'the use of a local partner' (p. 12) in a joint venture will be 'politically more costly for the government to target than a solely multinational enterprise' (p. 13).

The intellectual justification for this book is to test concepts from transaction cost economics, especially governance issues, within the context of the analysis of political risk facing MNEs in low income developing economies. The book is short at under 200 pages, and it consists

---

Journal of International Business Studies 34(2) (March 2003): 223–225.

mainly of three interesting empirical chapters (4–6) published recently in political economy journals. In addition, Chapter 2 is a brief literature review of Williamson-type credible commitments while Chapter 3 offers a new theory of TCE and governance contracts for MNEs facing political hazards in developing countries. Finally, Chapters 1 and 7 provide a brief introduction and conclusion respectively.

Chapter 3 is co-authored with Oliver Williamson and is reproduced from the new journal, *Business and Politics*. It provides the theoretical basis for the book, which can be summarized as follows. In a TCE model where there are three 'alternative modes of private ordering – principally markets, hybrids and hierarchies' (p. 30) there will be three different rates of adaptation to contractual hazards, where the latter principally mean challenges to MNE property rights due to imperfections in the host country political regime. There can be positive 'shift parameters' for hybrids and market forms if there is an improvement in host country contract law and enforcement. This will reduce transaction costs and somewhat reallocate the entry mode for an MNE into a host nation, varying the amount of 'partnering' (i.e. joint venturing) against hierarchical ownership by wholly-owned subsidiaries. This theory is nicely summarized in two simple but elegant microeconomic-type diagrams relating transaction costs to contractual hazards. The second diagram argues that incremental direct (government-related) political hazards will shift the transaction costs of ownership whereas indirect (private sector) political hazards will rotate the transaction costs of contract.

Henisz states that the desirability of MNE-local organization partnering depends on the asset specificity or opportunity cost of the underlying investment. The nature of the transaction itself can affect the benefits and costs of partnering to reduce political hazards. For example, with high asset specificity there is a risk that the MNE's partner may use its political connections to redirect potential rents to themselves away from the MNE. Such risk may offset the benefits of having the local partner work to reduce host country political hazards. Henisz argues that this is a new theoretical insight. Indeed, the major strategic implication from this model is that MNEs really do need to consider partnering with a host nation organization (in the form of a joint venture) in order to reduce the transaction costs of host country political risk, but there are contingencies that will alter the optimal amount of partnering versus ownership.

The three empirical chapters are of uneven quality. The one which actually tests the theoretical model best is Chapter 6 which is focused on the potential opportunism of the local partners of U.S. manufacturing MNEs. Depending on the nature of the project, the MNE needs to trade off the opportunism of its joint venture partner against the political benefits the partner can bring in terms of mitigating an unfavorable host country political system.

In Chapter 4 a 'structurally derived measure of political constraints' (p. 71) is developed. This is basically a measure of the political credibility of the host country institutional environment and the feasibility of policy change. Henisz has worked very hard to construct this new 'POLCON' dataset, which contains more objective measures for country risk ratings than the traditional country risk assessments. The Henisz measure combines analysis of the political institutions of a country with the preferences of the key actors there. It shows, for example, that the systems of Canada and the United States have lower political risk hazards than countries like Paraguay, Sudan and Zambia. Despite its innovative nature the new measure is still highly positively correlated with the more subjective International Country Risk Guide index (at 0.78 for one measure and 0.64 for another) (p. 64). The new measure is tested in regressions, and it is 'a significant predictor of cross-national variation in economic growth' (p. 76). Regimes with frequent policy changes experience lower economic growth.

Chapter 5 then uses this empirical analysis to study one key infrastructure sector, namely telecommunications. Here asset specificity is an issue and MNEs face what Ray Vernon called an obsolescing bargain if host governments change the rules of the game after the large initial investment. It is key for MNEs to be able to assess the credible commitments of host country governments. Again, Henisz finds 'cross-national and international variation in this measure for explaining variation in telecommunications infrastructure investment' (p 138). Political hazards result in less investment by MNEs in telecommunications.

As Henisz does not do this I feel that it is important to set the book within the context of international business theory and MNE strategy. While there is a specialist literature dealing with MNEs and political risk, mainly identified with the work of Louis Wells, Stephen Kobrin and others, this has never been fully integrated with a TCE/internalization viewpoint of the field. This is surprising as a very basic overview of this issue appears in my I.B. textbook of 1985, based on my internalization theory book of 1981. There I discuss the government-imposed 'unnatural' market imperfections as conceptually equivalent to Williamson-type 'natural' market imperfections as motivations for internalization by MNEs rather than markets. The senior managers of the MNE are required to act strategically in response to government-imposed regulations and political risk in the same manner that they do with asset specificity, bounded nationality, information asymmetries, opportunism, and related natural market imperfections.

While Henisz now goes into greater depth in terms of using political hazard models he does not build on this earlier work. I think that I know the reason. In effect, Henisz has the MNEs acting strategically to partly endogenize the political process in developing countries. They not only respond to government regulations, but can also attempt to change the structure of the political system by being an inside player, working with a local partner to limit political hazards. In my early work, I was careful to model government policy as exogenous and then analyze how MNEs respond, anticipate and otherwise take it into account in their strategies. Partly this has been influenced by my work with CEOs. They tell me that, provided they know the rules of the game as set by governments, then they can make intelligent investment decisions. It is when governments change the rules, or there are no rules, that MNEs have trouble. This is why trade agreements, like NAFTA, now incorporate the national treatment provision for foreign investments – to limit the ability of host governments in changing the rules affecting MNEs in a discriminatory manner.

The existence of national treatment, contracts, and the rule of law, is a type of 'public good' for MNEs. If these are lacking in some developing countries then the MNE will usually prefer joint ventures to wholly owned subsidiaries, and it will, indeed, try to act strategically to influence the host country political process. But this is a second best outcome to the first best one of a stable set of rules established and enforced by responsible host country governments. It is not surprising that the vast majority of MNE activity is in such regimes, and it is really the responsibility of developing country governments to bring their regulations in line with world norms if they expect to attract MNEs. For developing countries lacking such stable regimes, the Henisz model helps MNEs to assess political hazards, but it is not necessarily the most efficient way to inspire economic development in such countries.

Part II

International Finance and International Economics

Introduction to Part II

The book reviews in Part II deal with topics in international economics and international finance. In order to integrate this part into the book I have chosen to use the famous framework popularised by Chris Bartlett and Sumantra Ghoshal. In this framework the vertical axis deals with aspects of economic integration, sometimes mistakenly called global integration. In the next part, on globalisation, I shall discuss the fact that economic integration has certainly occurred, but mainly within each broad region of the triad, rather than globally. However, for our purposes in this part we can simply refer to the vertical axis as economic integration.

The beautiful point about the Bartlett and Ghoshal matrix is that the horizontal axis captures a new managerial dimension. It conceptualises the manner in which managers can respond (within the firm) to host country differences. Thus, the axis is called 'national responsiveness'. This is a pure management axis; it shows how managers can respond to the economic, political, cultural, social, and religious differences between their home country and the host countries in which their firm operates. The logic of the axis is that a firm with superior national responsiveness can beat other competitors purely through a managerial competence based on this international dimension.

The Bartlett and Ghoshal matrix is illustrated below in Figure 2. The ideas behind the twining of economic integration and national responsiveness can be traced back to work by Yves Doz (1976 and 1986) and by Doz and Prahalad (1993). The tension between integration and fragmentation goes back to early thinking in international business by Fayerweather (1960). Fayerweather explicitly says that managers need to tailor operations to the unique characteristics of each country and that a firm must develop good relationships with host country leaders. In other words, Fayerweather as early as 1960 argued that a successful strategy of internationalisation requires that the firm adapt its foreign operations to respect the political, cultural, and other distinctions of host countries.

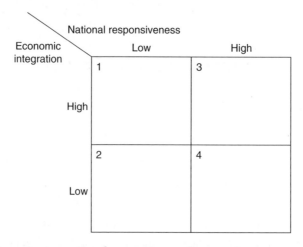

Figure 2 **Integration vs. national responsiveness framework**
Sources: Adapted from: C.A. Bartlett, 'Building and Managing the Transnational: the New Organizational Challenge', in *Competition in Global Industries*, edited by M.E. Porter. Boston, Mass.: Harvard Business School Publishing Corp., 1986; C.A. Bartlett and S. Ghoshal, Managing across Borders: the Transnational Solution, 2nd ed. Boston: Harvard Business School Publishing Corp., 1998; and A.M. Rugman and S. Collinson, International Business, 4th ed., Harlow, Eng.: Pearson Education, 2006.

However, his work was not influential, and it had to be rediscovered by Bartlett and Ghoshal in 1989, see Rugman (2002).

In Figure 2 we have cell 1 where only economic integration is important. The firm will develop capabilities based entirely upon international expansion and efficiency. Such advantages include the development of economies of scale and the selling of a brand product or service across additional economic space (into foreign countries). Basically all of the books reviewed in this part discuss and analyse aspects of cell 1. The reason is that many of these books were written and reviewed in the 1970s and 1980s. At that time international business was largely conceived of in terms of international economics and international finance. The theory of the MNE was not really understood until well into the middle of the 1980s. This was about 10 years after the breakthrough work by Buckley and Casson (1976), as discussed in the introduction to Part I of this book. As only country factors were being considered, the ability of the firm to develop non-economic capabilities was not widely understood.

We can better understand this issue with reference to cell 4 in Figure 2. The logic of cell 4 is that a firm can outcompete other firms solely on the basis of its capabilities in national responsiveness. As can be seen, there are no benefits of economic integration in cell 4; only the benefits of national responsiveness exist. In cell 4 the firm can develop excellent relationships with host country governments in order to minimise political risks. Or it may have excellent human resource management policies to build a good host country work force. Or it may understand other aspects of the local cultural and religious situation, such that it adapts its products and services and gains a better marketing foothold than is available to rival firms.

The attainment of cell 4 firm specific skills in national responsiveness is not easy. Marketing research, investment in host country analysis, and the training of senior managers are all necessary investments by a firm seeking to develop capabilities in national responsiveness. Indeed, the entire organisational structure of the firm may need to become decentralised and more responsive to host countries. This results in greater autonomy for foreign subsidiaries, and it is not easy for large MNEs to change their organisational structures due to their administrative heritage, which is a kind of 'sunk' cost facing corporations.

The field of international business is distinguished from international economics and pure strategic management since it regularly analyses both axes of Figure 2. In particular, cell 3 can only be addressed in a rigorous manner by using the concepts of modern international business management. In cell 3 there is an interaction between the benefits of economic integration and the benefits of national responsiveness. Multinational firms seeking to reconcile these twin attributes need to be flexible in their organisational structures (often using a matrix structure) and need to be willing to invest in ongoing training of senior managers. The MNEs need to develop network structures in which knowledge generation can take place in subsidiaries as well as in the parent firm.

In contrast, in cell 1, where only economic integration matters, a firm can be centralised, hierarchical, or ethnocentric and thereby be able to treat foreign subsidiaries as branch plants. Such firms ignore the potential knowledge generation of foreign subsidiaries. These MNEs were indeed characteristic of US firms in the 1960s and 1970s, and Japanese and European firms in the 1980s.

In cell 4 the resource based view of strategic management fully explains how firms can develop capabilities. The twist is that these are unique due to international country differences. However, the resource based view has not been fully developed to explain cell 3 attributes. There is relatively little literature on the dynamic capabilities required by MNEs to succeed in cell 3.

The book by Bartlett and Ghoshal is one of the most influential studies in international management ever published. In Review 25 the book was summarised for a Canadian managerial audience. The key contribution of Bartlett and Ghoshal is to use their framework of global economic integration and national responsiveness in an insightful manner to analyse the strategies and organisational structures of a set of nine large MNEs across three important industries and also across the triad of Europe, North America, and Asia. Unlike most of the economics related books reviewed in Part I, the Bartlett and Ghoshal book is focused upon strategic management. It relates in many ways to the topics discussed in Parts III and V.

Their work is an essential linkage between the economics based theory of internalisation with its focus upon FSAs and how such FSAs are embedded within the organisational structure of the MNE. Over the past 20 years the field of international business has moved on to research the internal mechanisms by which FSAs are generated and transferred within the internal networks of MNEs. Bartlett and Ghoshal argue that the managerial tensions between integration and responsiveness can be facilitated through a proprietary process of world-wide learning within the organisational structure of the MNEs. These aspects of international strategic management will be discussed later, especially in Parts III and V.

The literature in international finance and international economics was largely confined to work on the vertical axis of Figure 2. Starting with Review 26 through to Review 33 all of the books examined here dwell upon international financial markets purely in the country context. They are books by economics and finance professors dealing with issues in public policy. The implications of international capital markets and government regulations as they affect firms are a secondary focus of this literature. Some attention is paid to financial strategies of the MNE in Review 28 and in some of the essays in Review 29. However, all of the others see governments as the key actor, not firms. Most of Reviews 26 to 33 are sympathetic to the public policy orientation of the author.

However, in Review 33 I express strong disagreement with the naïve and ill informed views of the late Susan Strange.

Reviews 34 to 41 examine the literature in international economics which again is heavily biased towards government policy and the improvement of regulatory institutions. Fortunately, two of the reviews deal with books on transfer pricing which is an issue of MNE strategy examined by economists since the 1970s. In Reviews 37 to 41, which deal with trade agreements and the reduction of tariffs and non tariffs barriers to trade, there is more sophistication shown by economists in dealing with firms and strategic management. The reason is that in the negotiations of trade agreements, governments rely on the expertise of industry associations to formulate their platform on tariff reduction and investment policy. Thus, the role of the firm is indirectly entered into the development of the regulatory framework affecting international business operations.

It is only in retrospect that we can see that the framework of Figure 2 is now relevant to an understanding of this early literature on international finance and international economics. Over the last 40 years work in these areas has shown a gradual shift away from pure public policy and regulatory concerns towards a deeper understanding of industry and firm level strategy. Future books dealing with international capital markets must consider in detail the financial institutions and MNEs which engage in the international financial activities being considered. In tandem, future books in international economics must consider in depth the manner in which MNEs and other firms will undertake exporting, foreign direct investment, joint venture activity, licensing, and other modes of international business as they respond to liberalisation of goods and factor markets.

Overall, the academic interests of economics and finance specialists are now incorporating more aspects of MNE strategy. Much work still remains to be done in order to balance the prior focus upon the vertical axis of Figure 2 on economic integration with the horizontal axis with its focus upon firm level managerial skills in the benefits of national responsiveness.

References

Doz, Y. (1976) 'National policies and multinational management'. Unpublished doctoral dissertation. Harvard Business School.

Doz, Y. (1986) *Strategic Management in Multinational Companies*, Oxford: Pergamon.

Doz, Y. and Prahalad, C.K. (1993) 'Managing DMNCs: A search for a new paradigm'. In S. Ghoshal and E. Westney (eds), *Organization Theory and the Multinational Corporation* (pp. 24–50), New York: St. Martin's Press.

Fayerweather, J. (1960). *Management of International Operations: Text and Cases*. New York: McGraw Hill.

Rugman, A.M. (2002). 'The Influence of "Managing Across Borders" on the Field of International Management'. In M.A. Hitt, L. Joseph and C. Cheng (eds), *Managing Transnational Firms: Resources, Market Entry and Strategic Alliances* (pp. 37–56). Oxford: Elsevier.

25 Managing Across Borders: The Transnational Solution

Christopher A. Bartlett and Sumantra Ghoshal
Boston: Harvard Business School Press, 1989, xiv, 274 pp.[*]

Now that we have free trade, how will Canada's multinationals make out in the big leagues of global business?

For guidelines about the current state of play in global competition, this book is a useful starting point. It grows out of research and executive case teaching by the authors at Harvard Business School.

Mr. Bartlett is a business policy professor at Harvard and Mr. Ghoshal a business professor from MIT and the French business school, INSEAD. The book builds on their analytical skills and is based on interviews of 236 top managers in nine of the world's largest multinationals.

The nine companies are chosen in a very clever way, three each from the United States, Europe and Japan. The companies are also drawn from three interesting industries: consumer electronics (General Electric, Philips and Matsushita), telecommunications switching (ITT, Ericsson and NEC) and branded packaged goods (Procter & Gamble, Unilever and Kao).

The authors apply modern concepts of competitive strategy in a global context to analyze the performance of these companies. One of the key findings is that a successful global company needs to manage two elements simultaneously. First, companies need to operate to achieve the efficiency benefits of global integration (the process of 'globalization'). Second, they need to respond to national market needs (the process of 'national responsiveness').

Bringing together these twin pressures of globalization and national responsiveness leads to the development of a matrix in which the industry and company strategies can be examined. Successful multinationals are those that achieve both globalization and national responsiveness. This is a powerful concept; one readily applicable in Canada. For example,

---

[*]*The Globe and Mail* (Toronto, Canada) (October 9, 1989): B2.

in the free-trade debate it was argued that business in Canada needed the benefits of economic integration with the United States in order to achieve size efficiencies. It was also argued that the many exemptions from national treatment in the agreement (for health, culture, social services, etc.) maintained Canadian sovereignty, a type of national responsiveness.

Harvard Business School is training managers to be sensitive to both the economic, political and cultural aspects of management. Here in Canada we should recognize how the better multinationals are being organized and how it affects our policies. Canada's business leaders have seen this vision of the duality of economics and sovereignty and the last election endorsed it.

Messrs. Bartlett and Ghoshal build upon the globalization and national responsiveness framework by careful research on the nature of organizational structure in their nine multinationals. Most of their book reports on the administrative processes used to implement competitive strategies. A major conclusion is that implementation of strategy is critical to the success of a global company. However, this is not easy as a firm's 'administrative heritage' often makes managers reluctant to change.

They advocate a new organizational form, called the 'transnational,' which can manage structural change. The transnational company must 'manage complexity, diversity and change.' Once a company embraces the dynamics of change its structure itself then becomes a source of competitive advantage.

Although the authors ignore Canada, we can apply this thinking to Canadian-owned multinationals. Northern Telecom would do well in the Bartlett-Ghoshal matrix. It has emphasized both globalization and the marketing aspects of national responsiveness. There is also some evidence that its senior management is capable of changing Northern Telecom's internal structure. Their recent focus upon the efficient management of time is an example of change in the internal structure of the organization.

Some other Canadian-owned multinationals are making efforts to revise their internal structures and operate globally. Molson, Alcan and Nova come to mind. Others, like Labatt, Noranda and Domtar seem to be closer to the older 'unidimensional, symmetrical and static' structures, derided by Messrs. Bartlett and Ghoshal.

But these are just impressions. I wrote a book about Canada's 20 largest 'megafirms' a few years ago. Since then I have seen little serious process research being done by business professors on Canada's multinationals.

Messrs. Bartlett and Ghoshal spent over five years doing the groundwork for their nine-company sample. They received abundant financial support from Harvard and MIT for this type of expensive, interview-based fieldwork.

If Canadian companies are serious about doing business in the 21st century they need to work much harder with Canadian-based researchers to develop comparable skills in our business schools. Otherwise Canadian managers will be left wondering how much of the thinking at Harvard is really applicable in Canada, since there will be nothing else available.

Even with free trade, Canadian managers need research which is 'nationally responsive,' not just globalized.

The Floating Canadian Dollar: Exchange Flexibility and Monetary Independence

Paul Wonnacott

*Washington, DC: American Enterprise Institute for Public Policy Research, 1972, 95 pp.**

To what extent can a small open community pursue an independent monetary policy when there is highly mobile international capital? The answer suggested by Professor Wonnacott's examination of the postwar Canadian experience is the familiar one that flexible exchange rates permit greater independence for Canadian monetary policy than do fixed rates. In addition it is essential that the authorities follow appropriate economic policies.

The book should be extremely popular with students and others interested in this topic. Wonnacott gives a clear summary of postwar monetary policy in Canada, and his observations on the operation of the exchange rate are full of useful insights. He integrates a high level of theoretical sophistication with a concise historical description of the three main postwar periods: flexible rates in 1950–62 (Chapter three), fixed rates in 1962–70 (Chapter four), and flexible rates since the float of June 1, 1970 (Chapters five and six). In Chapter one there is a brief summary of recent theoretical work on fixed and flexible rates ranging from Mundell to the Caves and Reuber study, but excluding the recent contributions by Floyd.

The specialist in monetary theory and its application to an open economy may find this book of limited value. No original research is reported, nor are new statistical techniques used to analyze this familiar period. Wonnacott has written an interpretative essay which is similar to Robert M. Dunn, Jr.'s *Canada's Experience with Fixed and Flexible Exchange Rates in a North American Capital Market*, sponsored by the Canadian-American Committee and published in 1971.

Canadian Journal of Economics 6(1) (February 1973): 140–141.

In this limited review it is impossible to report and comment on all the points made by Professor Wonnacott. He is as much concerned with an analysis of postwar Canadian stabilization policy as with the exchange rate itself. The management of aggregate demand has been constrained by external pressures, and this situation was not improved when contradictory economic policies were followed. Two examples illustrate this. Firstly Wonnacott repeats an argument he made previously that flexible exchange rates operated well from 1950–58. The difficulties of 1956–61, which led to the abandonment of flexible rates, were not due to problems 'in the exchange rate mechanism, but rather in the inappropriate monetary policies which Canada followed' (p.38). These tight money policies were misguided in a period of high unemployment and led to an unstable foreign balance. Secondly, the excessively restrictive monetary policy followed recently in 1969–70 led to upward pressures on the fixed exchange rate because the widening Canadian-US interest rate differential induced short-term capital inflows, leading to the frustration of the anti-inflationary policy. The upward float of the exchange rate in June 1970 was associated with a decline in the rate of inflation, although the causes of this temporary price stability remain debatable.

Finally, a warning. It is tempting to apply the Canadian experience to other countries, especially Germany. Wonnacott cautions against this, for while the high level of integration of US and Canadian financial markets may have foreshadowed an integrated US-European capital market, Canada is a unique case study. It has 'exceptionally close ties to the predominant US economy' (page 93) which make it somewhat risky to apply the lessons to other countries.

International Monetary Policy: Bretton Woods and After

W.M. Scammell
London: Macmillan, 1975, 262 pp.

Professor Scammell has completely rewritten his famous textbook on international monetary economics. This version is based on the previous edition of 1957 and 1961 but has been reorganized and updated to incorporate recent changes in the Bretton Woods system. The major improvement is in the development of theoretical principles as they apply to international monetary problems. In the theoretical section, Chapters 2 to 5, Scammell draws heavily upon the work by Alexander and Harry Johnson on the absorption approach. He does this rather well. He also reports the Swan and Mundell models on internal and external balance but his treatment of these is somewhat cryptic. His analysis of the demand and supply for international reserves is not very good and in this connection the reader may wonder at the somewhat artificial distinction made between the 'optimal' level and the 'desirable' level of international reserves (page 23ff.)

Most of the book is descriptive. On page 36, Scammell says that he is 'concerned with institutional facts rather than theoretical analysis' and indeed this is the approach throughout the book. This can lead into analytical problems. For example, Scammell is too kind in his discussion of controls. On page 134ff. he argues that they were justified in the postwar reconstruction phase, but such an argument ignores the distortions and welfare costs imposed by such measures. In this section he should remember his discussion of controls on page 69 where he states that they only suppress the underlying adjustment problem. Professor Scammell also lays too much stress on the necessity for asymmetrical changes in world exchange rates and is too easily led into the belief that an expansion of SDRs will solve the problem of international liquidity. He does not incorporate the recent theory of optimum currency areas

---

Kyklos 29(1) (1976): 180–181.

into his discussion of the problems of implementing a European common currency. Neither does he make use of the recent literature on short term capital flows and completely omits any mention of the Eurodollar market. Portfolio theory and stock flow models are also excluded. Despite this lack of recent theory many of Professor Scammell's observations are interesting, for example, that the snake in the tunnel is a 'half-baked' approach to exchange stability on the part of the European nations (page 235).

The best part of the book is the analytical section on the Bretton Woods model, that is, Chapters 6 to 9. Here the record of the Bretton Woods system is critically examined in a close weaving of institutional, historical and theoretical writing. The major feature of the Bretton Woods system was the system of fixed exchange rates, or more accurately, managed flexibility. In practice the United States dollar was the lynchpin of the post-war gold exchange standard. It is clearly explained by Scammell that the International Monetary Fund was the creature of the Americans, that they controlled it (as voting strength was proportional to currencies accredited to the Fund, the great majority of which were American) and used it as an instrument of political policy.

Scammell discusses at length the three interrelated problems of the Bretton Woods system; liquidity, confidence and adjustment. These three problems are the familiar stuff of international monetary textbooks. Here they are treated with refreshing vigor and with the benefit of a recent perspective. The use of the pound sterling and American dollar as key currencies, used to supplement gold reserves, led to the intensification of each of these problems. It becomes clear that the Bretton Woods system contained the seeds of its own destruction. Specifically there was too much American influence and an unwillingness to adjust to dynamic changes in the world economy, with a fatal neglect of the promotion of other currencies as international trading vehicles. There was also a reluctance of surplus nations such as Germany, France and Japan to allow their currencies to be used in this manner. The Bretton Woods system was unable to respond to the changing postwar environment not only because it did not permit real adjustment through flexible exchange rates but also because the institutional structure was itself insufficiently flexible.

Financial Policies for the Multinational Company: The Management of Foreign Exchange

R. Aggarwal

*New York: Praeger, 1976, distributed by Martin Robertson & Co., ix, 161 pp.**

A basic premise of this book (but one which is not tested) is that the recent floating of exchange rates has increased their instability. This is alleged to lead to a greater exchange risk and to complicate the financial management of a multinational corporation (MNC). The use of traditional accounting procedures, which evaluate the fixed assets of overseas subsidiaries at historical exchange rates, may lead to an incorrect valuation of the MNC. Aggarwal favors an accounting method which places more weight on the use of current exchange rates, and in Chapters 4 and 5 he presents the 'earnings power principle' and 'control-limit' model to offer a practical method for calculating the exchange rate exposure of the MNC. To use these techniques the MNC will require information on expected movements in exchange rates, and while Aggarwal foresees the development of an in-house forecasting capacity it is just as likely that independent consultants, such as Forex, can supply such predictions. The book is weak in its awareness of economic theory and would benefit from a better treatment of hedging, stock-flow relationships, and the full implications of portfolio theory for risk reduction by the MNC. The main fault is a complete lack of empirical work. For example, it would seem necessary to know if the earnings and share valuations of MNCs have varied under regimes of fixed or flexible rates. Despite these shortcomings, Aggarwal has produced an innovative introduction to the problems of exchange risk and the accounting procedures of an MNC. His book will be useful reading for courses in international business and to students of the MNC.

---

*The Economic Journal, 87(347) (June 1977): 403.

29 International Capital Markets

Edwin J. Elton and Martin J. Gruber (eds)
*Amsterdam and New York: North-Holland/American Elsevier, 1975,
xvi, 387 pp.**

A new subfield of international finance has been developing over the last few years. In this the modern theory of finance is applied in new and imaginative ways to the traditional issues of international capital flows, foreign exchange risk, and regulation of the balance of payments. The essays in this book report on some of the latest research (mostly empirical) in this area. Every author makes use of the principles of portfolio theory first developed by Markowitz and most attempt to extend the capital asset pricing model (CAPM) in an international context.

The editors have grouped the research papers into three sections. In Part I there is a survey of empirical studies on capital markets by Granger, followed by six empirical studies on the performance of security markets in European nations. These latter studies test the CAPM for each nation individually, but while the results are of interest and the research is competent, there is little attempt to examine international aspects of risk. This is done in Part II of the book in a brilliant series of papers which are discussed below.

Part III consists of four papers on financial decision making in multinational corporations (MNC). Shapiro and Rutenberg attempt to introduce foreign exchange rate consideration into the financial management decisions of MNC's. Their efforts serve only to illustrate the primitive nature of such work. Adler and Dumas advance a two country behavioral model of the MNC which applies portfolio theory to several assumed states of the international capital market, namely when it is segmented or has imperfections and taxes. They find that if a segmented international stock market exists then financing decisions by the MNC may offer a substitute for individual international portfolio diversification.

Journal of Finance 32(4) (September 1977): 1382–1384.

The main contribution of this book lies in Part II where international versions of the CAPM are set forth and tested. There is an excellent introduction to the international use of the mean-variance model in the paper by Levy and Sarnat. They calculate efficient international portfolios and examine the influence of foreign exchange rate risk on these portfolios. In particular they estimate efficient portfolios which allow for recent devaluations in the U.S. and Israel.

The paper by Bruno Solnik is a brilliant exposition of the advantages of international diversification. He shows graphically that the systematic risk remaining in an efficient domestic portfolio can be reduced by holding foreign securities. International diversification also lowers risk more than industry-wide diversification within any domestic market. Solnik's most provocative finding is that the U.S. systematic risk of 27 per cent can be reduced to 11.7 per cent by holding an efficient portfolio of international stocks. The gains in risk reduction are even greater for German and Swiss investors since the market risk of well diversified portfolios is greater in those nations than in the United States. Solnik's findings hold up even when allowing for no hedging against foreign exchange risk. If hedging is assumed then the gains from risk reduction are marginally greater.

Part II also contains two interesting empirical papers by Don Lessard of MIT, an out of place theoretical contribution by Subrahmanyam, a good article by the editors on the estimation of stock correlations and an examination of international mutual funds by Farber. Lessard applies the CAPM in a conventional manner and assumes that a world market factor can be constructed by weighting national stock market indices in various ways.

The main theme running through the book is the question of whether international capital markets are segmented or whether the users of an international CAPM can assume an integrated world capital market. The tendency has been to adopt the latter view despite observable barriers to capital flows imposed by governments as they attempt to manipulate their balance of payments accounts. All of the empirical work in this volume follows this course and uses the CAPM without much regard for its theoretical properties. For example: what is a suitable international risk free asset and what is a proper world market factor? To this writer it seems necessary to use a different approach; one which focuses on the rates of return of the shares of multinational versus non-multinational firms. The motivation for foreign direct investment is at the firm level and the multinational firm may well offer a substitute vehicle for the private foreign investment discouraged by government barriers to international financial capital flows.

The book is highly recommended since it gathers together recent research papers from a new sub-field of international finance. Most of the papers have been published in journals but this is the first collection. If further volumes are published in this series of studies in financial economics it is hoped that the editors will work a little harder. There should be a proper introduction which adequately summarizes the papers and an index should be added. The present volume is lacking the editorial standards of a Machlup and this does a disservice to the high quality of the contributions.

30 The Failure of World Monetary Reform, 1971–74

John Williamson
Sunbury-on-Thames: Thomas Nelson & Sons Ltd., 1977, xviii, 221 pp.

The Evolution of the International Monetary System, 1945–77

Brian Tew
London: Hutchinson & Co. Ltd., 1977, 254 pp.*

The tableau for Professor Williamson's monograph is the period of international monetary crisis heralded by the formal collapse of the Bretton Woods system in 1971. The reasons for the collapse are reviewed in the first two chapters, with the balance of the book exploring the labyrinthal negotiations of the Committee of Twenty (C20). For the early part of this period Professor Williamson was employed by the IMF, so he is able to present an insider's view of the negotiations. Fortunately his capacity for economic analysis has not been constrained by any residual feelings for official diplomacy, and he fires a heavy broadside at both the process and end results of the negotiations. His criticisms need to be taken seriously, since it is clear from the high quality of the writing that Professor Williamson has a good grasp of theoretical international monetary economics without being committed to any one school of thought. The balanced perspective resulting from a wide knowledge of the literature is combined with a feeling for political reality rare in most economists.

Professor Williamson is pessimistic about the outcome of C20. The reasons for regarding their efforts as a failure he explains in this manner: 'In comparison with the initial objectives of writing a new monetary constitution for the world these results were meager. There was no agreement on a set of rules for assigning adjustment responsibilities, no

---

*Economica, n.s. 45 (180) (November 1978): 421–422.

design of a viable adjustment mechanism, no introduction of an SDR standard, no substitution and no curb on the asymmetries' (p.73). The central theme of this statement, and others like it in the book, is that the final Jamaica agreement of 1976 did not introduce a new world monetary 'system' with adjustment and exchange rate obligations on its members. In retrospect this is not surprising, since the participating nations are not able to engage in effective domestic monetary policy, let alone agree on a set of international constraints. In the Western democracies there appears to be a built-in political bias towards inflation. Therefore it is unlikely that these nations will accept any international system which requires real internal adjustment. Today we have neither the automatic discipline of truly flexible exchange rates nor the policy adjustment required by fixed rates. Instead, internal adjustment can be postponed and world inflationary pressures are the external reflection of failures of domestic monetary policies.

Here I would take issue with some of the points made in Chapter 7 on the causes of failure. Professor Williamson argues that attempts to restore the adjustable peg, passive technical advice by the secretariat of the C20, and the unwillingness of the Europeans to accept US proposals for reserve indicators were the three major reasons for failure. To this reviewer it seems that all parties suffered from a lack of recognition of the theoretical advantages of adjustment by flexible exchange rates.

Professor Tew has revised his well-known textbook, but it does not compare very favorably with the standard economics texts now available by authors such as Grubel, Caves and Jones or Scammell. There is almost no account of recent theoretical developments, and this basic flaw is most apparent in the new Part Four, which is a mere catalogue of the events of 1971–1977. A little more analysis is present in the first three parts but even here the theory of Chapters 4–7 is not integrated into the chronicle which comprises the major sections of the book. Consequently, while a freshman student in university economics may find some basic details of what has occurred in the international monetary system, he or she will find little explanation of why the system has been so unstable. My advice to any serious student of international monetary economics would be to consult Williamson rather than Tew.

31 New Means of Financing International Needs

Eleanor Steinberg and Joseph A. Yager, with Gerard Brannon
Washington, DC: The Brookings Institution, 1978, 256 pp.*

The basic premise of this book is that the 'international community' has to mobilize a greater amount of money to meet the present and future needs of poorer nations. The authors interpret the new international economic order as 'calling for a massive, assured and continuing transfer of resources from the rich to the poor nations of the world' (p. 3). Given this interpretation of the central problem facing the world, the book proceeds to search for methods of financing the international redistribution of income. Allied to this basic premise is the assumption that the vehicle for world income redistribution should be international agencies such as the United Nations. It is hoped that some of the taxation systems to be considered by such world bodies will also have secondary benefits in reducing the present large amount of environmental degradation. Apparently the authors believe that the major environmental problems of oil spills, pollution of the oceans and atmosphere, and nuclear waste, can all be relieved by appropriate tax policy. This is most unlikely to happen and the authors should not have mixed up environmental concerns with their major theme of world income redistribution.

Two of the chapters are devoted specifically to environmental taxes. Chapter Four comes out strongly in favor of an effluent tax on polluters of the marine environment. It is thought that a tax of ten dollars a ton on ballast spillage from tankers will prevent most of the present oil spills. The authors also believe that annual revenue of between twenty-two and one hundred million dollars a year could be raised by this tax, or that the tax will induce tanker owners to adopt better technology and prevent spillage. In the latter case there is a social gain since that

---

*Kyklos 31(4) (1978): 738–739.

projected expenditure of twenty-five million dollars a year on cleaning beaches (plus that spent on preserving the world fishery) will be released for other international objectives. In Chapter Five it is argued that the future development of manganese nodules on the ocean floor will yield economic rents of as much as two hundred million a year. These rents are assumed to exist once the joint products of the nodules (namely nickel, copper, cobalt and manganese) are extracted for commercial use. Given the high risk of ocean mining and the uncertain nature of future world metal prices I doubt if the rents will be a great as anticipated. It is unwise to expect taxation of ocean resources to yield reliable international income in the future and consequently this method of raising revenue to help in world income redistribution should be forgotten.

Major errors of economic analysis occur in Chapter Three which was prepared by Professor Gerard Brannon. It examines several international revenue taxes, the first of which is a general tax on international trade. It is shown that an *ad valorem* tax of 0.1 per cent on world trade can yield a billion dollars of revenue. On the other hand, taxes on trade in energy materials, or on foreign investment income, would not yield nearly as much and would be more difficult to administer. It is concluded that 'the general trade tax is probably the best of the lot' (p.98). This is a terrible mistake. A tax on international trade, even a small one, will lead to distortions of relative prices of goods and factors in the tradable and non-tradable sectors and will severely disrupt potentially optimal patterns of exchange. It is necessary to foster free trade, as attempted in the efforts of GATT to reduce tariff and non-tariff barriers, rather than to hinder trade by the imposition of a general tax barrier. Another conceptual error occurs on page 87 where the authors assume that multinational corporations have untapped profits which can be siphoned off by a new international tax. They should contrast this mistaken view with their summary of an article by Professor H. G. Grubel on page 228. He finds that there is a net social loss to the United States on its international investment since tax credits are allowed on foreign taxes paid. Clearly a new international tax would have adverse effects on foreign investment.

Overall this is a very poor book. It suffers from a lack of application of basic international trade theory. It confuses equity and efficiency. Consequently we can have little faith in its conclusion that new international taxes will provide enough revenue for world income redistribution. Some of the taxes proposed, especially the general trade tax and tax on foreign investment, will reduce world welfare. Other taxes proposed, such as the shadow tax on GDP, taxes on the use of the international commons, and charges for pollution of the seas, make a little more economic sense.

32 A Framework of International Banking

Stephen F. Frowen (ed.)

*Guildford, UK: Guildford Educational Press/Philip Thorn Associates, 1979, xiv, 273 pp.**

The papers on international banking published in this book were first presented at a summer school for bankers held at the University of Surrey in England in July 1978. Its speedy publication is to be welcomed. The volume is edited by Stephen Frowen, a lecturer in monetary economics at that University. He appears to have chosen to let the papers stand as they were delivered, that is in the form of lecture material rather than as tightly edited research papers. This format should make the contributions easily accessible for the type of students who would be exposed to an introductory course in international banking, although it will not attract too many professional scholars. While the latter will look to journal articles for their sustenance, it is clearly of great value to have the essence of the recent literature on Eurocurrency markets distilled for a student audience, as the papers in this volume attempt to do.

Professor David Llewellyn contributes three excellent chapters on the theory and practice of international banking. Like other enlightened writers on the Eurocurrency market, such as Dufey and Giddy,[1] he explains that the process of international intermediation is similar in principle to domestic financial intermediation. The Eurodollar market 'has similar effects at the international level as do non-bank financial intermediaries (NBFIs) at the domestic level' (p. 7). He finds that Euro banks can operate on a narrower spread than domestic U.S. banks, since the former are not subject to regulation of interest rates or reserve requirements, have lower fixed costs and benefit from scale economies. Empirical evidence confirms that in recent years there exists a narrower spread between Euro-dollar borrowing and lending rates rather than between U.S. ones. Llewellyn finds that 'the Euro-dollar market is in truth an adjunct to

Southern Economic Journal 46(3) (January 1980): 990–991.

the New York money market and frequently Euro-dollar market transactions have a counterpart in the Federal Funds market' (p. 10). It is an inter-bank market and is an efficient mechanism for international financial intermediation. He states that the efficiency of the new international banking sector was demonstrated by the successful recycling of the OPEC financial surpluses via the intermediation of Euro banks.

Next are two statistical chapters by Geoffrey Dennis. These present tables and data on external bank positions, on the size of the Eurocurrency market, and on external bond and Eurocurrency credits in the private sector. Steven Davis contributes some more practical insights in his chapter on techniques in international banking and is especially good on the syndication of Eurocurrency loans and in his awareness of risk. There is also a rather out of place chapter on the debt servicing and other development problems of poorer nations. It is found that there 'is no magic formula awaiting discovery that will transform the debt problem of the LDCs overnight' (p. 173) and that 'the lending decision on any proposal will of necessity involve balancing risk against return' (p. 182). Paul Bareau is still around and he contributes the type of chapter on the evolution of the international monetary system that a former financial journalist would be expected to write. His reminiscences go back to the gold standard, through the Great Depression and Bretton Woods system up to the floating rates of today. Like several other chapters in the book it is rather redundant since relatively little economic analysis is used and the institutional details or history of events will be familiar to most readers, including the bankers and young financial executives for whom this book is designed.

In two chapters which are a little more analytical, Ray Shaw looks at the U.K. money market and the role of London as an (international) financial centre. He studies in Chapter 9 the development of six new money markets over the last fifteen years, namely: the Local Authorities market; the sterling inter-bank market; the Eurodollar market; the finance house market; the certificates of deposits markets in dollars and sterling; and the inter-company loans market. He finds a high degree of integration between the traditional sterling discount houses' market and the newer complementary money markets. Whatever problems for domestic monetary policy the new markets may create, the author concludes 'that the problems have been accentuated by the introduction of the new monetary controls' (p. 235). In Chapter 10 Shaw evaluates the net benefits for London as the world's major international banking center. He finds the relative advantages of London over other centers such as New York, the Bahamas and the Cayman Islands are in its excellent communications, its time zone location, and its historical banking structure. It is less attractive on the grounds of taxation and sterling exchange controls. Yet there is, in general, a 'liberal regulatory framework' (p. 237) and no controls on Euro bank operations. Shaw states that the Bank of England 'authorities have not found it necessary for monetary reasons to impose controls on banks' international foreign currency (Euro-currency) operations' since 'the Euro-currency market is regarded as fundamentally an efficient and useful international transmission mechanism for funds' (p. 238). There is a final chapter on the financing of North Sea Oil by R.J. Walton, a bibliography and an index.

The overall quality of the book is somewhat disappointing. None of the contributions contains any really new analysis or empirical work on the many Eurocurrency market hypotheses that need testing yet remain unresolved today. The book is written for and geared towards a British audience. The heavy institutional detail of the London money markets and the repetitive nature of several of the contributions on the Eurocurrency market will make the book of relatively limited value for North American students. But while it is not a great book, it is a competent one. It will be popular with bankers and students of international finance seeking an introduction to the ever changing subject of international banking.

Note

[1] Dufey, Gunter and Giddy, Ian H. *The International Money Market*. Englewood Cliffs, New Jersey: Prentice-Hall, 1978.

33 Mad Money: When Markets Outgrow Government

Susan Strange
Manchester, UK: Manchester University Press, 1998, 221 pp.[*]

As a founder of the field of international political economy, Susan Strange leaves an unrivalled legacy. No student of international affairs can afford to neglect her original insights into the political economy of post-war international institutions, in particular the international financial system. This is the focus of her latest book, a sequel to *Casino Capitalism*. Strange repeats her theme of an unregulated and volatile international financial system, badly in need of governance mechanisms. She updates events over the last decade and reports on the exploding academic literature in this area. There are good and bad parts of this book. The chapters of interpretation (principally 1, 8, 9, 10 which argue for regulation) are much weaker than those which stick to a descriptive narrative of the basic facts of innovations (2), creditors (3, 4, 5), debtors (6) and tax havens (7).

Chapter 2 is on product and process innovations in financial markets, due to 'computers, chips and satellites' (p.24). The coverage of derivatives (of which 98 percent are in contracts for foreign exchange currencies or interest rates), leveraged buyouts and junk bonds is mainly anecdotal. Strange blames 'non-decisions' of governments and 'deregulation' (p.36) for the excesses of these three instruments. Her key finding is that 'the roots of international money and financial policy can often be traced to the domestic politics of the United States, especially inasmuch as these relate to banking and finance' (p.40). She says that the proposition is not well known in the field of international relations. I agree, but note that those of us teaching in business schools developed this point 25 years ago to explain the emergence of the Eurocurrency market.

In Chapter 3 on the U.S.-Japan axis I liked the section in which Strange condemns Laura Tyson and the Berkeley Roundtable's advocacy

---

[*]*International Affairs* 75(2) (April 1999): 414.

of strategic trade policy as 'a euphemism for a more protectionist attitude towards Japanese imports into the U.S. market' (p.52). In Chapter 4 she argues that the Euro will be a source of volatility in currency markets at least until 2003. This uncertainty is essentially caused by 'the domestic politics of France and Germany' (p.60). As a result of these events Strange argues that, today, there is no hegemonic leader to provide global governance in financial markets. Instead, a type of collective leadership is required to regulate markets. Chapter 6 is on the Mexican peso crisis of 1994 and the contagion effect of the Asian financial crisis. Her analysis of the African debt trap and the institutional underfunding of Eastern Europe (for which there is no 1990s equivalent of the Marshall Plan of the 1950s) is balanced and insightful.

In Chapter 8, Strange reviews the regulatory policies of national governments and finds them to be deficient, especially in Britain and France, or country-specific as in the United States and Germany. Strange states that national governments are unable to regulate greed and fear – 'the two human emotions most evident in the day-to-day behavior of the international financial system today. *Mad Money* is the result!' (p.139). In Chapter 9 the two international institutions which attempt to regulate financial markets are considered; the BIS and IMF. Strange states that the emerging strategy of the BIS is to let the bankers regulate themselves, supported by technical advice. At the IMF there is more emphasis on arranging intergovernmental cooperation. Given the perceived, and actual, failure of a global governance system Strange's last chapter is an anti-climax. She presents several 'scenarios', none of which involves a realistic international institutional response to the perceived problems of volatility and deregulation of the world's financial system. Strange has made us aware of a problem which apparently has no solution.

34 Price Elasticities in International Trade: An Annotated Bibliography

Robert M. Stern, Jonathan Francis and Bruce Schumacher
*London: Macmillan for the Trade Policy Research Centre, 1976, 363 pp.**

This will become a useful reference manual for economists (and their research assistants) engaged in empirical work in international economics. It will be helpful in the area of commercial policy and in predicting the effects of exchange rate changes on the balance of payments. The annotated bibliography records price and income elasticities for all major nations at an aggregated and often a disaggregated level. Summaries are provided of about 130 articles and books, published over the period 1960-1975, in which any estimate of an international price elasticity has been observed. The summaries contain a presentation of the main empirical results of the study, together with a brief description of the theory (if any) behind the measurements, the functional forms specified and the techniques of estimation. There are no critical comments on the articles, and no attempts at synthesis except for a short introduction of twenty pages. The bibliographical indices are ordered by country or region, by commodity group and are arranged alphabetically.

The main findings are that for total imports the national figures for price elasticity range between –0.5 and –1.5. The estimates are generally higher for manufactured goods than for raw materials and semi-manufactures. There are considerable differences between price elasticities for different groups of goods on a more disaggregated level. The results tend to support the general view that a devaluation could be expected to improve the balance of trade for the devaluing country. Modern econometric work on price elasticities thus tends to refute a pessimistic view of the stability of the international price adjustment mechanism. Another conclusion is that when trying to forecast the effects of tariff reductions on the structure of trade and production, and thus comparing expected

---

*Kyklos (1977) 30(3): 570–571.

tariff effects for different product groups, it is essential to compute both the size of the tariff cuts and the individual price elasticities.

There is no general discussion in the book of the theoretical background, the econometric methods and the data available for these kinds of studies. Most of the articles are based on a fairly conventional model in which the quality of imports is either a linear or logarithmic-linear function of relative import price (the ratio of import price to the price of other domestic products) and of real income in the importing country. This equation is then estimated by ordinary least squares technique on time series data. This approach however is subject to certain econometric sources of error, which are generally supposed to tend to bias the elasticity estimates downwards. To overcome the drawbacks of the simple OLS approach, several studies have used more refined econometric techniques, in particular simultaneous equation estimation methods, and the introduction of lagged variables to allow for the time pattern of the response of imports to price changes. There are also studies which use other models, such as some type of trade flow model. Another problem is the quality of the data. Most studies use unit values as measures of prices in international trade, but these are generally held to be of very poor quality.

The bibliography is mainly based on work reported in academic journals. A certain amount of empirical estimation of import and export price elasticities is not covered. In particular, elasticity estimates that are part of bigger forecasting models employed by public agencies are missing but these omissions probably do not affect the general picture of the results. In conclusion, provided that due regard is made to their parentage, the elasticities reported here can be incorporated into research projects which attempt to evaluate the output and sectoral employment effects of proposed tariff cuts, changes in non-tariff measures, and exchange rate adjustments.

Fiscal Transfer Pricing in Multinational Corporations

G.F. Mathewson and G.D. Quirin
Toronto: University of Toronto Press, 1979, 162 pp.*

This is a rigorous theoretical and empirical treatment of transfer price manipulation by multinational corporations (MNCs) operating in Canada. The authors first develop a model with Cobb-Douglas production functions for several intermediate processes used in a final product sold in two countries. They calculate costs of labour and capital for these processes and find that in 1970 labour costs are a little lower in Canada than in the USA, but that the cost of capital is significantly higher, reflecting a greater perceived risk of the Canadian economy. Next they introduce tariffs and taxes and it is found that 'transfer pricing erodes the effect of the tariff,' and that the MNE can use internal prices to minimize the distortions of international tax rate differentials. Extending the model to three countries does not change these findings. The authors' empirical work is based upon the more general constant elasticity of substitution (CES) production function, which tends here to produce the same results as the Cobb-Douglas functions. Due to lack of company data on transfer pricing practices of MNCs the authors are forced to assume parameter values for their empirical analysis. The data problem is compounded by the difficulty of setting a price for intangibles and managerial services which are provided within the internal market of the MNE, but do not exist on a regular (competitive) market. The authors state that as many as 25,000 cases have been examined using their CES-based computer programme. The more interesting results are reported in the detailed appendix. On the basis of this exhaustive theoretical and empirical research work the authors conclude 'that multinationals have a relatively restricted scope for transfer price manipulation'.

---

* *The Economic Journal* 90(358) (June 1980): 460.

Transfer Pricing and Multinational Corporations: An Overview of Concepts, Mechanisms and Regulations

Sylvain Plasschaert

Farnborough, UK: Saxon House, 1979, 120 pp.*

This is a brilliant synthesis of the recent literature on transfer pricing. With no empirical work or elegant model to report, Professor Plasschaert is free to make a clear and definitive statement of the transfer pricing practices of multinational corporations (MNCs) within the context of the theory of internalization, which is being developed by economists associated with the University of Reading. Consistent with internalization theory, Plasschaert emphasizes the point that transfer pricing is a response of the MNC to exogenous market imperfections such as tariffs, international tax rate differentials, exchange controls, and tax havens. Such government-imposed market imperfections complement natural externalities in the areas of knowledge and technology. These international externalities act as inducements to the MNC to create and use its own market, in which transfer prices are merely the internal prices required to make this market work efficiently. As a result the MNC needs to have centralized financial management which uses internal pricing to ensure that the joint costs of ongoing, indivisible research and development are charged to all divisions of the MNC, rather than being borne by the parent alone. The continuous increase in the internalization ration makes these central insights of great relevance. Being one of the first authors to apply the Reading theory to the emotional issue of transfer pricing, Plasschaert is able to make valuable criticisms of the few existing empirical studies since they have neglected internalization theory He is also critical of much of the existing public policy in this area and suggests that transfer pricing be viewed in less pejorative terms by governments. This challenging analysis of the theoretical rationale for transfer pricing should be required reading for economic advisers and government bodies which deal with multinational corporations.

---

*Economic Journal 90(358) (June 1980): 460–461.

Measurement of Nontariff Barriers

Alan V. Deardorff and Robert M. Stern
Ann Arbor, MI: University of Michigan Press, 1998, 137 pp.*

This is a rather thin book, perhaps best classified as a literature review of the theoretical and empirical work on the measurement of non-tariff barriers to trade. As is characteristic of the distinguished dual author team, the book offers an incisive and comprehensive state of the art review. The authors have, of course, contributed to this area in the past and they build on their 1985 book, *Methods of Measurement of Non-Tariff Barriers*.

Chapter 2 uses a standard neo-classical partial equilibrium diagram to analyze the characteristics of non-tariff barriers in a manner similar to the analysis of the costs of the tariff. Chapter 3 reports on conceptual methods to measure non-tariff barriers to trade. This covers both general methods, as well as specific purpose and special measures. The authors favor price comparisons over quantity measures but caution that both approaches face severe practical empirical difficulties. An appendix provides useful formulas for measuring non-tariff barriers, given the problems involved.

Chapter 4 summarizes the empirical work of others as they have attempted to calculate non-tariff barriers in countries such as Australia, Canada, Germany, Norway, the E.U. and the United States. This includes work in Canada which has measured anti-dumping measures as non-tariff barriers. Finally, Chapter 5 is a brief set of conclusions with recommended procedures for measuring non-tariff barriers.

While no original empirical work is reported by the authors, their masterly summary of the literature on the methodology for measurement of non-tariff barriers will make this a useful book for many researchers in the years to come.

**The Economic Journal* Book Notes webpage listed 1999–July 2000 www.res.org.uk/ecojbknotes/default.asp

Rags and Riches: Implementing Apparel Quotas under the Multi-Fibre Arrangements

Kala Marathe Krishna and Ling Hui Tan
Ann Arbor, MI: University of Michigan Press, 1998, 255 pp.*

This book brings together a series of empirical studies and research projects headed up by the co-authors. The research began at the World Bank and half of the chapters have been published previously in refereed journals. The chapters test the rent sharing and quota implementation practices of the Multi-Fibre Agreement (MFA) across key exporting countries such as: Hong Kong, Korea, Indonesia, India, and Mexico.

The MFA began in 1973, but can be traced back to the cotton textile agreement of 1961. The MFA sets quotas on the exports of apparel and textiles by developing countries to developed countries, principally to the United States. Basically the MFA puts in place a set of negotiated imports to the US market by as many as 33 developing countries. It is planned to phase out the MFA by 2004. The allocation of quota licenses is in the hands of the exporting countries, thus permitting any rents to be retained by the developing countries. In practice, some rents may have to be shared with large importing organizations of the developed economies. Tests are conducted of such rent distribution. It is found that exporting countries do not receive the full quota rent suggested by the standard competitive model.

Due to data problems, only MFA exports to the United States are evaluated and this is done across ten apparel groups. There is considerable theoretical development and discussion of appropriate methodologies. The authors argue that this work on the MFA can be applied to other regulated markets, such as pollution permits and immigration quotas. Their findings on the MFA suggest that 'direct intervention can easily become a nightmare...' (p. 209) due to massive problems of implementation when markets are regulated. So while most of the

**The Economic Journal* 111(2000) Book Notes webpage, www.res.org.uk/ecojbknotes/default.asp

empirical research is about rents the authors are well aware of the welfare effects of inefficiencies due to quotas.

Unfortunately, the book is badly written. For example, the second sentence of the overview chapter is 81 words long. Even longer sentences occur thereafter. The contingent clauses make this a very difficult book to read. Luckily, there are lots of tables, equations and diagrams acting on a strong parallel text. But only specialist empirical trade economists will find this a useful study.

Trade Rules in the Making: Challenges in Regional and Multilateral Negotiations

M.R. Mendoza, P. Low and B. Kotschwar (eds)

Washington: Brookings Institution Press/OAS, 1999, xiii, 546 pp.[*]

The twenty-one essays in this book explore the economic, political, and legal aspects of a Free Trade Area of the Americas (FTAA). The papers were prepared for a 1988 conference sponsored by the Organization of the American States (OAS) and World Trade Organization (WTO). While the US political drive for the FTAA has been stalled by the lame duck Clinton administration, the book provides compelling background evidence of the benefits to the Western Hemisphere of an FTAA. It is also shown that an FTAA would be a form of regionalization compatible with the multilateral trade liberalization of the WTO.

The editors report that the essays have been written for policy makers and practitioners and that theoretical questions are not addressed. However, the command of institutional, especially trade law, detail shown by the majority of writers is impressive. The result is a state of the art review of the case for an FTAA.

In part I of the book authors such as Robert Z. Lawrence, demonstrate that a regional agreement, such as the FTAA, will be complementary to multilateral trade and investment liberalization. The regional agreements are drivers for multilateralism. For example, both the North American Free Trade Agreement (NAFTA) and the Southern Common Market (Mercosur) substantially lower tariffs and apply national treatment provisions for investors. Using NAFTA and Mercosur as building blocks for the FTAA will mean that article XXIV of the General Agreement on Tariffs and Trade is satisfied, i.e. that trade restrictions on 'substantially all' trade are removed and trade barriers are not raised against third parties.

---

[*] *The Economic Journal* 111(469) (Feb. 2001): F162–F163.

It is also argued in Part II on preferential trade and regional agreements that the FTAA will be of great benefit to the smaller countries of the Americas. For example, Barbara Kotschwar states that Caribbean and Central American countries will have better and more secure access to the large markets of North American through the FTAA, compared to the current fragile unilateral preferences.

The strongest set of chapters appears in the eight chapters of Part III on enhancing trade rules. Of particular interest are the findings by Brian Russell on the use of antidumping actions as new quasi-protectionist devices and by trade lawyer Gary Horlick on the abusive and weak legal rationale for anti-dumping investigations. Instead of this failed system, Murray G. Smith advocates the replacement of antidumping, and their legal brethren, countervailing duties, by a system of safeguards, i.e. temporary import relief measures outside of the appellate systems of the WTO.

The 'new issues' of the WTO are addressed in six essays in the last part of the book. Given the dominant role of multinational enterprises as drivers of international business, perhaps the most important is the one by Maryse Robert and Theresa Wetter on why rules for foreign direct investment need to be an integral part of the FTAA. They advocate the principle of national treatment and argue that most countries now adopt this non discriminatory legal standard already, as in NAFTA and Mercosur. There are also two chapters on competition policy (one by Monty Graham), one on government procurement, one on labor rights, and a final chapter by Gary Sampson on trade and the environment. Overall, economists will find this book rich in institutional detail, especially on the vital legal aspects of trade policy.

Globalisation and International Trade Liberalisation: Continuity and Change

Martin Richardson (ed.)
Cheltenham: Edward Elgar, 2000, 204 pp.[*]

The interesting papers in this book were first presented at a conference at the University of Otago in July 1999, just before New Zealand hosted the annual Asia Pacific Economic Community (APEC) Conference. Most of the papers are by economists familiar with the trade and investment pressures on smaller open, trading economies. Thus, in the discussion of globalization that pervaded the conference, the most striking paper is that by Canadian John Helliwell. He reports on provincial data for British Columbia, showing that it has twenty-one times more trade with Ontario than with U.S. border neighbor Washington, a result previously demonstrated for Canadian provinces at large, by John McCallum in his 1995 *A.E.R.* article. This reflects the tighter institutional and social fabric of trade within Canada, in contrast to U.S.-Canada trade, which lacks such historic and institutional depth.

In his insightful rapporteur's commentary, Tim Hazledine takes up this finding to conclude that 'national borders really do matter' (p. 187) and that a simplistic view of globalization as economic integration is not justified. However, he does not hit on the main reason for this – namely that the great majority of world trade and foreign direct investment is clustered in the intra-regional triad blocks of the E.U., North America and Japan, as I have demonstrated in my recent book, *The End of Globalization*. In a co-authored paper, Douglas Irwin argues that there is today a far greater degree of goods and capital market integration than a hundred years ago, particularly due to the importance of multinational enterprises. He also concludes that the IMF and its 'financial safety net may create moral hazard, but it at least prevents financial catastrophe' (p. 40) – an interesting contrast to the policy of the new U.S. Bush Administration.

[*]*Business Strategy Review* 12(2) (Summer 2001): 74.

The other insightful paper is by David Robertson, who accurately forecasts the disaster of having non-governmental organizations (NGOs) set the agenda for trade organizations like the WTO, instead of democratically elected governments. The members of the civil society are seen by Robertson to lack legitimacy and transparency. Writing before the WTO Seattle fiasco of December 1999, he stated that 'the threat that NGOs pose to a new round is real.' He also noted the slippery slope followed by the WTO appellate body in accepting two *amicus* briefs from NGOs in the shrimp-turtle case of 1998. But despite the excellent analysis and warnings of economists such as Robertson and myself, it is apparent that some trade lawyers have made a deal with the devil in supporting *amicus* briefs at the WTO and in regional agreements such as NAFTA. The real danger facing trade and investment liberalization in the future is the increasing influence of trade lawyers when compared to the competent economists contributing to this book.

Free Trade under Fire

Douglas A. Irwin.

Princeton, N.J., and Woodstock, UK: Princeton University Press, 2002, 270 pp.[*]

In a refreshing and well-written book, Douglas Irwin advances a modern defense of free trade and globalization. Soundly based in economic theory and using recent empirical research, he demonstrates the efficiency advantages of free trade and its potential to alleviate income disparities. The reason that free trade has not yet reduced world poverty is due to institutional constraints, political lobbies and other non-economic factors that are being exacerbated by the role of non-governmental organizations (NGOs). Irwin criticizes self-serving protectionists and environmental groups and the contingent protection of 'fair' trade. He examines the North American Free Trade Agreement (NAFTA) and the trade dispute mechanisms of the World Trade Organization (WTO) in an open and incisive manner, rebutting the wrong-headed criticisms of many NGOs.

The focus of the book is on U.S. trade policy. In Chapter 1 data are presented showing how trade has been of increasing importance in the U.S. economy since the 1970s. In 2000 U.S. exports were 7.8% of GDP and imports 12.3% of GDP. Yet as the U.S. economy has shifted from manufacturing towards services (especially health care, housing and education) the share of exports to manufacturing production has shot up from 15% in 1970 to 40% in 1999. In addition, there is now more trade in services; in 2000 U.S. service exports were 3.1% of GDP, moving total exports of goods and services up to 11.0% of GDP (imports are 14.7% of GDP). Over the same period, U.S. foreign direct investment (FDI) increased from 6% of GDP in 1960 to 20% in 1996, whereas inward FDI stood at 6.3% of GDP in 1998. Much of this is in the form of two-way trade in intermediate products (which facilitates outsourcing and vertical specialization). This yields even higher degrees of economic integration

[*]*International Affairs* 78(4) (October 2002): 909–910.

(for example between the United States, Canada and Mexico under the NAFTA provisions).

Chapter 2 reviews the theoretical and empirical case for free trade, or its converse, the costs of protection. There are gains in economic efficiency with free trade, provided that there also exists private property rights and a market mechanism. There are also substantial gains in productivity due to free trade. Despite these benefits in efficiency and productivity there are always rationales for protection. The employment rationale is described in Chapter 3 where it is found that any jobs saved by protection are lost elsewhere in the U.S. economy. Further, jobs in import-competing industries are generally low-skill and low-wage jobs. Chapter 4 derails the popular U.S. support for anti-dumping (AD) protection for domestic producers. Irwin states that the administration of AD is biased towards domestic plaintiffs and is inefficient as a result.

Chapter 5 reviews the history of U.S. trade policy while Chapter 6 looks at its relationship to the World Trade Organization. Since the 1936 Reciprocal Trade Agreements Act the United States has generally favored free-trade policies over protectionist ones, and it has pushed this agenda through post war multilateral institutions and now the WTO. In Chapter 6 the criticism of the WTO by environmentalists is examined, especially the dispute settlement cases such as tuna-dolphin and shrimp-turtle. These legal cases are badly misunderstood by NGOs and Irwin throws cold water over their muddled thinking on these cases. Overall, the book is a refreshing alternative to the recent anti-globalization literature; much of which Irwin demonstrates is at variance with the evidence.

Part III

Globalization and Economic Integration

Introduction to Part III

A large academic literature in the international business field suggests that multinational enterprises (MNEs) are the key drivers of globalisation. Yet many popular books on globalisation fail to recognise the nature, extent and business reality of MNEs as leaders of globalisation. Perhaps the most influential of these books is that by New York Times journalist, Thomas Friedman, *The World is Flat*. It has been reported that over three million copies have been sold, yet this book is based upon a faulty understanding of globalisation. It lacks any insight and balance into the underlying empirical context of world business.

Basically, Friedman makes one point in his book, namely, that today a large proportion of international business takes place through offshoring. There are two main sites for offshoring. First, much manufacturing and cost innovation takes place in China. Second, many service sector activities, especially in information technology sectors, take place in India. While both types of offshoring certainly exist (and are explained by factor cost conditions) it is apparent that Friedman vastly exaggerates the importance of offshoring beyond the information technology related area. His book largely consists of interesting and well-written anecdotes referring to this particular sector.

Friedman's model can be summarised in Figure 3 He develops an argument that today the world is characterised by globalisation 3.0. This is a situation where individuals are empowered to run global businesses. They can process information and organise activities with the use of personal computers and the Internet. This type of globalisation has replaced globalisation 2.0 in which multinational enterprises organised international activity. During this era of globalisation 2.0 which lasted from 1800 to 2000, MNEs grew and benefited from falling transportation costs (the development of railroads, bulk shipping lines, jet aircraft) and falling telecommunications. Previous to this type of globalisation, according to

Globalisation 1.0 1492–1800 Labor costs and natural resources	Country level
Globalisation 2.0 1800–2000 Multinational enterprises Falling transportation costs Falling telecommunication costs	Firm level
Globalisation 3.0 2000 to date Personal computers and Internet	Individual level

Figure 3   **Friedman's Flat World Model**

Friedman, there existed globalisation 1.0. This lasted from 1492 to 1800. International exchange was organised across and between countries. International trade was largely explained by labour cost differentials and the existence of natural resources (see Figure 3).

The theoretical logic behind Friedman's flat world model (to the extent that there is any theory) would be as follows: globalisation 1.0 is largely explained by international economics and the principle of comparative advantage. Countries specialise in the export of goods which use intensively their abundant factor (e.g., cheap labour or mineral deposits). Globalisation 2.0 is explained by theories of international business (MNEs internalise knowledge advantages and control these firm-specific advantages within wholly-owned subsidiaries). Globalisation 3.0 essentially has no theoretical support. It appears to assume that information exchange is free and that there are no barriers to entry in doing business anywhere in the world. Clearly globalisation 3.0 presents many challenges, and these are discussed in more detail later.

In Figure 4, these three types of globalisation are synthesised in a new matrix. On the horizontal axis I put the Internet which is available to a low or high degree. On the vertical axis I present the presence of multinational enterprises, again, to a low or high degree. In cell 2 Friedman globalisation 1.0 appears; neither MNEs nor the Internet are important. In cell 1, globalisation 2.0 appears. Here the role of MNEs is predominant, while the Internet is unimportant. In cell 4, globalisation 3.0 appears. Friedman argues that only the Internet matters and that MNEs have been replaced by individual business activity.

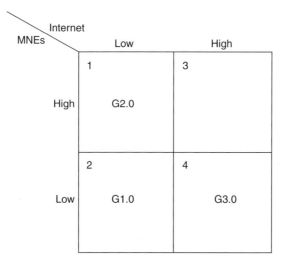

Figure 4 **Friedman's three types of globalisation**

In Friedman's book cell 3 is not discussed, yet this is clearly the cell where international business activity now takes place. In reality, individuals lack the financial resources, institutional learning advantages, and managerial expertise to build global businesses. Instead, in cell 3 both MNEs and the Internet are important. MNEs are better equipped than individuals to overcome the remaining frictions which constrain world business. These are in the form of government regulations, cultural and religious differences, and the persistence of historical and nationalist tendencies. While the Internet provides information on these issues it does not provide a mechanism to overcome them. In contrast, the MNE is better equipped to analyse and respond to such persistent differences. As shown below, the business world is largely divided into three broad regions of the triad. Doing business between the triad regions is extremely difficult. Only MNEs are able to tackle these triad barriers.

Building on this analysis, it is useful to reinterpret Friedman within the basic model used in the field of international business. This is the matrix relating country to firm factors, as first developed in Rugman (1981), and discussed as Figure 1. Recall that in Figure 1 country-specific advantages (CSAs) are shown on the vertical axis and firm-specific advantages (FSAs) on the horizontal axis. It is incorrect to generalise the country effect (the CSA axis in Figure 1) and make it the sole explanation of globalisation.

Instead, the firm effects need to be brought together, as in cell 3 of Figure 1. It can be seen that Friedman's book is mainly about cell 1 of Figure 1. He presents no evidence of the way FSAs can be developed such that CSAs in China and India are transformed by emerging economy MNEs into cell 3 firm-specific attributes.

This analysis counters the simplistic notions of writers such as Thomas Friedman. The world is not flat. International business suggests that there remain strong barriers as a business attempts to cross the boundaries of triad regions. It is pointless to assume globalisation; instead, it is necessary to investigate the manner in which a firm's business model may need to be adapted such that its FSAs can overcome the liability of inter-regional foreignness.

The Lexus and the Olive Tree

In an earlier influential book, *The Lexus and the Olive Tree*, Thomas Friedman uses the Lexus as a symbol for economic integration. In contrast, the olive tree is a symbol for the historical, political, religious and social aspects which present obstacles to economic integration. Therefore, the logic of the Lexus view of globalisation would fit on the vertical axis of Figure 5, whereas the olive tree would be assigned to the horizontal axis representing a need for national responsiveness. Friedman himself

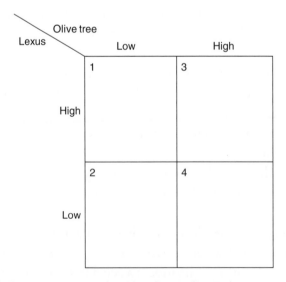

Figure 5 **Globalisation (Lexus) and Nationalism (Olive Tree)**

discusses the extreme cases of the Lexus in cell 1 and the olive tree in cell 4. However, based on our analysis of Figure 5 it is apparent that cell 3 represents another interesting case where both globalisation and national responsiveness are equally important. (This is the same as the earlier Figure 4). The other point is that Figure 5 is a strategy diagram to be put into operation by managers of MNEs (or other firms). Therefore, it is the interpretation of the Lexus and the olive tree axes which is important for strategic management. A potential for strategy in cell 3 of Figure 5 would require that an MNE is able to organise itself to cope with both axes.

Regional versus global integration

The final problem with Friedman's naive concept of globalisation is that it is refuted by the empirical evidence. In terms of integration, Friedman is partially correct in arguing that financial capital, ideas, knowledge and technology are now moving more quickly across countries. In particular, there is a faster rate of exchange across these dimensions between the core triad economies of the United States, Japan, and the EU on the one hand and the emerging economies of India and China on the other. However, empirical evidence indicates that these transfers largely occur within the home regions of the broad triad, rather than globally. If we look at the major vehicles for globalisation, namely MNEs, we can see from the summary data in Table 1 that the world's 500 largest firms average 76 per cent of their sales in their home region. Intra-regional sales in the manufacturing MNEs average 65.6 per cent while in service firms (which have always been thought to be more home oriented) they average 84 per cent. Furthermore, there is no discernible trend away from intra-regional sales and towards globalisation over the 2000 to 2006 time period.

Table 1 also shows in panel B that the world's 500 largest firms have 78 per cent of their foreign assets in their home region of the broad triad (defined as North America, East Asia, and the EU). Again, manufacturing is slightly more global with manufacturing assets averaging 71 per cent in the home region whereas services are very parochial, averaging 84 per cent of their foreign assets in their home region.

The conclusion to be drawn from this analysis of the best selling work on globalisation is that Thomas Friedman vastly exaggerates the nature

Table 1 **Intra-regional sales and assets of the largest firms in the service and manufacturing sectors**

Panel A. Intra-regional Sales				
Year	Number of firms	Intra-regional Sales (%)		
		All industries	Manufacturing	Services
2000	437	77.2	67.3	84.2
2001	511	76.7	66.0	84.3
2002	514	76.5	65.9	84.1
2003	513	76.5	65.6	84.3
2004	526	76.1	65.3	84.1
2005	529	75.5	65.1	83.3
2006	503	74.8	64.6	82.6
Weighted Average		76.2	65.6	83.9

Panel B. Intra-regional Assets				
Year	Number of firms	Intra-regional Assets (%)		
		All industries	Manufacturing	Services
2000	358	78.4	70.9	84.5
2001	413	77.4	70.4	83.3
2002	427	77.7	70.5	83.8
2003	431	78.0	70.9	83.9
2004	452	78.3	71.0	84.3
2005	461	78.3	71.2	84.1
2006	435	78.0	71.1	83.8
Weighted Average		78.0	70.8	84.0

Source: Annual reports for 2000–2006. Sample firms are included if they appear on the list for any year of the *Fortune* Global 500 during 2000–2006.

and extent of globalisation. The data indicate that the world's largest 500 firms (which account for over 90 per cent of the world's stock of foreign direct investment and half the world's trade) perform on a regional rather than a global basis. Since these large firms are often the flagship firms in business clusters to which many small and medium sized enterprises are affiliated it is highly likely that the entire business system is regional rather than global. While Friedman is correct in noting the increase in economic integration he fails to understand that this internationalisation has taken place on an intra-regional basis, not a global one.

For more discussion of the regional nature of multinational enterprises, see Rugman (2005). A related book by Ghemawat, which also finds a lack of Friedman type globalisation appears as Review 59 in this part. Readers interested in a book which largely supports Friedman can see Review 56 of the book by Govindarajan and Gupta. While this book has many excellent implications for strategic management, especially its focus on the business unit, there is a lack of rigorous empirical work and an over-reliance on case studies, some of which are misinterpreted. For example, as argued in my review, the Wal-Mart example is actually a study of frustrated globalisation since the firm has only succeeded in international expansion in North America. Wal-Mart has not adapted its business model to the realities of the triad markets of Asia and Europe. In summary, it is very important to always examine the empirical evidence before jumping on the bandwagon of globalisation.

The literature on globalisation exploded in the 1990s. Before that the field of international business actually dealt with the topic of globalisation, but did not call it that. Here two reviews numbers 42 and 43 deal with issues in economic development and the role of MNEs in fostering it (Review 42) or hindering it (Review 43). Review 44 looks at the role of small business using the experience of Germany as an example. This book was an early signal that the research on 'born globals' in the area of international entrepreneurship was likely to be at variance with the basic empirical data. Although the author of this book extolled the high export propensity of German small business, I found that virtually all exports went to Germany's immediate neighbouring countries in the European Community. Germany's small business had almost no 'international' trade outside of the institutional framework of the EC. This was an early indication of the regional nature of both big business and the small and medium sized enterprises associated with MNEs in localised clusters.

Reviews 45 to 53 were written while I was a research fellow at Templeton College, University of Oxford. The book by Anthony Giddens is typical of the superficial thinking and empirical ignorance portrayed by modern critics of the process of globalisation. Giddens and some of the other authors of the books reviewed (46 to 50) show a consistent neglect of the nature and extent of MNE activity and the regional manner in which it is conducted. Indeed, Giddens seems to assume that globalisation only consists of the actions of US MNEs. He does not understand the nature of the triad and the offsetting presence of large European and Japanese MNEs. While I believe that analysis of globalisation needs to understand the basic mechanisms of worldwide economic integration, and the precise nature of MNE activities, I am sympathetic to other views which examine the sociological, cultural, and political aspects of globalisation. Yet, here again, much of the literature appears to ignore the basic data relevant to these areas.

Overall, reading the set of books on globalisation published over the 1999 to 2000 period reveal basic errors in the use of empirical data and a general lack of understanding of the principles of international business, as I point out in my reviews. Fortunately, some of the other books reviewed here, 51 to 59, reveal more sophistication in their treatment of globalisation. I respond more favourably to insights in these books, especially to the thinking of Ohmae in Review 54, Spar in Review 55, and Ghemawat in Review 59. The only book drawing serious criticism is Review 57 which discusses the 2002 book by Joseph Stiglitz, which I summarise as 'vastly disappointing'. The reason is that throughout his criticisms of the World Bank, IMF and other institutions, Stiglitz fails to discuss MNEs and their role as key agents in economic development. This is a book which would fall into the old style category of economics books from the 1960s, previously reviewed in Part II. Stiglitz needs to realise that international institutions and the country effect are at best half of the answer to economic development. The other half has to be the agent which actually does business in developing countries, namely the MNE. My conclusion is that work on globalisation needs to thoroughly embed analysis of the MNE; otherwise a book on globalisation is likely to report half-baked ideas at best and nonsense at worse.

References

Friedman, T.L. (2003) *The World is Flat*. New York: Farrar, Straus and Giroux.
Rugman, A.M. (2005) *The Regional Multinationals*. Cambridge: Cambridge University Press.

Between Dependency and Autonomy: India's Experience with the International Computer Industry

Joseph M. Grieco

*Berkeley: University of California Press, 1984, x, 224 pp.**

This is a beautifully written account of an important case study of the transfer of technology between multinational enterprises (MNEs) and developing countries. The case study deals with the bargaining between India and the international computer industry, especially IBM, over the 1960–80 period. It is carefully researched and blends key elements of both economics and political science with a detailed historical analysis of the nature of the computer industry in India at a critical stage of its planning for self-reliant development.

Joseph Grieco's primary thesis is that there has been a shift in power away from MNEs toward host-nation governments, including some 'assertive' developing countries. His evidence is based entirely on the role of the computer industry in India. Grieco demonstrates that the ability of the Indian central government to negotiate successfully with MNEs such as IBM increased over the period being examined. The result was a transfer of technology in which India 'enlarged its share of the benefits resulting from interactions between the country and the industry' (p.1).

In Chapter 2 Grieco views India's experience in data processing and with computing MNEs over the 1960–80 period. He states that in 1966 the Indian government set an explicit goal of national self-sufficiency in computers, built on a state-supported enterprise, ECIL. This objective of computer autonomy was not fully achieved, but India was able to restructure its relationships with foreign computer firms to make them more consistent with its policy. An important demonstration of this policy was the forced exit in 1978 of IBM from the Indian market, in which it had held the major share until 1973. Grieco is, however, critical of the central government's handling of this industry leader,

*Business History Review 59(3) (Autumn 1985): 533–535.

stating that 'the government's inflexibility with regard to IBM did lead to the imposition of several unnecessary costs on the country's ability to meet its own computer objectives' (p.46). He also finds that the target of increased computer autonomy was achieved only because of the unanticipated success of several private indigenous computer firms, which compensated for the relative failure of ECIL to produce a sufficient number of modern computer systems, a deficiency made up by imports.

In Chapter 3 Grieco develops the argument that India's bargaining power with the MNEs was partly improved by the increasing international competition among MNEs. In turn this resulted from the breakdown of entry barriers to the international computer industry following the introduction of mini- and microsystems and peripherals, with the consequent spread of component manufacturing to smaller firms than the original integrated mainframe MNEs. In subsequent chapters, Grieco shows that India was able to modify its computer policy by changing to a systems-engineering approach, using imported components to substitute for ineffective domestic production by its 'national champion', ECIL. The Indian government was also able to attract Burroughs to the country on favorable terms, that is, in a joint venture, and to retain the presence of ICL, even after increasing local equity participation and management. This was probably due more to the decentralized nature of ICL than to any specific attribute of Indian policy.

Grieco feels that the successful Indian experience with MNEs can be generalized to other 'assertive' upper-tier developing nations, such as Brazil, Mexico, Colombia, Indonesia, Nigeria, and Venezuela. Yet clearly India's protectionist stance toward MNEs should be contrasted with the positions of the newly industrialized nations of Southeast Asia, whose trade-assisted growth has been phenomenally successful compared with India's.

Grieco's empirical findings (in Chapters 4 and 5) suggest that the dependency school of thought is analytically inferior to the bargaining school, which argues that the long-term balance of power can favor developing nations rather than MNEs. Members of the bargaining school, such as Robert Keohane and Joseph Nye, Raymond Vernon, Charles Kindleberger, and others (mainly economists), are said to believe that the initial technological and knowledge advantages of the MNEs are gradually eroded as contact with the host nations increases over time.

The Indian experience with the computer industry appears to confirm the thesis that prolonged exposure to the MNEs improves the ability of developing nations to negotiate and manage their relations with such firms.

Grieco's work offers major support for the bargaining-school viewpoint, since computers are obvious examples of high-technology products, over which MNEs should possess strong firm-specific advantages. Related evidence is coming from the pharmaceuticals industry about the power of host governments to compromise such knowledge advantages. If host governments can indeed exert control over the high-tech MNEs, then clearly resource-based MNEs, and MNEs in mature industries (with no risk of knowledge dissipation) are even more vulnerable to bargaining pressures. Yet what are the efficiency effects of such distributional controls and regulations?

I do not feel that Grieco pays enough attention to efficiency issues in his analysis. He certainly does not produce any measures of efficiency losses resulting from bargaining over the distribution of technological advantages. While India may have achieved more autonomy and increased its bargaining power over MNEs, these distributional gains have been attained only at a considerable cost in lost efficiency. The exit of IBM is a case in point. As an MNE concerned with its social responsibility, IBM has a corporate strategy of running a balance of trade by nation. The forced exit of IBM in practice worsened India's balance of technological payments, thereby offsetting many of the alleged benefits of self-sufficiency, which could not be achieved in any case, given the nature of interdependent global technological developments. The lessons are not new: protectionist policies always have welfare costs and no nation is an island unto itself. Policymakers in advanced as well as in developing nations need to wrestle with the twin objectives of distribution and efficiency, neither of which can be achieved without repercussions on the other.

43 Transnational Monopoly Capitalism

K. Cowling and R. Sugden
Brighton, UK: Wheatsheaf Books, 1987, vii, 178 pp.[*]

The objective of this book is to extend the analysis of monopoly capitalism to the multinational enterprise (MNE). Cowling and Sugden call an MNE a 'transnational corporation'. This is an example of a basic tenet of industrial organization scholarship known as product differentiation. It is also an example of the authors' ability to call a spade an 'expletive deleted shovel' whenever possible. Footnote 1 tells us that the book should have been called 'Oligopoly Capitalism' as the models apply to 'the quite general, perhaps ubiquitous case where markets are dominated by a few corporations...' (p. 7).

It is stated that the book is addressed to the 'new imperialism of free trade orchestrated by the transnationals...' (p. 2) and that the 'central focus...' is '...on the consequences of the evolution of the monopoly capitalist system for the distribution of income...' (p. 2). Allegedly MNEs earn '...a rising profit share...' which implies '...a secular stagnation tendency' and the undemocratic '...imposition of a world cultural homogeneity...' (p. 2, 3). This book admirably meets its objectives. Yet, why any serious student of the MNE would wish to read this sixties nonsense is a puzzle. In this review I shall comment on some of the more blatant Marxist biases in the thinking of Cowling and Sugden. Readers of this work can identify their own favorites.

The relentless pursuit of distributional dogma leads the authors to the development of hypotheses clearly at variance with the facts. For example, in Chapter 5, the argument is made that a cause of deindustrialization is an increase in the militancy of organized labour, which leads to a wage-price spiral causing capital to migrate to lower-cost economies offshore. This thesis is applied to explore recent British experience where it is

---

[*]*Economic Record* 68(190) (September 1989): 314–315.

alleged that MNEs have gone elsewhere to escape high labour costs. In doing so, MNEs escape the true social costs of such alleged capital flexibility at the expense of labour rigidity. The nomadic nature of capital is said to define MNEs as undemocratic institutions. Hymer said all this nearly 30 years ago.[1]

The logic of this is all wrong, as was Hymer. If the British (or 'foreign') capitalists experience wage distortions due to militant unions then this problem should be corrected at its source, i.e. in the labour market. A critique of the MNE, which responds to such environmental parameters is out of line. The authors' hang-up is in treating the MNEs as 'capital.' Instead, the MNE is better viewed as a hierarchy replacing a market.[2] The MNE embodies real, rather than purely financial, assets and it is a complex microeconomic actor rather than an input into the production function. In any case, sovereign governments, such as Thatcherite Britain, would appear to have solved such factor market distortions. Further, MNEs are not carpetbaggers; they are valuable contributors to host country employment, investment and wealth. They exhibit corporate social responsibility and operate subject to home and host country regulations, standards and controls. Frequently, they face sunk costs and other exit barriers. The nature of business–government relations is interactive and not the simplistic 'MNEs as nomads' picture painted by Cowling and Sugden.

What do the data actually show? Britain has lost some MNEs, principally American; it has gained others, notably European and Japanese. The most overwhelming fact of modern MNE activity is the incredible amount of two-way direct investment in advanced industrialized nations including Britain. Even the United States, now the world's largest debtor nation, still receives vast inflows of direct investment. Today, in North America, amounts of inward and outward direct investment both increase as the dynamic nature of global competition unfolds. The same is true within the European Community, and increasingly, in Japan. In these seats of triad power MNEs from home bases in Europe, American and Japan compete abroad for global market shares yet, simultaneously adapt their product lines to service local tastes and meet sovereign regulations and standards.

The reason for today's two-way flows of direct investment lies in the complex nature of modern MNEs, especially the 'services' component of much of their activity. In Canada, 70 percent of all jobs are in service industries, many of them in the MNEs. Canada would be 'deindustrialized' in the Cowling-Sugden model, but Canadians would be better off as a result. The children of farmers, miners and mill workers are now well paid bankers, social workers and economics professors. Occupational mobility into service industries facilitates the mobility of capital in MNEs which are both home and host-country based.

Cowling and Sugden fail to recognize that, today, MNEs compete with each other for global market shares. In a dynamic and interdependent global economic system the successful MNEs are simultaneously efficiency seekers and nationally responsive. They are concerned with economies of scope not just economies of scale. The ability to adapt their products and services to national tastes and regulations involves internal governance costs which largely offset any perceived economic rents. Cowling and Sugden have it all wrong; the successful MNE is observed to be responsive to national regulations. The MNE, today, has to be everyone's friend and neighbour. The true nature of managerial decision making in the MNE cannot be captured in any realistic manner by antiquated models of international monopoly capital.

Notes

[1] Stephen H. Hymer (1960) *The International Operations of National Firms*. Cambridge, MA: MIT Press. (Reissued in 1976.)

[2] Alan M. Rugman (1981) *Inside the Multinationals: The Economies of Internal Markets*. New York; London: Croom Helm: Columbia University Press.

44 Juggernaut: The German Way of Business

Philip Glouchevitch
*New York: Simon and Schuster, 1992, 238 pp.**

President-elect Bill Clinton will probably make the U.S. trade deficit with Japan the cornerstone of his trade and industrial policy. But if he were guided by *Juggernaut: The German Way of Business*, he'd see the tremendous economic and political power of Germany as no less significant. Says the book: 'While we should not view German business as a menacing power determined to destroy everything in its path, it would be naïve for Americans to ignore the fact that the Japanese are not the only economic threat we face. We do ourselves a disservice to ignore Germany's increasing economic – and political – power.'

As the quote illustrates, this book is written from an ethnocentric American viewpoint. That's not unreasonable, given the author's intended audience and agenda. But even if we can't demand that Glouchevitch be conscious of Canadian sensibilities or of the Canada–U.S. free trade pact, it still gets tiresome to read that 'we' need to learn about the German threat, when Canada's economic relations with Germany are quite different from those of the U.S.

Despite this, *Juggernaut* offers three interesting ideas to Canadians thinking about Clinton's likely global economic policy.

First is the nature of the small- and medium-sized German companies called the Mittelstand. Daimler-Benz, Bosch, Hoechst, Porsche, Siemens and Volkswagen are all familiar names. Their global success depends largely on the partnerships they have built with the Mittelstand. These are the core of the German business system, which some Canadian experts believe could be role models for our own firms.

Unfortunately, the social and historical reasons that have given rise to these obsessively secretive, family-run companies are extremely unlikely to be replicated here. The role played by the German banking system, with

Financial Times of Canada (December 12, 1992): 23.

131

its close ties to business, is illegal in Canada. The lack of disclosure and limited partnerships characteristic of the Mittelstand are also unlikely to occur here. Another recurring theme is Germany's alleged social consensus. Much is made of the German model of worker participation, collective bargaining and social equity. While there is some truth to this view, the actual practice is much more complicated; indeed, it is too specific to Germany for Canada to copy. For example, Glouchevitch notes that the family-run Mittelstand operate in a paternalistic and anti-union manner: 'Many companies function more like patriarchies than like corporations.'

They practise what might be called 'village capitalism' with a clear hierarchy from owner down to worker. The superficial observation that the owners work hard, often down on the factory floor, does not overcome the German tradition of learning to follow orders through the apprenticeship system. In a society with great respect for wealth and power, one owner's 'social responsibility' is another worker's paternalism.

The third theme of relevance to Canadians in Germany's place in the EC; the fact that most of its trade and investment is with EC partners is a major reason for its spectacular growth. The author states that 'companies with fewer than 500 employees and sales under DM 100 million generate half the country's national production, employ two-thirds of all working citizens and account for over two-thirds of all exports.'

The primary lesson for Canada offered by *Juggernaut* is that we need to access to a triad market. The FTA, and proposed NAFTA, give Canadian business the same opportunity to build successful global industries that Germany has had from its presence in the EC. Yes, German business is a juggernaut. But it is of much less concern to Canadians than the juggernaut to the south.

Runaway World: How Globalization Is Reshaping Our Lives

Anthony Giddens
*London: Profile, 1999, xiii, 104 pp.**

Giddens himself defines globalization too broadly: 'Globalization is polit-ical, technical and cultural, as well as economic' (p.10). He states that globalization is 'new' and 'revolutionary' and is mainly due to the 'massive increase' in financial foreign exchange transactions. This has been facil-itated by the dramatic improvement in communications technology, especially electronic interchange facilitated by personal computers. The trouble with this very broad perspective is that the key drivers of glob-alization, the MNEs, are badly misrepresented. International trade and multinationals have existed for two millennia. They have not led to deterritorialization and the nation state has developed and continues to flourish, setting laws and regulations that affect business.

In his first BBC Reith Lecture for 1999, Anthony Giddens painted a vivid portrait of all that is wrong with globalization. His views are representative of those of other recent critics of globalization such as Susan Strange (1998) and others. The pace of science, technology and electronic interchange has increased risk and given people the feeling that they are not in control of their lives – that it is a runaway world. Globalization is said by Giddens to be led by the West as it 'bears the strong imprint of American political and economic power' (p.4). With this statement, Giddens is today still making the mistakes of writers in the 1970s who argued that the power of the nation-state was being eroded by the MNEs. Giddens states that he agrees with the radical statement that nations have lost most of the sovereignty they once had.

Yet even the data on the triad-based disposition of the world's 500 largest MNEs are not all well understood by the critics of globaliza-tion. For example, Anthony Giddens states that 'many of the most visible cultural expressions of globalization are American – Coca-Cola,

Business Strategy Review 12(2) (Summer 2001): 69–70.

McDonald's, CNN' and that 'most of the giant multinational companies are based in the US too' (p.15). Yet only 185 of the world's largest 500 MNEs are American while 256 are either European or Japanese-based. Basically, the facts disagree with Giddens. His misunderstanding of these most basic data makes one wonder about the value of other statements.

Globalization and Culture

John Tomlinson
Cambridge: Polity Press, 1999, 238 pp.*

The word 'globalization' is much abused and presents a problem for scholars across the social sciences who define it from the viewpoint of their own discipline. For an economist and business school professor such as myself, globalization can be defined as 'the activities of multinational enterprises engaging in foreign direct investment to create foreign subsidiaries which add value across national borders.' For sociologists, such as the author of the book, the definition is much broader. John Tomlinson argues that an economic definition of globalization is too narrow, instead it is multidimensional, best 'understood in terms of simultaneous, complex related processes in the realms of economy, politics, culture, technology and so forth' (p.16). John Tomlinson's book is out of the Anthony Giddens publishing stable and, for obvious reasons, Giddens is quoted frequently, appearing 38 times in the index with entire paragraphs being reproduced from his numerous self-published books. Despite the unnecessary jargon from the academic literature of social theory the book is clearly written with numerous contemporary examples.

There are six chapters in the book. The first defines globalization and culture in the broad manner discussed above. The second, on 'global modernity' discusses social and cultural aspects of the process of the 'lived experience' of the 'complex connectivity' of global modernity. This builds on Giddens' argument that, with globalization, social relations are no longer local but stretch across time and space. In Chapter 3, the linkage of global modernity to global culture is discussed. This contrasts the power of multinational enterprises to distribute a 'global capitalist monoculture' with a more sceptical 'realist' viewpoint about the highly regulated and divided world system in place today. Tomlinson concludes that 'there is

**International Affairs* 75(4) (October 1999): 837.

little here to support the view that a single, unified global culture in any conventional sense is about to emerge' (p.105). Earlier, culture was defined as 'the social production of existentially significant meaning' (p. 21). Chapters 4 and 5 introduce a second major theme, namely that 'deterritorialization' of culture is occurring due to the hybridization of cultures. This process is being speeded up by global mass media and communications technologies. Tomlinson's conclusion is that a complex, deterritorialized, globalized culture is emerging rather than a simplistic, monolithic, global culture. The complexity exists because culture is not linked to local nation states – it is deterritorialized. This, in turn, links to a cultural process of enforced proximity and cosmopolitan politics, the subject of the last chapter.

Future Positive: International Cooperation in the 21st Century

Michael Edwards
*London: Earthscan, 1999, 302 pp.**

Michael Edwards has worked for Oxfam, Save the Children and the World Bank. Based on his experience in international development efforts, he has rediscovered the need for a middle way in economic development – 'between heavy-handed intervention and complete laissez-faire' (p.vi). He is quite critical of today's global 'system', which fails to distribute growth and incomes on an egalitarian basis. He states that globalization has costs as well as benefits. He advocates measures to 'humanise capitalism', but is not in favor of government planning. His solution is to have more effective international co-operation, based on a stakeholder model of capitalism. Agencies like Oxfam should 'spearhead a global movement for change' (p. 231). This will provide, suggests Edwards, quicker and better responses to humanitarian emergencies and global poverty by the 'great powers' (p. 225). I am not so sure that Edwards' views are as balanced as he thinks. For example, he is critical of 'irresponsible lending' and states that 'the point of global governance is not to organize world affairs for the benefit of speculators, but to promote reforms that are in the common interest, and despite the claims of economists there is no guarantee that markets will do this better than governments' (p.170). This is followed by criticism of a Multilateral Agreement on Investment, which has excluded poor countries, and the trade liberalizing efforts of the GATT and WTO, whose appellate procedures are criticized as mechanisms which 'accelerate the international transmission of inequality' (p. 173). These are not middle of the road views but sadly misinformed ones. However, as this book is well written in a non technical style, and contains some engaging examples from Asian and African countries, it may be of some interest to left of centre students and community activists.

International Affairs 76(1) (Jan. 2000): 151–152.

48 Globalism and the New Regionalism

Bjorn Hettne, András Inotai and Osvaldo Sunkel (eds)
Basingstoke: Macmillan, 1999, 312 pp.[*]

'New' regionalism is defined in this book 'as a multidimensional form of integration which includes economic, political, social and cultural aspects...' (p. xvi). It goes beyond the 'old' regionalism of a quarter century ago which was concerned only with the economics of free trade regimes and customs unions or the politics of security alliances. However, the new regionalism is a complement to globalization, not a substitute for it. It complements the mostly economic aspects of globalization by adopting a broader, multidimensional challenge to the Westphalian nation-state. In new regionalism there are multiple stakeholders and a multipolar global order.

The EU is the only core region with a formal political organization, since North America (with the North American Free Trade Agreement (NAFTA)) and the Asia-Pacific (with APEC) lack a regional political order although they are pursuing increased economic integration. There are intermediate regions being drawn into these three core regions, a process which has the appearance of globalization, but one which is quite different. In some cases (US–Canada in NAFTA) new regionalism is replacing bilateralism; in others (South Asia) it is not. Hettne argues that new regionalism is supposed to contribute to the three preferred outcomes of peace, development and ecological sustainability. Percy Mistry argues in Chapter five that new regionalism can support a new multilateralism; other contributors have little faith in this development.

New regionalism is a big tent. It can accommodate the moderate liberal views of Hettne and Mistry with the extremist rhetoric of Samir Amin (who defines globalization as the five monopolies over technology, finance, resources, media and weapons of mass destruction) and Richard

---

[*] *International Affairs* 76(1) (January 2000): 146.

Falk's long list of aspects of 'negative globalism.' These papers were developed at conferences over the 1994–6 period and their impact is somewhat diminished by the long delay in publication. Most of these ideas have been discussed in the journals and at other conferences for the last several years.

Globalisation and the Asia-Pacific: Contested Territories

Kris Olds, Peter Dicken, Philip F. Kelly, Lily Kong and
Henry Wai-chung Yeung (eds)
*London; New York: Routledge, 1999, 293 pp.**

This is the second book published by the Centre for the Study of Globalisation and Regionalisation at the University of Warwick. The Centre, directed by Professor Richard Higgott, has received £2.5 million from the Economic and Social Research Council. It states that it has an interdisciplinary agenda and it defines globalization as multidimensional. As this reviewer has argued, especially in my recent, *The End of Globalization*, such a broad definition leads to the agenda being diverted from hard analysis of the economic activities of multinational enterprises (the drivers of globalization, or in reality triad-based regionalization) towards more philosophical navel-gazing by sociologists, political scientists and geographers, among others.

This book of 14 essays is no exception. It is based on papers presented at a conference in Singapore in 1997. The editors attempt to set the book against the economic background of the Asian financial crisis of 1997–8, but almost immediately concludes that the 'Asian Miracle was never just about economics, and debates over its causes and consequences have always been interwoven with discussions of cultural identity, political reform, environmental impacts and human development' (p.10). This indeed becomes the agenda for the book and a carte blanche for critics of global capitalism, such as Dirlik, Jessop, Sassen, Mittelman, Schiller and Kong.

No clear message emerges from the book despite the attempt of the Warwick team to address the pressing issues of globalization and economic development in the Asia-Pacific. The reason is that the disciplinary blinkers of the writers blinds them to look at the symptoms of globalization – its alleged convergence towards social and cultural

---

International Affairs 76(4) (October 2000): 904.

homogenization and its threat to political regimes, rather than at the economic causes of globalization. The impact of globalization stems from the economic benefits of foreign direct investment (FDI) by multinational enterprises. Yet only three of the 14 essays address these topics: the chapter by Dicken and Yeung on Asian firms investing abroad; the chapter by Thrift on business knowledge; and the chapter by Paderanga on FDI and the Philippine economy. Dicken and Yeung provide convincing aggregate trade and FDI data to show that Asian firms now operate interregionally rather than globally. While Japanese FDI flows in East and South-East Asia were 36 per cent of its total, Hong Kong had 94 percent as intraregional, Singapore 57 per cent, Thailand 55 per cent, South Korea 43 per cent and Taiwan 39 percent. Coming at the issue from a different perspective, Higgott, in a somewhat rambling essay, also eventually recognizes the strength of regionalization: 'East Asia will be at the core of the new regionalism' (p.105). While these are useful papers, the majority of writers add little to our knowledge about either the process of globalization or the economics of the Asia-Pacific region.

Globalization and Its Critics: Perspectives from Political Economy

Randall D. Germain (ed.)
Basingstoke: Macmillan, in association with the Political Economic Research Centre, University of Sheffield. 1999; New York: St. Martin's Press, 292 pp.*

This is a collection of ten essays on globalization, broadly defined, by a set of political scientists. The original versions of the papers were presented at a conference in June 1996 convened by the Political Economy Research Centre at the University of Sheffield. The editor states that in this book globalization 'is viewed as defining social life rather than being one dimension within its broader perspectives' (p. xiv). The contributors, indeed, discuss globalization as a complex phenomenon that is not necessarily leading to convergence and homogeneity but rather is diverse and variable in its effects on social life. They are interested in developing abstract arguments about the philosophical foundations of globalization. To do so they use the jargon and methodology of political science, for example in chapters by John MacLean, Randall Germain, Timothy Sinclair and Barry Jones, and of sociology, for example in a good chapter on culture by Nick Stevenson and one on technology by Michael Talalay. Another chapter on technology, by Ngai-Ling Sum is, unfortunately, written in 'techno-babble.'

I found three essays to be particularly interesting. In Chapter 4, Philip Cerny discusses the 'Competition state' in an era of economic globalization. He finds that 'political globalization' results, which leads to major changes in the role of the state across economic, social and cultural dimensions. In Chapter 6, Jonathan Perraton examines the markets versus hierarchies literature in a useful essay that discusses the recent development of business networks and strategic alliances. In Chapter 5, Ronen Palan recognizes the importance of trade/regional blocks, or 'hybrid political giants' as he calls the EU, NAFTA and APEC. But even this paper reflects the abstract, theoretical, tone of the book, which offers little of practical relevance to the reader.

**International Affairs* 76(4) (October 2000): 868.

51 The Challenge of Global Capitalism: The World Economy in the 21st Century

Robert Gilpin

*Princeton, NJ: Princeton University Press, 2000, 385 pp.**

This is a thoughtful and beautifully written account of the political aspects of economic globalization by one of America's leading thinkers. The result is a balanced perspective on the overall, but fragile, economic benefits of globalization coupled with a sympathetic treatment of the complementary concerns about perceived income inequalities and social injustices. Gilpin is an enlightened liberal who thinks that these problems of global capitalism can be solved by renewed and more effective US leadership and better international institutions. 'Global capitalism and economic globalization have rested and must continue to rest on a secure political foundation' (p. 13).

The major topics explored are the familiar ones – the rise of the 'triad' regional economies of the European Union, NAFTA and Japan; problems of multilateral trade liberalization without US leadership and its lack of 'fast-track' approval from the Congress; the power of multi-national enterprises as an offset to their undoubted economic benefits; volatile financial flows and international capital market instability; the problem of income disparities in less developed economies; the increased power of non-governmental organizations and populist discontents about globalization.

Gilpin discusses the success of the 'New American Economy' with enthusiasm. He is also able to articulate the economic benefits of global capitalism and the need for open markets. Yet, like most political scientists, he gets it half wrong. Gilpin argues that the international economic system is unstable and that current international institutions are inadequate to regulate it. 'Improved governance and management have become imperative' (p. 9). New rules are needed. In the global economy, 'the most important factors are and will be political' (p. 50). In contrast, an

International Affairs 77(1) (January 2001): 200.

economist would argue that the benefits of open world markets, even if instability occurs, need not be offset by global regulation. Indeed, effective regulation of world markets is probably impossible. Yet Gilpin still sees the nation state as the unit of analysis; an international concordance of national governments could regulate global capitalism. This is like the search for the holy grail – a vision which haunts us still.

52 The Political Economy of Globalization

Ngaire Woods (ed.)
Basingstoke: Macmillan, 2000, 230 pp.[*]

This set of essays offers a balanced perspective on globalization that will make it useful reading for students in international relations. The papers were previously published in a special issue of the journal, *Oxford Development Studies* and the editor has produced two good introductory and concluding chapters which not only synthesize the other seven chapters, but also build upon them. She offers the pragmatic conclusion that globalization has not reduced the role and power of the nation state but that stronger international institutions are needed to generate more effective global governance.

One of the strengths of this book is its focus on the activities of multinational enterprises (MNEs) as the key agents of globalization. In an excellent empirical chapter, John Dunning explores the geography of foreign direct investment flows, finding the largest growth to be in Asia in the 1990s. Dunning also provides useful analysis of business strategies of MNEs and their development of worldwide business networks. Another interesting empirical chapter, with more of a macroeconomic perspective, is that by Geoffrey Garrett of Yale. He finds that the greater openness of world markets has not reduced national autonomy, thus rejecting one of the key beliefs of anti-globalization writers. This is echoed in a chapter by Tussie and Woods on the continued importance of regionalism rather than globalization. Other excellent analytical chapters include Benjamin Cohen on money, Thomas Biersteker on the new thinking required by international institutions and Jan Aart Scholte on global civil society. Overall, this is one of the few recent books on globalization to provide an educational service with a focus on facts and analysis rather than on unsubstantiated rhetoric.

---

[*]*International Affairs* 77(1) (January 2001): 200–201.

Global Transformations: Politics, Economics and Culture

David Held, Anthony McGrew, David Goldblatt and Jonathan Perraton
*Cambridge: Polity Press, 1999, 527 pp.**

This sweeping literative survey and synthesis is, apparently, already popular as an introductory textbook on globalization. It is very clearly written, and the four authors have managed to cover the waterfront. There are eight very long descriptive chapters on what are considered by the authors to be the core subject areas of globalization, very broadly defined 'as the widening, deepening and speeding up of worldwide interconnectedness in all aspects of contemporary social life, from the cultural to the criminal, the financial to the spiritual' (p. 2). As a result the eight long chapters deal respectively with: politics; military 'organized violence'; global free trade; finance; multinational corporations and networks; migration; culture; and the natural environment.

The chapter on multinational enterprises is a finely balanced narrative showing some good analytic insights into the strategic management literature, as well as the economic basis for foreign direct investment. The chapter on free trade is also well done. Paradoxically, the weakest chapter is the introduction, which presents an unnecessary model of four types of globalization which may well turn off otherwise open-minded students.

A problem with the book is that it does not appear that the four authors of the eight chapters have spent much time talking to each other. For example, whoever wrote the excellent chapters on trade and multinationals (Chapters 3 and 5 respectively) must surely wonder what happened in Chapter 8 on the environment. In this superficial chapter, where environmental 'degradation' is assumed to be an historical process caused by development there is no discussion of the activities of multinational enterprises. Yet recently, a literature has sprung up in the management sciences testing to what extent firms engage in sustainable development, do or do not use pollution havens, internalize the external

---

*International Affairs 77(2) (April 2001): 434.

social costs of pollution, etc. It would help students if this literature could be integrated. As it stands, I could not advise any student to read Chapter 8 on environmental catastrophe, as it is too biased; maybe other instructors will have different views and overall, the book is bustling with data, ideas, viewpoints and references to more detailed reading.

The Invisible Continent: Four Strategic Imperatives of the New Economy

Kenichi Ohmae
London: Nicholas Brealey, 2000, 262 pp.[*]

As one of the gurus of globalization, Kenichi Ohmae continues to bring a sharp analytic focus to the issue of our times. His latest book is based on the real life insights he has gained as a McKinsey consultant and, now, a Japanese businessman. His major theme is that the era of the nation state is over, and the old economy system of power, based upon ownership of land, machines and capital, has been replaced by the new economy. Ohmae calls this the 'invisible continent', and he means more than the Internet and cyberspace. The four dimensions of the invisible continent are: first, a visible dimension of bricks and mortar; second, a borderless dimension of global production and distribution; third, a cyber dimension of the Internet and flexible services; and fourth, a dimension of high multiples, fueled by pension funds and highly mobile international investors.

The most powerful idea in the book is Ohmae's discussion of global 'platforms'. A platform is a universal standard; it can be 'financial, techno-logical or cultural' (p. 30). The English language is said to be the platform for the Internet and gives an advantage to U.S. business over Japanese. The U.S. dollar is another platform, while corporate ones are: Visa and MasterCard for electronic financial commerce; Windows for personal and business computers; Fed Ex; Amazon.com; and some emerging telecom systems. Ohmae says that 'on the invisible continent platforms are deter-mined by customers' (p. 34). These customers are worldwide, and there is little role for government to facilitate competitiveness except by dereg-ulation and enhancing flexibility to respond to worldwide trends. The platforms cannot be regulated and so reform of the world's financial and trade architecture needs to be driven by deregulation thinking, not by the Keynesian thinking of the old economy.

[*]*International Affairs* 77(3) (July 2001): 715–716.

In an interesting discussion of country-specific policies, Ohmae takes Ireland as an example of the successful new economy model, using English as a platform for efficient call centres, tuned into the invisible continent. Other successful city-state regions are: Singapore; Bangalore; Barcelona/Catalonia; Hong Kong; and some of the Chinese coastal cities. In contrast, Russia, China, Japan, Malaysia and Indonesia (among many others) are berated for old economy nationalism and ineffective economic policy. The globally competitive regional city-states generate new waves of knowledge workers and benefit from recent decentralized regional governments yet local autonomy does not lead to wasteful duplication (such as a theme park in each Japanese prefecture) as there is a loose federation of power which facilitates universal platforms. The United States is seen as the most successful model. It has developed a base for the 'Godzilla' multinational corporations like Microsoft, Dell and Cisco. It has a 'zebra-like' structure where there are bands of successful regions in contrast to older, uncompetitive areas. Investors favour regions with platforms, not countries as such. For international relations scholars this means use of a sub-regional unit of analysis.

Another example of failure to adapt to the invisible continent is the Asian financial crisis of 1997. This 'took place because most of the Asian countries refused, in one way or another, to go through the long tunnel' (p. 160). By long tunnel, Ohmae means the successful 1980's Reagan-Thatcherite process of deregulation and privatization, which unleashed the entrepreneurial, technological and e-economy boom in the United States and United Kingdom. In Asia, in contrast, a set of old economy autocratic leaders held back economic reforms and built their expansion on a speculative financial bubble. Ohmae is particularly critical of the lack of deregulation in Japan, and he even blames the Clinton Administration for encouraging wasteful Japanese public works programs instead of insisting on Japanese banking and business reforms. Overall, this is a profound and provocative book.

Ruling the Waves: Cycles of Discovery Chaos and Wealth from the Compass to the Internet

Debora L. Spar
New York: Harcourt, 2001, 418 pp.*

Debora Spar's main thesis is that the Internet will follow the path of earlier technologies and end up being regulated by governments. The incentive for such rules will come mainly from commercial enterprises using the Net that will need to establish property rights and enforce standards. Eventual regulation will follow historical patterns of business/government interaction that have gone on since the pirates of post-Elizabethan England were eventually brought to heel by the power of the British Royal Navy and other state-run military forces. Such state-sponsored regulation is usually the result of demands by business leaders whose commercial viability is threatened by 'pirates' in the periods of anarchy that occur as new technologies move from the innovation to the commercialization stage.

In other words, Professor Spar is of the Douglass North view that states are required to make markets. Like North, Spar argues that only governments can provide the rules and institutions required for the successful sustained commercial development of a new technology. In the case of the Internet, nation states appear to be too location bound to avoid effective regulation, so Spar argues that national government will eventually set effective rules by setting standards and enforcing property rights. As a scholar of international business, Spar understands the power of multinational enterprises, such as Microsoft, but she also argues that national governments have an offsetting countervailing power, even in the global arena.

Rich in historical anecdotes, this book argues that there is 'a dance of regulation' along the technological frontier (p. 8) that takes place as

**Business Horizons* 45(2) (March–April 2002): 84–85.

commercial enterprises (firms) replace the innovator and entrepreneurs of the earliest stage of a new technology. The firms interact with governments (usually national states) to set rules that regulate the use of the new technology. Governments and their rules thwart the use of 'pirates' who would otherwise not only appropriate a large chunk of the rents, but would also reduce efficiency by slowing down the commercial development of the new technology by their nefarious activities.

Professor Spar makes a convincing case that there are four phases of 'life along the technological frontier' (p. 11). These are: (1) innovation, (2) commercialization, (3) creative anarchy, and (4) rules.

In phase one, the new technology is created by inventors and there is no role for government, unless the military sees a potential national security use of the technology, as happened with radio and TV in their early days.

In phase two, entrepreneurs and pioneers try to get big fast by growing the overall market size, and seeking large slices of it for themselves. This then attracts pirates, as a reaction more to the commercialization of the technology rather than to the novelty itself. The pirates are impossible to police and an unstable equilibrium ensues which leads to the next phase.

Phase three is one of creative anarchy. Firms try to establish standards and obtain property rights for their investments in development of the new technology. This leads to the standard managerial challenges of centralization and coordination of control (to obtain standards) versus the need for competition (to ensure efficiency). The usual pattern is for the pressures of standardization to lead to a dominant player, a monopolist, but then for the monopolist to drag its feet on future innovation. This leads to the need for government regulation and rules for the new technology.

In phase four the government charges to the rescue and imposes rules for business to operate efficiently and fairly. 'In general,' argues Spar, 'rules get created because private firms want them' (p. 18). But NGOs can also help create them. In the end, Spar concludes, it is simply more efficient to have the state set the rules, and police them, rather than for firms to try to do it themselves.

Spar's first, and most powerful example of the need for rules, is her historical discussion of how the British East India Company, started in 1600, eventually petitioned the British government to start up the

Royal Navy to police the high seas and stamp out the prevalent piracy that was a major threat to its trade and commerce.

Indeed, the historical chapters that illustrate Spar's four phases are well chosen and brilliantly written. She melds a nice degree of business school scholarly analysis with historical accuracy (and abundant footnotes) and a storyteller's writing skills. Her first wave of technology (in Chapter 1) is about the improvement in navigation, the compass, that literally launched international trade and commerce in the new and better-engineered ships of the sixteenth century. She moves on to discuss Samuel Morse and 'the code makers' in Chapter 2; Marconi and radio in Chapter 3; Rupert Murdoch and satellite (Sky) TV in Chapter 4; cyberspace and encryption in Chapter 5; Microsoft in Chapter 6; and online music in Chapter 7. She concludes with Chapter 8 on the role of government in setting rules.

This is a very readable book, and it will be enjoyed by managers as much as by academics and students. The high quality of the writing will enhance the book's acceptance in the market for ideas that is always of interest to managers and academics.

56 The Quest for Global Dominance

Vijay Govindarajan and Anil K. Gupta
San Francisco: Jossey-Bass, 2001, 319 pp.*

The Quest for Global Dominance: Transforming Global Presence into Global Competitive Advantage, by Vijay Govindarajan and Anil Gupta, is a well-written managerial version of the authors' academic research on the currently popular topic of how to develop a global strategy. The main insights in the book come from their extensive analysis of the strategies and performance of multinational enterprises (MNEs) such as Dell, Hewlett-Packard, IBM, Microsoft, Amazon.com, Yahoo!, Canon, Procter & Gamble, and several emerging Chinese and Indian MNEs. Despite the unfortunate timing of some company examples (the Enron and Hewlett-Packard stories predate recent events) the analysis is sound. For example, the fact that Amazon.com has been very slow to internationalize (the opposite of the so-called 'born global' dot.coms who have mainly died in childbirth) is an expected outcome given the authors' basic arguments.

There is much to commend this book to managers. Perhaps of greatest benefit is the authors' choice of the unit of analysis, which is the strategic business unit (SBU) rather than the MNE as a whole. Today's giant MNEs have dozens of SBUs in scores of countries. It is refreshing that Govindarajan and Gupta have chosen to focus their attention on the decision-making of these subsidiary units, rather than solely on the parent firm. The authors also state that they have based their research on interviews with SBU-level managers. Perhaps as a consequence of this exposure, the authors pay more attention than usual in such global strategy books to the need for strategies of 'national responsiveness.' This need is emphasized, for example, in the chapter on exploiting global presence. Of the six strategies discussed, the very first one is the national response related to 'adapting to local market differences.'

**Academy of Management Executive* 16(3) (August 2002): 157–159.

The key model of the book, is the 'star framework' wherein the authors plot a three-dimensional diagram of the drivers of global value. In this framework, 'locational competencies' are placed equally with 'global coordination' and 'activity architecture.' Readers from the management academic community will recognize that this is virtually identical to the well known Bartlett and Ghoshal framework of 'national responsiveness,' 'global integration,' and 'worldwide learning.' The focus of their model on the SBU-activity parts of the value chain makes the Govindarajan and Gupta book so relevant to managers.

Indeed, *The Quest for Global Dominance* is rich in its applications to business. The book contains in-depth analysis of the strategies of major MNEs. Yet the authors still manage to conclude strongly with a chapter on 'globalization in the digital age,' despite recent work suggesting that neither of these phenomena really exist in the simplistic forms first imagined and that management strategy based on such assumptions is not very useful. The authors expertly convey their knowledge about MNEs and their enthusiasm for their global models is readily apparent.

However, the authors' enthusiasm potentially distracts them from discussing a fundamental flaw in their assumptions about MNEs. That is, the authors simply assume that 'globalization' exists whereas their own data and examples suggest that it does not. Indeed, virtually all of the MNEs they study started operating on a triad/regional basis in the three great world markets of the European Union (EU), North America (NAFTA – the U.S., Mexico, and Canada) and Japan. Over 430 of the world's 500 largest MNEs are from the triad, and have been for the last 30 years. The authors claim that Chinese, Indian and Mexican MNEs will made the top 500 'radically different in twenty years'.

In addition, the authors use trade data to argue that there is 'global integration'. Yet 60 percent of all EU trade is intra-regional; 50 percent of NAFTA trade is intra-regional, as is well over half of Asia's trade. These data suggest that regional strategy matters, not global strategy. My book, *The End of Globalization: Why Global Strategy is a Myth and How to Profit from the Realities of Regional Markets* (2001, AMACOM) demonstrates that global strategy to a large extent is a myth. To solve the apparent disconnect between global and triad/regional strategy, readers should substitute the word 'international' for 'global' wherever it appears, and then think regional.

For example, the authors use Wal-Mart Stores as an example of 'building global presence,' yet their own data indicate that the company is not a global business. That is, while Wal-Mart Stores does have 1,004 'international' stores, 624 of these are in Canada and Mexico. So, rather than being a global competitor Wal-Mart Stores' international operations are primarily in the NAFTA region. Thanks to its nearly 3,000 'domestic' stores, the ratio of foreign to total sales for Wal-Mart is only 13.8 percent. The global retail competitor to Wal-Mart Stores used by the authors is French-based Carrefour. This business is even less global, having most of its sales in Europe where there is an economic union with intra-regional free trade. Yet the authors argue that Carrefour's 'international' profits are 62 percent of total profits without making any adjustment for home-based EU sites. My interpretation of these cases is that neither retail firm is truly global, as their retail sales are largely local or at least regionally located within the EU or NAFTA blocks.

The Quest for Global Dominance underscores the need for global mind-sets, global knowledge machines, global business teams, global strategy games, and the realization that firms today are increasingly selling goods and services beyond the borders of their home country. Govindarajan and Gupta suggest that developing a 'global' presence, having a 'global' mindset, and devising a 'global' strategy will lead to 'global' competitive advantage. Yet, their basic model of SBU activities in the value chain is just as applicable at the triad/regional level as at the 'global' level. Managers will benefit from this perspective since the authors have a remarkable capacity for reality and relevance. The book will be useful to MBA students interested in international business and managers seeking to better understand how business beyond their home country borders will likely occur.

Globalization and its Discontents

Joseph E. Stiglitz
*New York: Norton, 2002, 282 pp.**

This is a controversial book by a Nobel Prize winner in economics. In the book, Stiglitz endorses the popular criticism of globalization and launches into an extended attack on the current policies of the International Monetary Fund and World Bank. He argues that these international institutions are not succeeding in reducing world poverty or in helping the growth of developing nations; rather their market-based policies worsen the situation. As a former chief economist at the World Bank, he would be expected to offer some useful insider analysis of these international institutions. Sadly, this is not provided as the book lacks any solid analysis or even balanced insight with its unrelenting criticism of globalization.

The book is a polemic. It is well written, free of academic jargon, except for the repeated discussion of information asymmetries and their applications to monetary policy and the efficiency/distribution dichotomy. Yet the polemical writing comes at the expense of substance. For a distinguished economist, Stiglitz makes a succession of lightweight and debatable points including a simplistic criticism of globalization as having failed to end world poverty. The IMF is alleged to have worsened the Asian Financial Crisis, prevented Russian development and to have created poverty and inequality in Africa and Asia. International institutions are blamed for their market-based, efficiency-first, views, but local dictators and corrupt governments are not analyzed as the more likely causes of poverty and misuse of external loans. Probably this reflects the experience of Stiglitz at these institutions and his lack of insight into corruption and government maladministration as he flew around on a world tour of key political and economic trouble spots. In other words,

Long Range Planning 35(6) (December 2002): 654–656.

Stiglitz is the typical visiting expert who meets the leaders on their best behavior but fails to see what is really going on.

The weakest part of Stiglitz's book is his brief discussion of foreign direct investment and multinational enterprises. Here, no knowledge is displayed of the vast literature on the theoretical and empirical analysis of the performance, operations and strategies of multinational enterprises. When Stiglitz says that foreign multinationals quash local small business (p. 68) he displays ignorance of empirical and case studies of the benefits of networks, joint ventures and supply chains in international business. When he says that the abuse of strong local competition policy results in monopolies, and that local workers are displaced, he wrongly criticizes multinationals instead of the corrupt or inept local governments. In fact, the evidence of international business researchers suggests that foreign multinationals help to offset local monopolies, transfer technology, stimulate growth and improve the efficiency of developing countries. But for Stiglitz ignorance is bliss and ill-informed criticism of multinationals can be launched without any regard for the actual evidence on their performance and behavior.

In fact, Stiglitz does not address most of the real issues in globalization; besides the lack of analysis of multinationals there are no data on world income inequality, trade and development, the causes of economic growth, etc. Instead, his book is really a technical critique of policy at the IMF in the 1990s. He criticizes the high interest rate and tight fiscal policy applied as conditions to IMF loans to countries experiencing currency crises. He also attacks IMF and World Bank conditions favoring privatization before the institutions and legal frameworks were in place to make markets work. This is a reasonable point and growth, indeed, has been poor in countries like Russia, but not so bad in Asia. Thus his criticisms are really over financial timing and loan mistakes rather than a tight case against globalization. Indeed, Stiglitz has little evidence to back up his criticism of globalization. He appears to have been opportunistic in even using the word globalization in a technical book about IMF policy. Even his prescriptions for the future are weak; for example, in Chapter 9 two key reforms are called for: 1) improvements in global governance (where this really means reducing U.S. influence at the IMF); 2) greater transparency (this means less power for technical bureaucrats other than Stiglitz).

In short, Stiglitz is not really as critical of international institutions as the rhetoric implies. His real villain is the power of the United States to push its alleged free-market ideology through its control of the IMF and influence at the World Bank. In addition, U.S. ideas are said to be institutionalized in the senior bureaucracy of these Washington-based economic agencies. Finally, the U.S. Treasury is also too free market and pro-Wall Street for Stiglitz's liking, and he sees it as the root cause of U.S. free-market policy. All of this is far too simplistic, as economists at the IMF will perform in much the same way as economists anywhere, regardless of nationality. Where Stiglitz has a much better point is in his discussion in Chapter 6 of U.S. 'fair trade' laws on anti-dumping and countervailing duty actions. Here I fully agree that these are basically protectionist laws, captured by the domestic U.S. industry lobbies, giving, in practice, a form of administered protection.

Overall, this is a vastly disappointing book. Stiglitz is a liberal intellectual who is good at pure theory but bad at applied economics. His theoretical insights on market imperfections are valid, but his criticism of international institutions is badly misplaced. What is the alternative to the IMF and World Bank? Even more poverty? How can they be reformed to emphasize more equitable global governance without compromising their focus on efficiency? A reallocation of internal resources at these institutions may be needed, but a recommendation to radically reform these institutions is a misguided and naïve viewpoint. The book will add to the negative literature on global capitalism propagated by anti-global activists. Its level of insight is actually slightly above the average for such works, but is well below any minimum standards of academic objectivity and scientific research.

58 Governing Globalization: Power, Authority and Global Governance

David Held and Anthony McGrew (eds)
*Cambridge: Polity Press, 2002, 370 pp.**

The explosion of literature on aspects of globalization in the last ten years is leading to a second generation of quasi textbooks which attempt to integrate the often divergent viewpoints of authorities in the field. This book is one of the better attempts to offer synthetic essays on global governance by leading authors in this specialized sub-area of globalization. Eventually a third generation of fully integrated textbooks on globalization will emerge – this is a stepping stone towards that end.

There are sixteen chapters divided into three parts: 1) the global governance complex; 2) governing global problems; and 3) theories of global governance. The theme of the book is that a large number of international institutions exist and function in a complex manner and that effective global governance can be built on them through reform and adaptation, rather than by attempting to develop a completely new system of global governance. These basic institutions include: the United Nations and its agencies; the World Trade Organization; the International Monetary Fund; the World Bank; the summit meetings of the G8, APEC, the EU; and the international non-governmental organizations (INGOs) who attach themselves to these organizations and meetings like barnacles on a rusty ship. Also relevant are multinational enterprises, although these are hardly analyzed in this book.

The contributors include such well known political science professors as: Robert Gilpin, Robert Keohane, Phil Williams, and James Rosenall, as well as some younger scholars such as Jan Aart Scholte, Ngaire Woods, and Susan Sell. All of them have contributed to the literature on either economic globalization or political globalization, including some from a Marxist prospective such as Alex Callinicos or a feminist one such as Jill Steans. The book is predictably left wing and of use mainly

International Affairs 80(1) (January 2004): 139.

159

to already skeptical anti-globalization readers rather than ones with a more open mind. And, of course, none of the contributors seems to be aware of another literature on globalization in business schools that is focused on its efficiency aspects rather than on these regulatory and distributional concerns. The marginal returns to an economist from reading this book must be very close to zero, but the returns to a new student of international political economy in this area would be higher, especially as it serves as an alternative to reading the larger works of these contributors.

59 Redefining Global Strategy: Crossing Borders in a World Where Differences Still Matter

Pankaj Ghemawat

Boston: Harvard Business School Press, 2007, 268 pp.[*]

The theme of this book is that the world is not flat; rather it is characterized by 'semi-globalization'. As explained on page 30, this is a situation between zero integration and total integration, where the latter is the flat earth version of globalization. This concept is related to (but not identical to) the regionalization effect which I have observed in firm level and country level analysis. Professor Ghemawat provides abundant empirical evidence to support the existence of semi-globalization. He also provides substantial theoretical reasoning and insight into the dangers of simplistic global strategy and the predominance of intra-regional activity by the world's largest firms. He achieves the former with some useful tables of regional data mainly in the three chapters in Part One but also in Chapter 5. He does the latter mainly through an interesting set of theoretical arguments in the five chapters in Part Two of the book where he outlines his Triple A model. In this model 'Adaptation' is a form of local (national) responsiveness; 'Aggregation' is basically the achievement of economies of scale; and 'Arbitrage' is the exploitation of national differences. The Triple A model is well presented and is based upon a clear and incisive (but not comprehensive) understanding of the relevant academic literature which is summarized in sets of abundant footnotes.

Part Two of the book on the Triple A model is stronger than Part One in which Ghemawat persists with his somewhat simplistic 'CAGE' framework where: 'C' represents cultural distance; 'A' represents administrative (government regulatory) distance; 'G' is geographic distance; and 'E' is economic distance. Although linked in a useful manner to the gravity model all four of these are elements of the country factor, well known to the international business scholarly community. This renders

---

[*]*Journal of International Business Studies* 39(6) (September 2008): 1091–1093.

CAGE largely redundant as a new research concept and of limited value as a learning tool. CAGE is used later in Chapter 6 on Arbitrage. Part One also contains in Chapter 3 the so-called 'ADDING value scorecard' where there are six items in the ADDING acronym. Again, this score card is used later in the book. In general, both lists appear to be aimed more at the executive education and consulting markets rather than at a serious academic audience.

Notwithstanding these caveats, I am very pleased that this book has been written and published in this readable form as it should influence executives and students. Ghemawat brings a major academic name to the camp of those critical of flat earth/ pure globalization thinking and the misleading use of uniform global strategy. In doing so he provides both empirical and theoretical support for my research work demonstrating that the world's largest firms perform largely within their home region of the broad triad markets of North America, Europe, and Asia Pacific. While Ghemawat does not use the triad concept or the current regional terminology of the academic literature, this book (and his related publications) produces similar conclusions about the need for effective home region strategy, the liability of inter-regional foreignness, and the danger of the popular conventional wisdom concerning globalization. I shall raise some concerns about the depth of the academic research in Ghemawat (as is appropriate for a review in this scholarly journal); in doing so, I recognize that the primary audience for his book is the practicing manager and consultant keen to learn and to implement recent academic thinking.

In Chapter 1 Ghemawat presents useful evidence showing that across many industry sectors the degree of internationalization averages 10% rather than the 100% to be expected with pure globalization. This work could be improved if Ghemawat were to engage more forcefully with firm level data, rather than the industry level data which he seems to prefer. Using firm level data he could construct a ratio of regional to total sales, as shown in Rugman (2005). The (R/T) ratio represents a more useful metric for regionalization than the traditional internationalization ratio of foreign to total sales (F/T) behind Ghemawat's numbers. Furthermore, firm level data can be used to test the performance of firms according to their degree of regionalism or internationalization, as attempted in various chapters of Rugman (2007). In other words, the academic literature is marching ahead of Ghemawat partly due to its focus upon firm level rather than industry level data.

In contrast, the major strength of the book lies in Ghemawat's mastery of cases and practical examples. The opening example extending over the Introduction of the book is about the nature of football (soccer). Ghemawat argues correctly that soccer is not a global sport. Of course, this argument also appears in my 2000 book, *The End of Globalization*, and in recent editions of my textbook on international business. Ghemawat also discusses many other cases and company examples, some of which have been well worked over by other scholars. In general, he always adds value, for example, in the useful diagrammatic positioning of the profits of country divisions of Wal-Mart (on page 36). He also reprises in detail his excellent Harvard cases on Cemex, Star TV, Ericsson in China, Philips, Wal-Mart, Tricon, Embraer, Ranbaxy, Tata Consultancy, and Philips Medical. He also provides informed discussion of the problems that Google has experienced in emerging markets, similar to Microsoft in China. Chapter 5 on Adaptation is 30 pages of examples, perhaps the most practice-based chapter. The emphasis here is upon local (country level) adaptation, rather than regional adaptation. However, nearly all of Ghemawat's examples complement the insights to be gained from parallel regional analysis at firm level. The cases also bring out that the former focus on the globalization of markets now needs to be replaced by firm level studies of the globalization of production, where the latter can be partly solved by use of the Triple A model.

Of the five chapters in Part Two of the book my favorite is Chapter 5. In this chapter Ghemawat explicitly discusses regionalization. He presents data showing that the degree of intra-regional trade has increased between 1958 and 2003. These data parallel those reported in Rugman (2000), but for slightly different regions. The most striking point of agreement is that intra-regional trade in Asia has increased from 35% in 1958 to over 54% by 2003. Ghemawat also examines the nature of Toyota's regional (not global) strategy. He agrees with me that even large companies like Toyota need to build upon their home region and then expand very cautiously into another region. Ghemawat also discusses six types of regional strategy archetypes and gives excellent examples of firms in each of these six categories. Ghemawat also has a relevant discussion of regional head offices. This is partly based upon insights by Michael

Enright and others working towards the regional solution. This work provides a useful contrast to the now dated work by Bartlett and Ghoshal (1989). Their focus upon the transnational solution was based upon an explicit argument concerning 'global' integration. This needed to be offset against national responsiveness with both to be enhanced by worldwide learning.

In practice, few firms are potential candidates for the transnational solution. Indeed, Rugman and Verbeke (2004) found only 9 of the world's 380 largest firms to be truly global with 320 being home region based and needing a regional, rather than a transnational, solution to strategy and structure. Most of the examples in Ghemawat's book reinforce this finding and support the need for the regional solution to strategy and structure. For this reason Ghemawat's book is the most important book published by Harvard Business School Press since that of Bartlett and Ghoshal (1989). In particular, Ghemawat argues that a firm does not need to develop a special organizational structure (like the transnational) to do all three of the 'As'. He says managers need to: 'nail down at least one of the As and, with one in hand, possibly seek another, but be careful about pursuing the elusive trifecta' (p. 218). Hopefully, Ghemawat's work, aligned with the exploding related academic literature on regionalization, will generate a similar upsurge of research on regional strategy and structure similar to that produced for global strategy and structure nearly twenty years ago by Bartlett and Ghoshal.

The puzzle that I have with Chapter 5 is that Ghemawat's excellent discussion of regional strategy and structure appears in a chapter called Aggregation. Why does this thinking not also carry over to the chapters on Adaptation and Arbitrage? The analysis of regionalization is not confined to the focus on economies of scale as in the chapter on Aggregation. Ghemawat is, of course, correct to show that economies of scale can be achieved within a large region. In practice, this is normally the home region of the firm. But this thinking on the home region base also applies to the need for Adaptation when entry is made to another major triad region. There are inter-regional liabilities of foreignness. It is also relevant when exploiting national differences through Arbitrage. Yet, Ghemawat reintroduces his CAGE model in the Arbitrage chapter instead of extending the regional material to this leg of the Triple A framework.

My conclusion is that Ghemawat has not come to grips with the economic, cultural, and political importance of the triad. In my work on the regional effect I have distinguished between a 'core' triad of the United States, Japan, and the EU and a 'broad' triad consisting of NAFTA; the EU, and the largest six, eight, or twelve economies in Asia Pacific. Over 400 of the world's 500 largest firms come from the core triad, and virtually all of the 500 from the broad triad. For the 380 firms providing data on the broad region of their geographic sales they average over 77% of their sales in their home region over the 2001–2005 period, see Rugman and Oh in Rugman (2007). Ghemawat does (perhaps implicitly) use the triad, e.g. on page 28 he states that: 'Coke is one of only a dozen or so *Fortune* 500 companies that derive at least 20 percent of their sales from each of the three triad regions of North America, Europe and Asia-Pacific'. There is no citation here to the origin of the 20 percent figure in Rugman and Verbeke (2004), and Ghemawat misreports our findings which are for the *Fortune* Global 500, not the U.S. *Fortune* 500. It is the Global 500 which has the triad data. I would like to see Ghemawat engage more carefully with these triad-based firm level data and with the full implications of the triad concept in his future work on semi-globalization and regional strategy.

On a more technical note, many of the basic components of the Triple A model have also been previously developed elsewhere in the academic literature. For example, Rugman and Verbeke (1992) provide a clear distinction between Adaptation and Arbitrage. We distinguish between the national responsiveness elements of Adaptation (which we call location bound firm specific advantages) and the Arbitrage possibilities of exploiting national differences (which is one component of non-location-bound firm specific advantages). The other type of non-location-bound firm specific advantages comes from economies of scale (Ghemawat's Aggregation concept). These distinctions have been built upon in subsequent publications, and by other authors, and it is somewhat sad to note that Ghemawat does not seem to be familiar with this mainstream literature in international business. Despite this lack of academic bite, Ghemawat's book is highly recommended as a clever popularization of the new subfield of regionalization, semi-globalization, and regional strategy.

References

Bartlett, C.A. and Ghoshal, S. (1989) *Managing across Borders*. Boston: Harvard Business School Press.

Rugman, A.M. (2000) *The End of Globalization*. New York: Random House; AMACOM.

Rugman, A.M. (2005) *The Regional Multinationals*. Cambridge: Cambridge University Press.

Rugman, A.M. (ed.) (2007) *Regional Aspects of Multinationality and Performance*. Oxford: Elsevier, now Emerald.

Rugman, A.M. and Collinson, S.C. (2006) *International Business*. 4th ed. Harlow, UK: FT/Prentice Hall.

Rugman, A.M. and Hodgetts, R.M. (2002) *International Business*. 3rd ed. Harlow, UK: FT/Prentice Hall.

Rugman, A.M. and Oh, C.H. (2007) 'Multinationality and regional performance, 2001–2005' in A.M. Rugman (Ed.), *Regional Aspects of Multinationality and Performance* (Research in Global Strategic Management, v.13) Oxford: Elsevier.

Rugman, A.M. and Verbeke, A. (1992) 'A Note on the Transnational Solution and the Transaction Cost Theory of Multinational Strategic Management', *Journal of International Business Studies*, 23(4): 761–772.

Rugman, A.M. and Verbeke, A. (2004) 'A Perspective on Regional and Global Strategies of Multinational Enterprises', *Journal of International Business Studies*, 35(1): 3–19.

Part IV

Free Trade, NAFTA and Competitiveness

Introduction to Part IV

The focus of this part is upon international competitiveness. This is a concept which became popular in the 1980s and 1990s. In particular, this success of Japanese MNEs (in autos, consumer electronics) in the 1980s led to an intellectual reaction in the United States and Western Europe. It was felt that the Japanese government fostered the success of Japanese firms in the wealthy markets of North America and Europe. Some groups (such as the Berkeley Roundtable in the United States) argued that the US government should reduce its reliance on market based economics and move to support national champions in the United States. Similar thinking developed in Canada and in Western Europe where the French government in particular has always been supportive of their national champions, such as Airbus, Suez, Elf, etc.

In terms of international business, this was a troublesome development. In the late 1980s the basic thinking about multinationals was that their foreign operations served to transfer technology and upgrade host country macroeconomic infrastructures. In legal terms MNEs received national treatment. These were efficiency based arguments which were antithetical to the explicit subsidisation and discrimination required to support selected national champions.

Into this muddled academic and government milieu strode Michael Porter. His book reviewed here as Review 72 on *The Competitive Advantage of Nations* (1990) essentially set the terms of reference and policy making on this topic of international competitiveness. In his book Porter stated that there were four determinants of international competitiveness: factor costs, domestic demand, related and supported industries in the home country, and the amount of rivalry in the home country between leading firms by sector. He also said that government policy and the role of chance affected each and every of the four determinants. He also argued that the four determinants and two other determinants interacted as a system, see Figure 6 for a variant of this applied to Canada.

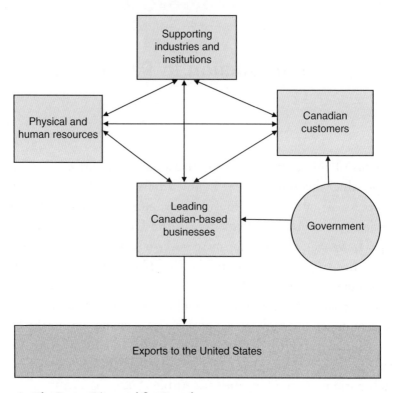

Figure 6 **The Porter Diamond for Canada**
Sources: Adapted from Alan M. Rugman, and Joseph R. D'Cruz, *Fast Forward: Improving Canada's International Competitiveness* (Toronto: Kodak Canada, 1991, p. 35); Rugman and Collinson, *International Business*, 4th ed. (Harlow, UK: Pearson Educational, 2006, p. 448).

Porter conducted some empirical analysis of country level trade data to find rankings of competitive industries across countries. Basically this showed that Japan was outcompeting the United States across most manufacturing sectors. Countries like Sweden and Canada were shown to depend on natural resource based industries.

Michael Porter only included 10 countries in his ground breaking book. He then offered to include other countries if the research was carried out by the consulting firm Monitor, with which Porter had an association. For example, Porter conducted a study of Canadian competitiveness, which cost over $1m, and this study was undertaken by the Canadian office of Monitor, under the overall supervision of Prof. Porter. They produced a report called *Canada at the Crossroads* which I review in number 73.

The major intellectual problem with the Canadian study is that the Porter single diamond home country model does not work for Canada.

In my own research, based on interviews with Canadian managers and a long-term understanding of Canadian business, I have developed jointly with my University of Toronto colleague, Joe D'Cruz, a double diamond model. In this the Canadian home diamond is stacked against the US diamond from the viewpoint of Canadian managers, see Figure 7. Since the US market is ten times bigger than Canada's a Canadian based business needs to fully understand the US diamond as thoroughly as its competitors based in the United States. Another way of saying this is that a firm from a small open economy such as Canada's is not restricted to developing firm specific advantages based on Canada's country specific advantages in natural resources. While some firms do this others can achieve success through the development of market based FSA and the development of brands which succeed in the US market. In short, there are multiple sources of competitive advantage; they are not restricted to the home country as in the Porter home model.

This double diamond framework and its associated thinking of course can be generalised to other small open economies besides Canada. Indeed,

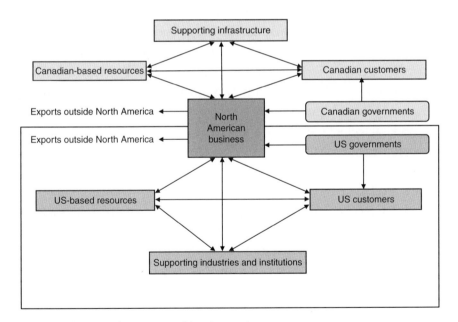

Figure 7 **The Canadian–US Double Diamond**
Sources: Adapted from Alan M. Rugman, and Joseph R. D'Cruz, *Fast Forward: Improving Canada's International Competitiveness* (Toronto: Kodak Canada, 1991, p. 35); Rugman and Collinson, *International Business*, 4th ed. (Harlow, UK: Pearson Educational, 2006, p. 448).

both theoretical and empirical analysis has built upon the double diamond and been applied to firms from Korea, New Zealand, Austria, Singapore, Australia, and many other non-triad countries, see Rugman and Verbeke (1995). Another way of saying this is that the Porter single diamond model probably explains the competitiveness of the United States and Japan but nowhere else. Even in the EU it is clear that a single diamond analysis for Germany, Italy, France, or the UK is not adequate. All these countries are now integrated in the EU which has a common set of government regulations, institutions, judicial, and administrative procedures.

As can be seen by a reading of the books reviews in this part there is still no academic consensus about the economic nature and politics of international competitiveness. Many of the Canadian books reviewed are arguing for the free trade agreement of 1989 which belatedly recognised the economic integration of the US and Canadian economies. Canadian firms had been hindered by protectionist policies for many years. Canadian manufacturing lacked economies of scale and was inefficient. Also, the Canadian tariff served to entice American firms into Canada, with the result that foreign direct investment increased and foreign control of the Canadian economy became a political issue in the 1970s and early 1980s. These themes of free trade and foreign ownership pervade readings 60 to 71. After the Porter work Canadian thinking took better account of business and management concerns and the Mulroney government succeeded in implementing both the free trade agreement of 1989 and NAFTA in 1994. These agreements served to provide institutional rules to conduct business across national borders.

The quality of research on free trade and international competitiveness in a Canadian context has generally been of the highest standard. Virtually all of the books reviewed from readings 61 to 78 are reviewed favourably. However, I include two reviews to illustrate the persistent anti-Americanism and naivety of many Canadian writers on these topics. Review 79 of a book by Linda McQuaig is a modern day version of the 1970s work on Canadian economic nationalism illustrated by Review 60. Only gradually has mainstream intellectual thought and academic analysis in Canada moved on from the mistaken concern about foreign ownership towards a more nuanced understanding of the realities of regional economic integration. Some of the books reviewed here were early pioneers in this improved thinking, such as Reviews 61 to 68, with the possible exception of Review 66.

To illustrate that Canadian thinking was not alone in being behind the times in its endorsement of national champions I include a review of a book number 69 by professors at the Harvard Business School which was just as nationalist and economically illiterate but this time making an argument for US national champions. Much more insight came from books 70 and 74 through 78 (with the exception of book 71 which is a poor attempt to analyse Canada's multinationals). Much insight into the nature of the free trade negotiations is contained in Review 76 and in my comments on the nature of governments' consultations with the business sector advisory committees of which I was a member.

Overall, a reading of the reviews of books in Part IV reveals the nature and extent of contributions to the literature on international competitiveness and free trade by several generations of Canadian based scholars. Canada's experience is highly relevant for other open trading economies. I believe that it is an essential counterpoint to literature prepared by university based scholars in the large core triad economies of the United States, Japan, and now the integrated European Union.

In conclusion, the debate on international competitiveness has now been resolved. Economic integration in the form of regional trade and investment agreements, such as NAFTA, have allowed businesses to develop efficiently and to expand abroad. Today, the majority of business is conducted intra-regionally (as discussed in Part III). From a Canadian viewpoint the issue of foreign control has disappeared. The Canadian economy is now integrated with that of the United States. At the time of writing (spring 2008) the Canadian dollar was at a premium against the US dollar. This is partly explained by Canadian exports of oil and gas to the United States, which are safeguarded under the provisions of NAFTA. Thus, the regional trade agreement has served to increase Canadian prosperity and improve relationships between the United States and Canada. Although, few books on Mexico are reviewed here, it is probable that the efficiency of Mexico's firms has also increased and that the United States benefits in a similar manner with a secure supply to

Mexico's natural resources. In short, international competitiveness today means regional economic integration.

Reference

A.M. Rugman, J. van den Broeck, and A. Verbeke (1995) *Beyond the Diamond.* Greenwich, CT: JAI Press.

The Great Canadian Stampede: The Rush to Economic Nationalism

Alan Heisey
Toronto: Griffin House, 1973, 148 pp.*

This book adds a new dimension to the conspiracy theory. Many nationalists and left-wing writers have argued that Canada is run in effect by certain corporate, financial and academic elite groups, all operating with a common interest in promoting Canadian growth and development with the aid of foreign investment. These groups foster their own interests at the expense of the majority of Canadians living on lower incomes.

Heisey's version of the conspiracy theory is that the Canadian media have influenced public opinion in Canada to the extent that the political leadership in all three major parties has adopted a nationalistic viewpoint. He is particularly sorry that the Progressive Conservative party has fallen into this error and suggests some 'fresher options' for that party and anyone else interested in listening. Most of these suggestions for reform of his party can be classified as libertarian, in particular his repeated emphasis on the need for unfettered foreign investment. Heisey is also in favor of the monarchy, supersonic aircraft, foreign travel for students in preference to travel within Canada, and a more internationalistic foreign policy, to list but a few. He argues for a North-American customs union in Chapters 6 and 16, and makes a reasonable summary of the economic advantages of such a free trade option. He believes that economic integration will inevitably be followed by political integration but, somewhat paradoxically, argues that Canada has in fact a strong negotiating position due to the unique character of Canadians and the strength of demand for Canadian resources. In this connection he refers with approval to the entry of Britain into the European Economic Community, and he argues that Canadian incomes will be higher if there is 'some new form of economic and political community in North America.'

**The Canadian Forum* 54(644) (Sept. 1974): 47.

Heisey is in favor of unrestricted investment and attributes the current moves by political leaders of all three federal parties to control foreign investment to the inspiration of the media, especially the beguiling influence of Walter Gordon of the *Toronto Star*. Lack of leadership shown by the Southam papers and other potential leaders of public opinion is criticized, and he hopes that the chartered banks (which have been protected from foreign ownership) may argue in favor of removal of such protection as they can now compete in a North American market.

Heisey's book is an intensely personal account of his feelings about the emerging nationalist consensus in Canada. This reviewer's use of the adverb 'intensely' is no exaggeration, a description that unfortunately cannot be applied to the author's style of writing. Heisey will not help to stop the stampede to economic nationalism with this poorly written book. Even the most sympathetic reader will wince at the poor taste of the author's recollections of early childhood in Chapter 1, and the rambling discussion of his contribution to the Ontario Tory party as described in Chapter 11. These personal recollections should have been edited out of the book as they considerably detract from the argument. The whole book, in fact, is badly disjointed and written in a highly aggressive style which is probably poor journalism, let alone good scholarly writing. The only sections which partially overcome the liability are Chapter 5 on the influence of the media and Chapter 16 on the Canadian-American option.

In his polemic Heisey does not attempt to evaluate the economic issues at any other level than gossip. For example, his argument in favor of a customs union for North America is mistakenly confused with an argument for free trade. They are not the same for while, on the one hand, it can be demonstrated that multilateral foreign trade is beneficial to all nations as they may then trade according to their comparative advantage, on the other hand it is well known that a customs union does not involve free trade, since a common external tariff barrier is erected in addition to the removal of internal tariffs. Secondly, most of Canada's trade is with the United States and if Canada wishes to end protection by removing tariffs and other barriers of trade it should probably attempt to diversify markets if a policy of free trade is to be implemented. Thirdly, a point not recognized by Heisey is that the tariff itself has encouraged foreign investment in Canada as multinational firms have set up branch plants in order to sell similar goods in the local Canadian market.

61 Canada-United States Free Trade and Canadian Independence

Peyton V. Lyon

Ottawa: Economic Council of Canada, 1975, 42 pp.[*]

This short monograph examines the political consequences for Canada of forming a free trade area with the United States. It is one of the background studies commissioned by the Economic Council of Canada to help in the preparation of its recently published report on free trade entitled 'Looking Outward: A New Trade Strategy for Canada'. A free trade area between Canada and the United States (which Lyon labels 'CUFTA') is only one of several possible free trade options considered by the Economic Council. However, it appears to have a greater probability of being adopted than options such as: multilateral free trade; free trade with Europe, Japan, and the United States; or various combinations of the latter. A study of the politics of a free trade area is a useful supplement to the predominantly economic issues considered in the other background papers for the Economic Council.

Professor Lyon, of Carleton University, engages in a sweeping review of the literature on political and economic integration. In this review he finds no support for the common Canadian fear that formation of a free trade area will eventually lead to political integration of the United States and Canada. There are no historical examples of such a trend and Lyon advances many arguments to show that Canadian independence will be greater than it is now once a free trade area is formed.

Prominent amongst these is the argument that Canadian independence is constrained at the present time by the large amount of foreign ownership in manufacturing and resource industries. Such foreign direct investment is attracted by the Canadian tariff as U.S. firms attempt to make sales by subsidiaries in Canada rather than by exports from home.

[*]*Canadian Public Policy/Analyse de politiques* 2(1) (Winter 1976): 124–125.

Lyon has picked up the suggestion that elimination of the tariff will reduce U.S. direct investment in Canada and replace it with increased trade in goods and/or factors of production. With less foreign investment it is assumed that there can be more independence. To this reviewer it seems that independence comes from trade diversification rather than greater concentration in one market.

Associated with the viewpoint above is the belief that a free trade area will increase real per capita income and that with a larger G.N.P. Canadians will be able to achieve more independence – a view which believes that independence is a luxury good. Lyon adds a new twist to this rather materialistic conception of human motivation by linking the increased income argument to anticipated cultural benefits stemming from the Canada-United States association being a 'disparate dyad'. This dyad is like an economist's small country assumption – it says that Canada is too insignificant for the larger United States to bother to influence, and that local Canadian concern for cultural 'disparities' can flourish in an atmosphere of indifference by the larger partner. Lyon refers with approval to the free trade area between the Irish Republic and the U.K. which he alleges has not reduced Irish independence. He seems to imply that Canada would be happy to be in a similar position to the Irish – a somewhat unfortunate example.

While the main theme of Professor Lyon's paper should be taken seriously many of his points are inadequately developed or are purely speculative, an example of the latter being on pages 26–29. Chapter 3 is poorly conceived since in it Lyon attempts to imitate economic jargon when this is not necessary. His use of abbreviations is unfortunate; for example NAFTA is used for the New Zealand-Australian free trade area rather than the North Atlantic free trade area advocated by Harry Johnson and others in a large and well known literature. Also CUFTA might lead the casual reader into the mistaken notion that a customs union is under consideration rather than a free trade area. An appendix by C.C. Pentland argues that free trade will eventually lead to political integration, although the writer seems to have a customs union model in mind rather than the free trade area option studied by Lyon.

In conclusion, this reviewer did not find that Lyon's study made acceptable justifications for his assertion that there are not negative political costs to a free trade area. It is probably more difficult to model the political side of the question than the economic, and consequently it would be advisable to leave the political debate open. The economic rationale for a free trade area is so strong that it should be considered on its own merits by those engaged in public policy.

Energy from the Arctic: Facts and Issues

Judith Maxwell
Montreal: Canadian-American Committee, 1973, x, 125 pp.*

It has become clear over the last few years that Canada is increasingly reluctant to export energy resources to her natural trading partner, the U.S.A. What factors have caused this recent aversion to continental free trade in general and energy trade in particular? How vital is Canada as a supplier of energy to the U.S.A.? What regulatory proceedings, environmental hearings and native land claims remain to be undertaken before a Mackenzie Valley pipeline can be constructed? The answers to these questions are not to be found in this slender volume, since an understanding of them requires detailed study and analysis of the Canadian economy and its institutions. However, Ms. Maxwell does provide an excellent introduction to these topics. Her diligence in gathering factual material is to be welcomed, especially as her recording of this information is not offset by an excessively partisan attitude either for or against trade in energy.

Ms Maxwell completed this study in the summer of 1973, before the Arab oil embargo and subsequent increase in the world price of oil. It was written on the assumption that the U.S.A. would face an energy crisis and that American policy in the late 1970s would be directed towards reducing reliance on Middle East oil, and increasing supplies of oil and gas from North American sources. Ms. Maxwell states that Canada is projected to be a vital source of energy supply for the U.S.A., providing about 10 percent of total American imports of oil and gas by 1985. This high cost energy from Arctic regions, once it is discovered in sufficiently large fields, can be transported to Midwestern and Pacific consumers by a Mackenzie Valley pipeline, provided the latter is approved. It is a tribute to Ms. Maxwell's grasp of the issues that she correctly predicts the problems which have befallen the Mackenzie Valley project in recent

**Journal of Energy and Development* 1(2) (1976): 352–354.

years. Her book considers these problems in logical order: the necessity for exploration to reveal fields of sufficient size to realize economies of scale in production (Chapter 2); the challenge of transportation by pipeline across the Arctic environment (Chapter 3); native land claims (Chapter 4); regulatory hearings (Chapter 5); and government attitudes towards the national benefits and costs of a present or future Mackenzie Valley pipeline (Chapters 6, 7 and 8).

The issues involved in the transportation of natural gas (but not oil) from the Mackenzie Delta to markets in the south focus upon the application by Canadian Arctic Gas pipeline Company Limited to build a 48 inch pipeline to deliver some 4 billion cubic feet per day of gas. This consortium of twenty seven companies active in the production and distribution of natural gas originally hoped to carry gas from the Prudhoe Bay oilfields in Alaska in addition to Canadian sources. The El Paso Company has a counter proposal to move the Prudhoe Bay gas via a gas pipeline to be built parallel to the Alyeska oil pipeline, and then by liquefied natural gas tanker to the Pacific coast. In addition, a 'Maple Leaf' group has applied to move Mackenzie Delta gas to Canadian markets, using a smaller 42 inch pipeline. These developments do not invalidate the informative chapters on native land claims and regulatory hearings in Ms. Maxwell's book, since these have carried on following the pipeline application by Arctic Gas.

The lengthy hearings and concurrent hardening of public opinion in Canada against an early start to the Mackenzie Valley pipeline have led to considerable delay in Northern energy exploration and production. Ms. Maxwell reports that Arctic Gas Co. had hoped to begin construction in the winter of 1976/77 but this has been held up by at least three years. The Canadian Department of Indian and Northern Affairs has set up the Berger Commission to examine the full economic, social and environmental effects of a Mackenzie Valley gas pipeline right of way. It began hearings in March 1975 and is funded until September 1976. In early 1976 a large Eskimo Land claim by the Inuit Tapirisat was filed with the Cabinet and is expected to take some times to settle. The National Energy Board has also been conducting hearings on the Arctic Gas Co. application. Its role in the Canadian structure of political decision making is outlined concisely by Ms. Maxwell in Chapter 5. The NEB is charged with examining the economic and technical viability of the proposal and in doing so must consider 'any public interest that in the Board's opinion may be affected by the granting or the refusing of the application' (p.68). This involves a long and costly process. The final decision on the pipeline application in Canada must be made by the federal Cabinet. Arctic Gas Co. must also obtain approval from the U.S. government for the pipeline on American territory. The major regulatory body involved in the United States is the Federal Power Commission, although Ms. Maxwell found that 'as many as sixty-five branches of the federal government have some influence on energy policy'(p.72).

In the last three chapters of her book Ms. Maxwell manages to use a little economic analysis. She deals with the benefits and costs to Canada of the Mackenzie Valley pipeline, and makes a good theoretical point by showing that an inflow of foreign (U.S.) capital to finance the pipeline will lead to an appreciation of the Canadian dollar with possible adverse secondary effects on domestic output and employment, depending upon the amount of spare capacity in the economy. She argues that the pipeline should satisfy two conditions, i.e. that the benefits to Canada exceed the costs, and that it strengthen the economic base of the nation. After some diversionary remarks on the difficulty of making reliable econometric forecasts, she gives a modest push in favor of arguments which advocate postponement of the pipeline. True, she does not argue for the option of postponing construction as strongly as does John Helliwell of the University of British Columbia, but it is clearly stated that the main benefit will be to guarantee that Canada is self-sufficient in energy in the future. It is also suggested that delay of the pipeline will make it easier for Canada to finance construction from domestic sources, as national wealth increases over time. Thus delay will help to avoid the anticipated appreciation of the dollar which may occur with an inflow of foreign capital to finance an early start.

This reviewer is not impressed by the foreign exchange rate appreciation argument. At most, the appreciation would be by a few cents, rather than the more dramatic changes forecast. The total cost of the pipeline is expected to be about $5 billion, which is only 3 percent of Canada's G.N.P. The construction will take place over several years, so the annual expenditures will run well under 1 percent of G.N.P. Canada is an open economy and historically has financed a current account deficit by a capital account surplus, with persistent net foreign investment.

Consequently Canada should not find it unusual to accommodate large capital inflows.

Another issue which deserves a more specific statement than it receives from Ms. Maxwell is the major role played by governments in actual energy production and development, as well as regulation. Today the actions of government agencies are probably the major element of uncertainty in energy policy. In Canada there is a major dispute between producing provinces, such as Alberta, and consuming provinces, such as Ontario and Quebec, over the price of oil and gas. Effective tax and profit rates on oil and gas exploration can be changed arbitrarily by legislation. The two price system for oil has produced major distortions in the economy. Government involvement in Syncrude and Petro Canada has increased the influence of the public sector relative to the private sector, and may eventually be decisive in leading to a Canadian policy of self-sufficiency in energy.

From this review we can see that many Canadians wish to delay construction of a Mackenzie Valley pipeline. They have become more sophisticated in their approach to the U.S. energy crisis and wish to insulate themselves from it. They are reluctant to trade in energy and are interested in conservation of resources for future self-sufficiency. In economic terms, Canadians have adopted a higher rate of social time preference. Government policy has responded by becoming more cautious towards energy development. The book by Ms. Maxwell is an excellent introduction to these changes in Canadian attitudes towards the development and marketing of energy from the Arctic.

63 Tariff and Science Policies: Applications of a Model of Nationalism

D.J. Daly and S. Globerman
*Toronto and Buffalo: University of Toronto Press for the Ontario Economic Council, 1976, 125 pp.**

There are three contributions in this recent essay on Canadian commercial and science policy. First, there is a good survey of the ever growing literature on the costs of the Canadian tariff. This goes beyond the usual aggregative proposition that the tariff serves to reduce the level of national income *per capita* by incorporating a discussion of its distributional and regional impacts. This distributional issue is taken up at length by a clever twist of the Stopler-Samuelson theorem. The authors assume that management is the scarce factor of production in Canada, relative to labor and other factors. This leads to the prediction that owners of knowledge and management skills gain from protection relative to workers and owners of capital and resources. Several interesting explanations of nationalism in Canada and implications for tariff and science policy follow from this insight. Thirdly, there is a good critical review of Canadian science policy. Here it is shown that present research expenditures on basic innovations would be better directed towards support of methods which speed up the diffusion of existing technology.

The three sections are integrated by constant reference to the Albert Breton–Harry Johnson model of economic nationalism. The authors state that this model predicts that the Canadian tariff reduces real national income, increases prices of goods to consumers and workers, but leads to extra payments for owners of the scarce factor. In Canada the scarce factor is human capital, especially management and research skills. This assumption is central to the basic theme of the book, which is that highly educated managers, bureaucrats and research scientists are able to earn higher relative incomes than would be possible under a system of free trade with its competition from outside rivals. This argument

Canadian Journal of Economics 11(3) (August 1978): 632–634.

is best developed in Chapter 3 and goes a long way in explaining the history of Canadian nationalism as it has manifested itself in commercial, science and immigration policies. These are all tinged by the self-interest of small groups of individuals, members of the Canadian intelligentsia, who articulate a rationale for nationalism. The impact of this trade theory insight by Daly and Globerman is that it provides a link between conventional economic theory and work on the Canadian elite by other social scientists such as Clement. It shows that even very neoclassical economists can develop a radical critique of the conventional politics of the Canadian establishment.

Condemnation of nationalism is continued by the authors in Chapters 4 and 5, this time in the context of science policy. Expenditures under present policy are said to favor basic research and innovations of new technology. This work is fostered by members of the science and research profession to increase their prestige and job responsibility. The authors favor a change in science policy, one which places much more emphasis upon the economic efficiency of technology. They suggest that such a new policy would favor adoption of existing techniques rather than invention of new ones. More attention should be devoted to the diffusion of technology in Canada, since it is allegedly slower than in the U.S.A. In support of their new science policy the authors provide some rather anecdotal evidence. Three examples of slow diffusion are reported, namely: innovations in numerical control for machine tools, the introduction of special presses for paper making, and the use of tufted carpets in the textile industry. The last example is used to advance a further point. Canadian manufacturers are often risk averse and are unwilling to adopt new technology since they are able to continue with inefficient production behind the tariff barrier.

Perhaps the main contribution of Daly and Globerman is to highlight the adverse impact of the tariff on the apparently unrelated area of science policy. The inefficiency of protection is felt throughout the Canadian economy with unexpected distributional consequences for managers and researchers. The formulation of science policy cannot escape from the vested interests of leaders in that field. These are challenging conjectures for national policy makers, although they will not surprise very many trade economists. The distributional aspects of the tariff can be extended to regional issues. The West and other areas peripheral to central Canada are often recognized as suffering net losses from the tariff since they buy manufactured goods at inefficient protected prices yet sell resources as world prices. When such adverse distributional effects of the tariff are added to its well known welfare losses for the nation as a whole, as confirmed by Young and the Wonnacotts, then the use of protection to foster Canadian independence is called into question. The virtue of this study is that it confronts the nationalist with some of the logical implications of tariff policy. Daly and Globerman have raised a valid issue and their work should stimulate further empirical research on this important topic.

The Effects of Energy Price Changes on Commodity Prices, Interprovincial Trade and Employment

J.R. Melvin

Toronto and Buffalo: University of Toronto Press, 1976, 106 pp.

This study of Canadian energy policy was commissioned by the Ontario Economic Council, an economic policy research group headed by Dr. Grant Reuber of the University of Western Ontario. In the last few years the Council has produced several excellent research studies in which economic theory is applied to a current policy problem in an effective manner. The present study by Professor Jim Melvin is in this spirit and is characterized by the imaginative use of international trade theory in the analysis of interprovincial trade in energy.

Readers of this journal will find the book of interest not only for its sound theory and informed empirical work but also because it brings out the policy conflicts between federal and provincial governments in Canada as they respond to sectional interest groups. This policy conflict within Canada is exaggerated by the loose nature of a confederation in which the competing interests of producer provinces, such as Alberta in the West, are set against those of consuming provinces, such as Ontario in the East, leaving little scope for the federal government to set a national energy policy. The lack of a consistent internal Canadian energy policy has been reflected in external problems as the Canadian and United States governments seek to reach an energy accommodation following increases in the world price for oil by OPEC. It would be useful if United States policy makers recognized the fragile nature of economic relationships within the federation of Canada, especially following recent political events in the province of Quebec.

Professor Melvin is concerned with tracing out the repercussion of a two-price system within Canada for petroleum and natural gas products. A divergence in energy prices can occur if a producer province increases the export price to other consuming provinces while keeping the costs

Journal of Energy and Development 2(2) (Spring 1977): 346–349.

to domestic users at a lower level. In effect, a provincial tax on exports is imposed by the producers of energy, which changes the intra-national terms of trade in their favor. It does not matter whether the oil firms or the provincial government increase the price, provided that the terms of trade move in favor of the producer against the consumer provinces. This conclusion is reinforced if oil is treated as an intermediate product, as there is an even greater fall in welfare for the consumer provinces.

The major analytical point made by Melvin is that such a system of differentiated provincial taxes on oil and gas is equivalent to a tariff since both have identical effects on relative prices and output. This equivalence of commodity taxes and tariffs, as first demonstrated by Mundell, is used to correct free market level. This implies that the best economic policy for Canada as a whole, and for Ontario as a consumer, is to set a uniform price for oil and gas across the nation. This will ensure the advantages of free trade in energy within Canada. Melvin does not explore the level of such a uniform price but presumably it should be set at the exogenously determined world price in order to avoid distortions and to reduce domestic consumption.

In the empirical chapters Melvin uses an input-output model for Ontario, which has 49 sectors, to examine the repercussions throughout the Ontario economy of a doubling in the price of energy products. In general the results reveal few welfare costs, namely, a modest fall in output, an increase in prices of under 3 percent overall (and only 1.6 percent in manufacturing), and a reduction in employment of between 2 and 4 percent – all of these results depending upon the assumptions used. The main adverse effect is upon the labor force, and this result stems directly from the fixed coefficients model used by Melvin. With the input-output model used in this version there is little or no possibility of factor substitution following the change in energy prices, despite common theoretical knowledge that relative prices of both factors and goods should alter, and thereby lead to general equilibrium effects.

Melvin is well aware that his empirical work using input-output tables with fixed coefficients is inconsistent with a theoretical neoclassical trade model in which substitution effects should occur in response to a change in relative prices. His defense is to suggest that the estimated changes in prices, output, and employment are the upper bounds of the true values, and that these are more valid in the short run than in the long run.

The major conclusion, that even relatively large increases in the price of energy have modest effects on the prices of other goods, is strengthened by this approach since it was obtained by a methodology which put all of the bias in an upward direction.

The other results are obtained using the same approach and all tend to be the extreme upper values. Doubling the price of hydrocarbon fuels raises prices in Ontario by 2.1 percent, with the largest increases of up to 5 percent in agriculture, plastics, and chemicals but with small increases in manufacturing. A uniform increase in prices of oil across the nation tends to harm Ontario less than other provinces, and Ontario exports are not adversely affected. There is an increase in unemployment in Ontario between 2 and 4 percent, depending upon the assumptions made about import demand elasticity. In general, Ontario does better than expected from a uniform oil price rise, and its policy should be to argue for one.

Melvin also examines the impact on the United States of a doubling of oil prices. His estimates are reported in [his] table 5 and reveal a small price increase of under 3 percent in total with even smaller increases for most sectors, even allowing for the indirect effects on prices of the impact of oil as an intermediate product. It is also found that if energy prices increase by the same amount in North America, there is a greater adverse effect upon Canada than upon the United States, and the Canadian dollar could fall in value by 1 percent. Melvin suggests that it may not be in Canada's interest to secure a uniform North American price for energy. In this context his figures could also be interpreted to show the relatively trivial benefits to Canadian industry of an energy price differential vis-à-vis the United States; the resulting small sectoral gains should be placed alongside the economy-wide gains from free trade.

In conclusion, Melvin's work can be interpreted as further evidence for the benefits of free trade in energy products, not only between nations, but also on an interprovincial basis.

Coal and Canada-U.S. Energy Relations

Richard L. Gordon
*Montreal: Canadian-American Committee, 1976, viii, 75 pp.**

Considerable doubts are expressed in this volume about proposals to make the United States more reliant on coal as our alternative energy source in future years. In the context of the country's internal energy policy it is argued that coal will be doing well to retain its present share of energy supply, just under one-fifth of the total. The reasons for this rather pessimistic viewpoint are outlined by Professor Richard Gordon, a mineral economist at Pennsylvania State University, in his book written well over a year ago, before the new energy policy of the Carter administration was announced. Consequently there are several assumptions about policy parameters which have been modified by subsequent events, but the book remains valuable for its comments on United States-Canadian energy relations.

In the external context the book is correct in emphasizing the interdependence of United States-Canadian trade in energy, in general, and coal, in particular. It is anticipated that free trade in coal will continue despite the increase in support in each nation for policies of self-sufficiency. The economic advantages of north-south trade in coal, and in other energy sources such as electricity and gas, are mainly explained by high transport costs for east-west movement. The economic advantages of free trade in coal are likely to outweigh any political benefits from self-sufficiency, with the gains from trade being mutual.

Prof. Gordon does not find any evidence to support the viewpoint that development of coal offers a potential alternative source of fuel to oil and gas for meeting the United States energy crisis. He concludes (p.67) that 'In general the longer-run prospects for a substantial shift towards greater use of coal in the United States must be viewed with considerable skepticism.' There are several reasons for this conclusion. First, Gordon

Journal of Energy and Development 3(2) (Spring 1978): 439–441.

is critical of coal reserve forecasts, since many of them make use of inferred or hypothetical reserves rather than actual reserves. The costs of developing even the identified reserves may be higher than anticipated. Second, a major increase in coal consumption would require relocation of industry with resulting expenditures on capital equipment and on the retraining of workers in the labor-scarce Western states. Alternatively, a breakthrough in transportation technology would be required, since high transport costs act as a constraint on the movement of coal. Third, the structure of United States public policy hinders coal development, especially since the passage of safety and health regulations in 1969 (which are alleged to have reduced productivity in mining) and recent legislation to control sulfur emissions and strip mining. Gordon anticipates that a strong environmental lobby will succeed in the maintenance of anti-pollution standards and conservation-minded legislation.

In practice it is possible for the United States government to trade off environmental standards for higher coal output, especially by the relaxation of controls on strip mining. If it does so, the government will be choosing to perpetuate the divergence between the private and social costs of coal production and will be giving an implicit subsidy to coal. There are other methods by which the government can change the cost parameters of the coal industry, for example, by increasing the price of competing energy sources through the removal of price controls on gas and oil. Although these policies are not considered by Gordon, he does stress the interrelationships of coal with other energy sectors, and the implications of this for external policy.

As in most other areas of economic life there is a considerable amount of interdependence in coal consumption and production between the two major North American countries. At first sight Canada appears to be a little more vulnerable than the United States to possible changes in the current policy of unrestricted trade in coal. Ontario Hydro imports a large proportion of its coal from the United States and this source of supply might be threatened by a United States policy of coal self-sufficiency. Upon deeper analysis it is found that Canadian vulnerability is less than it appears since there are alternative sources of coal supply in Western Canada, which could be made available at high, but not prohibitive, transport costs. Western supplies would make use of the railway system from Alberta to the Great Lakes, and use low-cost barges to Ontario. There appears to be enough Albertan coal to make Canada self-sufficient in coal, if required, while still leaving British Colombian coal available for export to Japan. In addition to the economic potential of coal self-sufficiency, Canada also has considerable political bargaining power in the wider area of energy policy. Large amounts of electricity are exported from Canada to the Midwestern states and this can be cut off if coal supplies are threatened. It would also be possible for Canada to restrict exports of iron ore to United States steel companies, and to withhold other types of resources.

Of course, none of these restrictions is desirable as all will impose welfare costs in terms of foregone economic efficiency. Presumably both nations realize the opportunity costs of policies of energy self-sufficiency and should be reluctant to incur them. The author suggests that an embargo on coal exports to Canada is unlikely to be imposed by the United States, for the above reasons, and also because exports of steam coal to Ontario Hydro are a small percentage of total United States coal supply. It can be concluded that there is a greater danger to Canadian-United States harmony in other areas of energy trade, such as oil and gas pipelines, than in the relatively non-controversial area of trade in coal.

Nationalism, Technology and the Future of Canada

Wallace Gagne (ed.)
Toronto: Macmillan of Canada, 1976, 167 pp.[*]

For the many diverse arguments made by the authors of the six essays in this volume it is possible to draw two themes. First, it is clear that the major constraint on Canadian nationalism is the heterogeneous structure of the country. This leads to different cultural patterns and attitudes across the nation, with local concerns of primary interest in each of the four regions. The search for a distinctive Canadian identity is always frustrated since there is no single central conception of national unity but several regional cultural areas instead.

The essay by Howard Aster deals with the philosophic basis of Canadian nationalism and advances the idea that the diversity of culture observed in the country is a basis for nationalist development. He favors the slow, organic growth of 'communitarian' or regional nationalism in Canada rather than the 'ideational' sort of federalism with its emphasis on power and territory. Here it is perhaps valid to realize that regional diversity is the unique feature of Canadian nationalism, and that heterogeneity can have cultural advantages which may offset the probable economic disadvantages. It is a pity that the essay on Quebec, by E. Cloutier, does not explore this theme. Instead it has a narrow viewpoint and merely outlines the (pre-1976 election) program of the Parti Québécois.

A second theme is the perception that Canadian independence is restricted by the pervasive nature of (U.S.) technology. This inverse relationship between the pace of technical change and the degree of independence is assumed by all six of the writers despite the debatable nature of the proposition. The opposite case could be made. In terms of conventional neoclassical theory an increase in technology will increase output and the absolute returns to factors of production. As wages and profits increase, there is greater scope for the pursuit of non-economic

[*]*Journal of Economic History* 38(2) (June 1978): 539–540.

goals such as independence. Here we see that independence is a luxury good. With greater wealth achieved through technical advance, Canadian consumers have more degrees of freedom rather than less.

In addition to these two major themes, some more specific points made in the book call for comment. The well-argued paper by Paul Phillips uses the Galbraithian model of society to focus upon the problems of Canadian unions in an economy dominated by foreign (U.S.) owned multinational corporations. Phillips does not believe that the large international unions can work for the interests of their Canadian members since they have a tendency to support U.S. legislation, such as the Burke-Hartke bill and DISC, both of which are designed to create jobs for U.S. workers at the expense of foreign labor. Phillips does not agree with Galbraith's view that modern corporations pose a threat to the unions. Instead he suggests that as technology advances there is a greater need for intellectual human capital in corporations and government departments. This development leads to the 'proletarianization' of skilled white-collar workers and in turn to their unionization. Phillips hopes that these new unions will strengthen the labor movement in Canada and that they may help to promote an independent Canadian labor movement which can attempt to reduce American domination of the economy.

The papers by Clarkson, Gagne and Woods all emphasize the colonial status of Canada. They reject a continentalist free trade policy (which would at least maximize welfare and increase real income) since it means more integration with the United States. They do not seem to realize, however, that historical reliance on tariffs has not promoted a healthy domestic industry but has only succeeded in encouraging foreign direct investment by U.S. multinationals. Perhaps one method to reduce foreign ownership of the Canadian economy would be to remove tariffs, permit investments by multinationals, but tax away any excess profits. Such a policy would distinguish between the efficiency and distributional aspects of nationalism – a distinction which has escaped the attention of the political scientists writing in this book.

The Impact of Free Trade in Canada

Roma Dauphin
*Ottawa: Economic Council of Canada, Supply and Services Canada, 1978, xii, 185 pp.** *

In this stimulating and provocative study Professor Dauphin of Sherbrooke University examines both the distributional and efficiency aspects of the Canadian tariff. The stimulating sections of the book are those, such as Chapter 4, which focus upon the regional aspects of protection. Dauphin provides some useful empirical estimates of the regional impact of free trade between Canada and the United States. He uses the 1971 Canadian input-output table, with 110 sectors, to calculate the effects of such a policy on wage rates and distribution of the labor force in five regions. He finds that the Western and Atlantic provinces may stand to gain relatively more than Quebec and Ontario from a policy of unilateral free trade. His model assumes that labor mobility is the safety valve which helps to minimize the adjustment costs of a free trade policy. Dauphin also provides, in Chapter 3, some very useful data on the net and gross rates of protection. These update previous studies on effective rates of protection and incorporate some Canadian non-tariff barriers to trade.

The discussion of the costs of the tariff in Chapters 1, 2 and 3 is somewhat more provocative. Dauphin refers to the 'astonishing results' of the well-known 1967 study by the Wonnacotts which found that a free trade area between Canada and the United States would increase Canadian real GNP by 10.5 per cent. He alleges that 'these estimates have since been refuted' (page 9) and refers to unpublished work by Powrie and Fortin to support this point. However, he then states that the scale assumptions of the Powrie paper are 'totally arbitrary and somewhat unlikely' without being able to substantiate this crucial criticism. It is the potential dynamic economies of scale and related gains from free

Canadian Public Policy 4(4) (Autumn 1978): 576–577.

trade that account for most of the net trade benefits calculated by the Wonnacotts and others. They should not be downgraded by the author.

In a similar fashion Dauphin misrepresents the more recent study by J.R. Williams. In the table on page 74 and in the accompanying text Dauphin states that 'Williams calculated, on the basis of a general equilibrium model, that elimination of the Canadian tariff would make it technically possible to increase the level of real income in Canada by about 1.4 per cent.' This is a complete misreporting of the Williams study, which fortunately has been published recently by the University of Toronto Press. On page 30 of Williams' book it can be found that in purely static terms the cost of the Canadian tariff alone is 1.36 per cent in terms of consumption goods, but is 5.33 percent in terms of investment goods. The cost of both the Canadian and United States tariffs (which is what the Wonnacotts measured) is 3.97 per cent in consumption goods or 9.12 per cent in investment goods. The latter figures confirm the Wonnacotts estimate of static costs. Of course, their final figure of 10.5 per cent for the costs of both tariffs together also includes dynamic elements. Williams himself realizes this and states that this figures are 'exceptionally conservative' and tend to underestimate the gains from free trade.

For Dauphin to fail to report the full results of the Williams study is misleading and exhibits an unscientific bias which throws doubt upon his other findings. For example, few readers will have confidence in Dauphin's main conclusion, which is that 'free trade achieved through a unilateral action might not increase income per capita by more than 2 per cent' (page 83). Before he could come up with this ballpark figure it seems that Dauphin had already struck out. It is a pity that the unsatisfactory work on the costs of the tariff may reduce that value of the author's very useful focus upon regional aspects of the tariff. This is a challenging book for those concerned with Canadian commercial policy. Its findings should be interpreted with caution.

Foreign and Domestic Firms in Canada: A Comparative Study of Financial Structure and Performance

Daniel Shapiro

*Toronto: Butterworth, 1980, vii, 142 pp.**

Professor Shapiro's new empirical study of the performance of foreign-owned versus domestic firms in Canada is a welcome addition to the literature of international business in general and of Canadian industrial organization in particular. The book is in the tradition of work by Safarian, Rosenbluth, Bloch, Caves, and other specialists on the structure of Canadian industry and foreign ownership.

Using a new database, Shapiro examines the interrelationships between the key variables affecting a firm's economic performance, such as size of firm, degree of foreign ownership, concentration ration and growth rate. Shapiro throws new light on previous studies in this area, which have been somewhat indecisive. In addition, he extends the analysis in a significant new direction by giving substantial attention to the financial characteristics of Canadian and foreign-owned firms. Here he builds upon the work of Pattison for Canada, and that of Robbins and Stobaugh on other countries and for multinational firms. Shapiro's integration of economic theory and financial analysis is more comprehensive than much of the previous work done in this area.

The book has seven chapters and a poor index. The introduction contains a good literature review which emphasizes the Hymer-Caves approach to multinational firms and identifies the internal market of multinationals as a firm-specific ownership advantage. There follows a crucial data chapter, and then four chapters testing the financial structure, profitability, determinants of profitability and growth of foreign versus domestic firms in Canada.

The main element which distinguishes Shapiro's work is his diligent exploitation of a novel database. The data are drawn from detailed corporation financial statistics collected for the Corporations and Labour

Canadian Journal of Economics 14(4) (November 1981): 739–741.

Unions Returns Act (CALURA). While aggregated CALURA data are published by Statistics Canada, Shapiro makes use of new unpublished disaggregated balance sheet information. These CALURA data are used at the three-digit level for the 1968–1972 period. The sample includes some 750 large firms in the manufacturing sector with assets of $5 million or more. These large firms account for 75 percent of all manufacturing assets. The numerous small firms excluded from the study are mainly Canadian owned, but the author argues that this fact is unlikely to bias the results, especially since he is mainly concerned with a comparison of the relative performance of three categories of corporations: American owned, Canadian owned, and other foreign owned. Data on some sixty financial and economic items are manipulated to analyze the performance of these three categories of firms.

Canadian-controlled firms are found to be slightly smaller than American- or foreign-controlled firms, although the difference is not statistically significant when size is measured by assets. Yet when measured by sales, American-controlled firms are significantly larger than Canadian- or other foreign-controlled firms. The correlation between assets and sales is 0.78 for all firms in the sample. The relatively strong support for the classic relationship between size and foreign control is not matched by support for a similar correlation between foreign control and the concentration ratio. Shapiro does not find a significant relationship between American control and high concentration, a result which is somewhat similar to that of Rosenbluth using data of an earlier vintage. Shapiro finds widespread differences in the financial structure of the three groups of firms. The American-controlled firms use retained earnings more than any other methods, while other foreign-controlled firms have more debt financing. When they do use debt financing American firms borrow mainly from affiliates. In a related study at a more aggregate level Pattison found that foreign controlled firms use retained earnings rather than debt, in contrast to other Canadian firms, a finding that is apparently biased by the inclusion of American-controlled firms along with other foreign-controlled firms as one group. Shapiro also finds that while American-controlled firms accumulate more inventories than domestic firms, they are still efficient in turning over inventories. The American-owned firms are not more liquid than other firms once inventories are netted out. They also tend to invest less in affiliated companies that the other foreign and Canadian firms, perhaps owing to remittance of funds to their parents.

In his model of the determinants of profitability, Shapiro generates significant coefficients for most of his independent variables; yet the explained variation is only about 20 percent. Variables positively related to profits are size, size squared, concentration ratio (as measured by the Herfindahl index), foreign control, leverage, turnover ratio, and growth. The variance of earnings is usually insignificant (86–7). Shapiro produces evidence to demonstrate that American-owned firms earn higher profits than other firms in Canada. The American firms also have less risk (measured by variance) in their earnings. The higher mean and more stable earnings of American firms hold across several measures of profitability and are probably due to the advantage of internalization. Shapiro does not find that size is positively related to profitability; indeed, across most size classes he says that 'increasing firm size brings with it neither an increase in profits rates, nor a decrease in variability' (p. 75). For Canadian firms profitability declines as size increases. Over the 1968–72 period of the study Shapiro notes that the American-Canadian differential in profitability persisted. Yet despite their profitability, Shapiro discovers that American-controlled firms do not necessarily grow faster than other firms.

Shapiro fails to include two important variables in his work; namely, the tariff and expenditures on R and D. The tariff is excluded due to a lack of detailed data at the three-digit level, but an attempt is made to capture some of the effects of the tariff by the use of dummy variables for thirteen industry groupings. The subsequent work reported fails to draw out fully the important implications of the tariff for profitability, concentration, and financial performance of the sample firms. Similarly the fundamental nature of R and D expenditures by parent multinationals and the undetermined impact of such R and D on the relative performance of subsidiaries versus independent domestic firms is not considered, again due to the lack of R and D data at the three-digit level. A little less concern for the virtue of the statistical data set in hand and more interest in the unresolved theoretical issues about the interrelationships between tariffs, foreign ownership, R and D, concentration, and all the other variables would have improved this study. As it stands, Shapiro's work is a significant advance in the continuing study of the influence of foreign ownership on the structure of Canadian industry.

69 U.S. Competitiveness in the World Economy

Bruce R. Scott and George C. Lodge (eds)
*Boston: Harvard Business School Press, 1985, 543 pp.**

In Canada industrial strategy is usually discussed by nationalists rather than managers. Arguments are advanced to reduce U.S. foreign ownership by a stronger role for governments in the economy. Sometimes it is suggested that high-technology sectors can be promoted, perhaps by discriminatory R&D grants to Canadians rather than to foreign-owned firms.

The nationalist, protectionist version of an industrial strategy for Canada is sometimes endorsed by business groups, which might benefit from such selective protection, government subsidies and/or tax breaks. With these exceptions, those to the left of centre usually advocate more state intervention with greater fervor than business leaders, or, indeed, most policy makers.

All of this may change. While managers of the subsidiaries of U.S. multinationals in Canada wrestle with the issue of protectionist sentiment versus free trade with the United States, at home the thinking of the managers in the U.S. parent firms is undergoing a dramatic change.

Faced with the immense success of Japan and the four newly industrialized countries (NICs) of South East Asia (South Korea, Taiwan, Hong Kong and Singapore) many U.S. firms and managers are making a reappraisal of U.S. trade policy. Questions are being asked about the costs of the traditional policy of comparatively free trade in an age when Asian competitors seem to benefit from government-assisted trade programs.

A new book[1] by professors at the Harvard Business School captures the current spirit of U.S. management thinking. Produced to commemorate the seventy-fifth anniversary of the world's leading business school, this

---

Policy Options Politiques (April 1985): 15–16.

200

book is a shocking reminder of the self doubt and malaise now prevalent in U.S. business circles.

The key theme of the book is that the United States needs to adopt a coherent and explicit industrial strategy, in which the state will work with business to restore the competitiveness of the U.S. business sector. Only by such a match of public and private interests can the United States meet the challenge to its export markets of the new high-technology products of the Asian nations.

The editors of this report on the declining nature of U.S. competitiveness argue that the United States already has an implicit industrial strategy. But it is the wrong one.

At present the United States, like the democracies of Western Europe, pursues a national policy which is 'distribution-oriented'. The governments (federal and state) make large expenditures on social welfare and related equity-type programs. The contributors to the book argue convincingly that the United States is now a *de facto* welfare state, since domestic social commitments have increased dramatically in the last 15 years.

In contrast, Japan and the four newly industrialized countries pursue a 'development-oriented' strategy. This emphasizes the growth and efficiency. It neglects social justice. The state works hand-in-hand with business to promote new industries and exports. Japan and the NICs have now developed sweeping man-made competitive advantages in high technology sectors.

While the success of Japan is legendary (it is now the second largest trading partner of the United States, after Canada) the phenomenal growth of the four NICs is less widely known. While Japan has used its large internal market for a blatantly protectionist policy to nurture its high-technology industries, the NICs have relied upon export-led growth.

The NICs are now the third largest trading partner of the United States, ahead of any single European nation. Most worrying, from the U.S. point of view, is that the NICs are now successful in trade in many high-technology product lines, the very ones where the United States itself used to enjoy world leadership.

The Harvard professors report measures of the decline in U.S. competitiveness. These show that the U.S. share of world markets in the higher-technology sectors is falling relative to the shares of Japan and the NICs. Already U.S. trade patterns are strikingly similar to those of the uncompetitive nations of Western Europe, which increasingly rely on exports of mature and lower-technology sectors.

The reasons for this decline in U.S. competitiveness are traced back to a national strategy which has emphasized consumption rather than investment. It is argued that U.S. savings and investment ratios are too low, and that these have been depressed by government fiscal and monetary policies which penalize the business sector.

It is further argued that the United States must break out of its distribution-oriented straightjacket and escape into the real world of competitive growth. Since national strategies can change comparative advantages, it is said to be necessary for the United States to have its own industrial strategy.

The U.S. industrial strategy envisaged will be protectionist and business-oriented. Expenditures on domestic social programs may be reduced. The United States may decide to modify its leadership position in the Western Alliance, in order to consolidate its international commitments.

With such a redirection of effort, it is argued that the United States can regain its competitiveness in world markets. The effect that a resurgent U.S. trade sector will have on other nations is not discussed in this very ethnocentric study.

What this means for Canada is trouble. The protectionist paranoia of the Harvard Business School study will leave Canadian business out on a limb, unless Canadian interests are explicitly incorporated into U.S. strategy, through a properly negotiated free trade agreement.

Even then the focus on exports alone will raise problems for a nation, such as Canada, which is so involved in foreign direct investment. The gravest analytical error of the Harvard team is their total misunderstanding of the value of foreign investment.

In a world of ever-increasing non-tariff barriers to trade, foreign direct investment is a substitute for exports. Part of the growth of the NICs themselves has been stimulated by U.S. multinationals using the cheap labor of the NICs for offshore assembly platforms. In turn, this leads to greater exports of the NICs. The Scott and Lodge measure of competitiveness is far too narrow. It picks up such intra-industry trade by U.S. multinationals as a threat to the U.S.

economy since the NICs export high-technology products financed by U.S. capital.

Yet clearly the United States benefits from ownership of offshore production plants. Dividends are received and these profits help to finance future U.S. growth.

In fact, this example illustrates the mercantilist perspective of the Harvard team's industrial strategy. Nations are not firms. While a corporation can attempt to increase its worldwide market share, for all nationals to do so becomes a zero-sum game.

Canadian policymakers should therefore read Scott and Lodge with caution. It contains misleading prescriptions for trading economies like Canada's. We cannot afford the luxury of such protectionist wishful thinking.

Note

[1] *U.S. Competitiveness in the World Economy*, edited by Bruce R. Scott and George C. Lodge Boston: Harvard Business School Press, 1985. 543 p. US$25

Weathering the Storm: Canadian-U.S. Relations, 1980–83

David Leyton-Brown
Toronto: C.D. Howe Institute and National Planning Association, 1985, xi, 82 pp.[*]

The structure of this policy study may grate a little with an academic audience. The approach seems to be derived from the principle of casting a stone into a pond, where the ripples radiating out from the core contain ever wider versions of the same message. Thus we have basically three introductions, plus a concluding chapter, all making the same underlying point that there were major tensions in the US-Canadian relationship over the 1980–1983 period, but that greater understanding of our interdependence can lessen such tension. Fortunately, the further into the study one dives the greater is the depth of knowledge displayed in making this important point.

Following the author's introductory chapter, there is a sketch in Chapter 2 of the underlying economic and political factors affecting the bilateral relationship. The economics picture painted is one of increasing international competitiveness and the aggravation of a 'nascent protectionism' in the clothing, footwear, and consumer electronics industries that are most affected by cheaper Asian imports. The political picture emphasizes the disparities in political philosophies in the 1980–1983 period between the market-orientated, deregulationist Reagan administration in the United States and the more state-oriented Trudeau government in Canada, which perceived itself to have an election mandate to 'increase government intervention in foreign investment, energy and industrial strategy' (p.14). Also noted is the greater pluralism in the United States and an asymmetric spillover impact of U.S. media on Canadians. Examples cited as evidence of the increasing complexity in managing the bilateral relationship are the East coast fisheries treaty of 1979, which the U.S. administration failed to have approved by the

[*]*Canadian Journal of Political Science* 18(4) (December 1985): 796–797.

Senate, and the trucking dispute of 1982, which arose from deregulation of the U.S. trucking industry, and was found to involve no international discrimination against U.S. truckers on Canada's part.

The crux of the book lies in the next three chapters each of which deals with a major bilateral dispute in the chosen period: Chapter 3 on the National Energy Program, Chapter 4 on the softwood lumber case, and Chapter 5 on the dispute over border television broadcasting. Finally, Chapter 6 draws lessons from these examples of tensions in the bilateral relationship. One of the key U.S. complaints against Canada's National Energy Program was its apparent violation of the national treatment principle under which foreign-owned firms should not face discriminatory treatment. Canada has signed the 1976 OECD declaration on multinationals which prohibits such discrimination. The United States complained to the OECD about this issue, but little appears to have been resolved, although in another multilateral forum, the GATT, the United States did succeed in having Canada's local content provisions of FIRA declared a violation of the GATT articles. It is also argued that the United States could not take any effective unilateral 'retaliatory action against Canada without jeopardizing its own interests' (p.38). However, the threats of such action increased tensions and may have harmed bilateral relations.

The manner in which U.S. trade law can now be used by producers' groups is examined in the softwood lumber case of 1982–1983 (not to be confused with the reopening of this dispute in 1985). In 1982 U.S. lumber producers filed a petition with the U.S. International Trade Commission and the International Trade Administration of the Department of Commerce, to seek countervailing duties against Canadian lumber imports. The ITC made a preliminary determination that U.S. industries were materially injured by Canadian imports, due to the implicit subsidy involved in the provincial system of stumpage fees. However, the ITA found that the estimated net subsidy for each lumber product was *de minimis* (that is, under .5 per cent of the value of the product) and the case was dismissed. As a footnote on page 53 aptly observes, 'the underlying problems have not gone away, however,' as U.S. lumber interests are still seeking redress in Congress.

The most troublesome aspect of the border broadcasting dispute, which started in 1976 with Bill C-58 when Canadian advertisements on

U.S.-owned television stations ceased to be tax exempt, is the successful manner in which this case has been linked to unrelated issues. For several years lawyers working for the U.S. border television stations lobbied Congress to prevent U.S. citizens from deducting the costs of attending conventions in Canada, a strategy that worked until December 1980 when deductibility was permitted. Next, attempts were made to link removal of Bill C-58 with fishing rights and with removal of tax deductibility on sales of Telidon in the United States. Leyton-Brown states that 'now the genie is out of the bottle' (p.70) and that as other disputes arise interest groups will continue to seek linkages to unrelated issues.

Leyton-Brown concludes that the bilateral relationship is in a state of transition. The traditional 'set of implicit rules of conduct that were widely recognized by scholars and policy-makers alike' (p.79) no longer applies. However, he expects a new regime to develop fairly quickly, due to the great interdependence of the United States and Canada. He does not anticipate a return to the old special relationship, but instead a great recognition that unilateral action by either country is less than optimal for both. Basically Leyton-Brown is saying that the transaction costs of the bilateral relationship need to be reduced by the principals involved in the partnership. This would certainly help to improve the efficiency of the relationship but even economists now recognize that governments do not live by efficiency alone.

71 Canadian Multinationals

Jorge Niosi

*Toronto: Between the Lines, 1985, 200 pp.**

This is a translation by Robert Chosos of a book first published in French in 1983. It is perhaps an apt comment on the segmented nature of French-English research in Canada that this reviewer had not come across the original book despite spending most of the last two years working on the same topic. Niosi is a sociology professor, but he chooses to undertake a basically economic analysis of the rise (and fall) of Canadian-based multinationals such as Brascan, Momenco, Inco, Falconbridge, Noranda, Alcan, Cominco, Seagram, Hiram Walker, Macmillan, Bloedel, Massey-Ferguson, Polysar and Northern Telecom. In general, the descriptive commentary on these multinationals and their positions in the Canadian and world markets is well done and informative. The data used are mainly drawn from annual reports and company histories, but appear to stop in 1980. Niosi also attempts to apply the theories of economists such as Hymer, Vernon, Wells, Buckley and Casson as well as the dependency school to explain what he considers to be a paradoxical group of multinationals.

The paradox is mainly due to Niosi's misinterpretation of mainstream multinational theory. He seems to believe that the firm-specific advantages of multinationals are always based on technological innovation. He finds (correctly) that Canada's multinationals tend to adopt US technological innovation rather than generate their own. He feels that Canada is a 'semi-industrialized' national as a result of its dependence on foreign technology, yet he also finds that most of these Canadian multinationals are successful firms. He attributes this to their presence in oligopolistic industries and he argues that only the leading firm in the group goes abroad as a multinational. It is concluded that the existence of these

Canadian Public Policy 12(1) (March 1986): 273–274.

non-technologically intensive, yet successful, multinationals from Canada presents a challenge to existing theories.

This is wrong. First, Niosi does not seem to have heard of Japanese multinationals, the most successful in the world today. These firms have adapted and commercialized existing technologies and engage in globalization strategies in which they couple distributional skills with efficient production methods. Japan has not generated many Nobel Prize winners but Japanese firms are far ahead of U.S. and European multinationals; there must be some lesson here for Canada. Second, the advantage of marketing skills completely escapes Niosi. Yet, the postulates of internalization theory demonstrate that firm-specific advantages need not just be technologically based (and built up by R&D). They can also include marketing advantages; indeed, my own study of Canada's megafirms finds that their marketing strengths are part of a three tier, value-added chain in resource extraction, processing and distribution which combine to place Canada's multinationals in a very strong, long-run, globally competitive position. Third, Niosi does not understand the concept of intra-industry foreign direct investment. It is perfectly logical for multinationals to engage in cross investment when government-imposed barriers to trade, plus natural market imperfections, lead to opportunities for product differentiation and the exploitation of distributional advantages in separate national markets. Niosi does not have a 'feel' for business and the manner in which managers of multinationals search for the market niches in which Canada's multinationals have settled comfortably.

Despite the failure of the author to grasp some of the subtleties of the recent theory of multinationals, this study at least recognizes the importance of Canadian outward foreign direct investment. Niosi's suspicions about the effects of international capitalism bring a different perspective to the debate. His work should also help to contribute to the growing awareness by policy-makers of the global significance of Canada's multinationals.

72 The Competitive Advantage of Nations

Michael E. Porter
New York: Free Press; Toronto: Collier Macmillan, 1990, xx, 855 pp.*

Michael Porter's blockbuster book, *The Competitive Advantage of Nations*,[1] has been elegantly summarized by Donald Thain in the Summer 1990 issue of *Business Quarterly*.[2] Unfortunately, the length and complexity of Porter's work means that it is probably doomed to be one of the most unread books on the managers' bookshelf. Therefore, Professor Thain's laudatory review may leave Canadian managers with a rather sanguine view about the relevance of Porter's book. While most of Porter's analysis would work for managers based in the U.S., the European Community or Japan, much of it is superficial and plain wrong when applied in a Canadian situation.

His work needs to be modified in order to analyze the issue of Canada's international competitiveness. These modifications are not simple extensions; rather they represent an entirely different way of conceptualizing and testing the nature of Canadian competitiveness in an integrated global economic system.

Concept of the diamond is brilliant

About 90% of Porter's book is accurate and potentially relevant for Canadian managers. This included the brilliant concept of the diamond, the identification of clusters and the four stages of economic development. Yet, as is well known, Canada is only one-tenth the economic size of the U.S. Unfortunately it is the very 10% of Porter's book that is most relevant for Canadians that is the questionable part. In particular, the sections of his book that are most debatable include Porter's treatment of inbound foreign direct investment and the role of Canadian multinationals.

**Business Quarterly* 55(3) (Winter 1991): 61–64.

In these vital areas Porter's lack of knowledge of Canada tends to devalue the application of his core model to Canada. Porter's focus on Canada's 'home country' diamond cannot explain Canadian competitiveness and, whereas Canada's successful clusters are resource-based, they have value added in them. Porter's statements in his book, to the effect that Canada is a stage one 'factor-driven' economy, simply is inaccurate and dangerously misleading as policy advice to Canadians.

Porter's Diamond Model

The Porter model is based on four country-specific determinants and two external variables: chance and government. Porter's four determinants and two outside forces interact in the diamond of competitive advantage, with the nature of a country's international competitiveness depending upon the type and quality of these interactions. He says the four determinants for a nation '...shape the environment in which local firms compete and promote or impede the creation of competitive conditions.' The four determinants are:

1. *Factor conditions*: the nation's factors of production, including natural resources and created factors, such as infrastructure and skilled labor.
2. *Demand conditions*: the nature of home demand for products or services.
3. *Related and supporting industries*: the presence or absence of supplier and related industries that, themselves, are internationally competitive.
4. *Firm strategy, structure and rivalry*: the domestic rivalry of firms and the conditions governing how companies are created, organized and managed.

Porter's two outside forces, chance and government, present interesting contrasts. Government is clearly of critical importance as an influence on a home nation's competitive advantage. For example, to penalize foreign firms, government can use tariffs as a direct entry barrier, or it can use subsidies as an indirect vehicle. In both cases domestic firms benefit from short-run competitive advantages. These discriminatory government actions can lead to shelter for domestic firms, where shelter actually prevents the development of sustainable (long-run) competitive advantages.

While there is a certain lack of originality in the components of Porter's diamond model, it has exactly the correct perspective by its focus on the strategies of firms rather than nations. Porter says, 'firms, not nations, compete in international markets.. To the extent that he brings together the firm-specific linkages between the four determinants and the two outside forces, his model is useful and, potentially, predictive. Porter's policy recommendations to restrict the nature of government industrial and strategic trade policy, and instead, to open markets and have no arbitrary restrictions applied on foreign investment, are also to be welcomed.

Porter's testing is conventional

To operationalize the model Porter constructs 16 industry clusters and tests the model across ten countries, although only eight are reported. The eight are: West Germany, Italy, Japan, South Korea, Sweden, Switzerland, the United Kingdom and the United States. Of these countries, in terms of its diamond, Sweden is closest to Canada and can act as a base to think about applying Porter's model to Canada.

For each of the eight countries reported, Porter divides their industries into the 16 clusters, which incorporate a conventional grouping into four upstream clusters, six clusters for industries and supporting sectors, and six clusters for final consumption of goods and services. The four upstream clusters consist of materials and metals, forest products, petroleum and chemicals, and semiconductors and computers. The six industry and supporting sector clusters include multiple business, transportation, power generation and distribution, office, telecommunications, and defense. The six industry clusters for final consumption expenditure include food and beverages, textiles and apparel, housing and household, health care, personal, and entertainment and leisure. While these 16 clusters are quite useful for international comparisons they are probably not the set that would be used to analyze Canada's situation. For example, defense and most of the six final consumption clusters are obviously geared up for local (Canadian-based) use and will not show up in export statistics as a source of competitive advantage. We already know the reasons for this – Canada-first protectionist policies. What can Porter tell us that is new?

Finally, Porter describes four stages of national competitive development: factor driven, investment driven, innovation driven, and wealth driven. The last stage is associated with a decline in international competitiveness. At several points in the book Porter makes the classic mistake of stating that Canada is stagnating in Stage 1, due to its reliance on resource industries.

Canada's most successful industry clusters

Based on conventional statistical analysis of export shares it can already be predicted that Porter will find that Canada's most successful industry clusters will be: materials and metals, forest products, petroleum and chemicals, and transportation. The first three of these which are upstream, will be determined by Canada's natural resources in minerals, timber and energy. There is, however, substantial value added due to managerial and marketing skills in these areas. The transportation cluster's competitiveness will be determined by the institutional device of the Canada-U.S. autopact, since nearly one-third of Canada's exports (and imports) are in autos and auto-related products. This will drive the data on international competitiveness based on exports and world market share. While Canada's telecommunications sector should show up as a successful cluster, the particular role of Northern Telecom may be missed in Porter's national data, but may perhaps be captured by an industry study. Other clusters that might be close to inclusion but probably will not make it based on their global market shares, are power generation and distribution, and food and beverages. In the other nine clusters Canada is highly unlikely to be internationally competitive according to Porter's approach, although there may be successful segments within some of these clusters.

Porter's diamond is flawed

The model developed by Porter fails to explain key issues in Canada's international competitiveness on its own terms, for a variety of interconnected reasons. The major conceptual problem with Porter's model is due to the narrow definition that he applies to foreign direct investment (FDI). Porter defines only outward FDI as being valuable in creating competitive advantage. He then states that foreign subsidiaries are not sources of competitive advantage and that inward FDI is 'not entirely healthy.' He also states that foreign subsidiaries are importers, and that this is a source of competitive disadvantage.

All of these statements are questionable and have long ago been refuted by Canadian-based scholars. All have demonstrated that the research and development undertaken by foreign-owned firms is not significantly different from that of Canadian-owned firms. The largest 20 U.S. subsidiaries in Canada export virtually as much as they import. (The ratio of exports to sales is 25% while that of imports to sales is 26%).

The work by Porter actually reveals a branch plant mentality. He sees foreign firms in Canada as simply micro-replicas of their parents that only exist because of unnatural entry barriers, for example the tariff. While he states that judgment is used in examining the competitive performance and managerial autonomy of foreign-owned subsidiaries he does not specify how this is to be done and then indicates that is does not apply to 'production subsidiaries of foreign companies.' This thinking then rules out the broader nature of the foreign-owned subsidiaries' contributions to the development of Canada's manufacturing base.

Foreign direct investment is two-way

The real weakness in Porter's book is its flawed understanding of the nature of two-way foreign direct investment. In the Canadian context, 70% of Canadian trade is done by 50 multinationals, with half of these being foreign owned. The methodology used by Porter permits only an examination of the exports and outward FDI of Canada's 'home' industries. Yet there is as much inward FDI as outward and the imports of the foreign-owned subsidiaries are matched by their exports. Indeed, Canada runs a slight surplus on the intra-firm trade of the sum of U.S. firms in Canada plus Canadian-owned firms in the U.S., demonstrating that foreign-owned firms act and play as significant a role as do the domestic-owned Canadian corporations.[3]

The views expressed by Porter on the role of natural resources are old fashioned and misguided. He argues that reliance on natural resources is as bad as reliance on unskilled labor or simple technology. In fact, Canada has developed a number of successful megafirms that have turned our comparative advantage in natural resources into proprietary firm-specific advantages in resource processing and further refining.[4] These are sources of sustainable competitive advantage. Canada's successful multinationals such as Alcan, Noranda and Nova, illustrate the methods by which value added has been introduced by the managers of these resource-based companies. Over time, Canada's resource-based industries do, in fact, have sustainable advantages.

True significance of multinational activity

Almost all of Canada's large multinationals rely on sales in the U.S. and other triad markets. Indeed, it could be argued that the U.S. diamond is likely to be more relevant for Canada's industrial multinationals than is Canada's own diamond, since, on average over 70% of their sales take place there. The Canada-U.S. free trade agreement reinforces this point. It rather devalues the entire approach of Porter's book to dismiss Canada's diamond in this manner, however.

We can conclude from this that tensions arise in Porter's model as soon as a serious effort is made to incorporate the true significance of multinational activity. It is questionable whether multinational activity can actually be added into any, or all, of the four determinants, or included as a third exogenous variable.

This weakness in Porter's model would not only apply to Canadian-based firms but to multinationals from all small open economies, that is over 90% of the world's nations potentially cannot be modeled by the Porter diamond. Besides Canada, other nations with their own multi-national enterprises based on small home diamonds include Australia, New Zealand, Finland and most, if not all, Asian and Latin American countries, as well as a large number of other small countries. The small nations in the European Community, such as Denmark, have been able to overcome the problem of a small domestic market by gaining access to one of the triad markets – a point somewhat neglected by Porter. Perhaps 'triad-based diamonds' should be constructed and analyzed.

The main point of this criticism of Porter's methodology is that a clear recognition of the need to model multinational activity correctly in a Canadian context is necessary if policy prescriptions and activities are to be properly defined and undertaken. This requires a deep and consistent understanding of the nature of the multinational enterprise in Canada, coupled with a rich empirical and practical understanding of the actual performance of multinationals in Canada. Porter's book does not demonstrate mastery of these twin requirements.

Canada needs a North American diamond

Canada's home country diamond does not have the answers to explain Canada's international competitiveness. Instead, as Canada is highly integrated already with the United States, it is much more useful to conceive of a North American diamond for Canada. Once individual Canadian managers and workers perform to North American standards they can take the next step, which is to perform at a global standard.

Most Canadian manufacturing is already being forced to compete globally. Therefore the North American diamond is much more relevant for both FDI into Canada as well as Canadian FDI into the United States. (Some small, multidomestic businesses are not globalized.) In sharp contrast, most of Canada's service sectors are not globalized; they still rely on Canada's own diamond. The few globalized service sectors include banking and business services.

Canada needs to play in the big leagues of international competition and this means having the North American diamond as the basic unit of analysis for Canadian business decisions.[5] Success in North America can then be used as a base for success in the global economic system. Thus the North American diamond must be interpreted as an intermediate step in the development of globally competitive Canadian business. Without success in North America, survival is unlikely for any Canadian business subject to global competition. Virtually all Canadian manufacturing firms and most service sector organizations are now in this position.

Misplaced policy initiatives possible

While it is useful for Canada's business and government leaders to seek advice and ideas from all over the place, including outside of Canada, it will only compound the problems of Canada's lack of international competitiveness if the wrong framework of analysis is adopted carte blanche. Porter's original diamond model is conceptually flawed and empirically unsound when applied unchanged in a Canadian context. The thoughtless application of his book to Canada could reap a whirlwind of discontent and misplaced policy initiatives.

Notes

1 Porter, Michael E., *The Competitive Advantage of Nations*, New York: Free Press; Toronto: Collier Macmillan, 1990.
2 Thain, Donald H., "The War without Bullets," *Business Quarterly* 55(1) (Summer 119): 13–19.
3 Rugman, Alan M., *Multinationals and Canada-United States Free Trade*, Columbia, SC: University of South Carolina Press, 1990.
4 Rugman, Alan M. and John McIlveen, *Megafirms: Strategies for Canada's Multinationals*, Toronto: Methuen/Nelson, 1985.
5 For discussion of this, see Rugman, Alan M. and Joseph R. D'Cruz, *Fast Forward: Improving Canada's International Competitiveness*, Toronto: Kodak Canada, 1991.

73 Canada at the Crossroads: The Reality of a New Competitive Environment

Michael Porter
Ottawa: Business Council on National Issues and Minister of Supply and Services, October 1991, x, 468 pp.*

The study described in the report, *Canada at the Crossroads: The Reality of a New Competitive Environment*, faithfully applies Michael Porter's 'diamond' framework to Canada. It was prepared under Porter's supervision by the Canadian office of his Monitor consulting firm, using precisely the same methodology and conceptual framework as for the eight countries actually reported in his 1990 book.[1]

In an earlier *Business Quarterly* article, I outlined some of the problems with such an approach.[2] The Porter/Monitor team has missed the opportunity to amend the Porter framework to make it relevant for Canadians. Their conclusions and recommendations are inconsistent with their own analysis.

Does Canada have a weak home base diamond?

The key result of the Porter/Monitor study is the finding that Canada's home 'diamond' is weak and leads to an inability of Canadian-based businesses to develop sustainable global competitive advantages, except in resources. But Porter states that resource-based industries are an essential part of Canada's 'old economic order,' which Porter thinks has no future. He says, in effect, that Canada's diamond is broken and that it needs to be upgraded to improve Canada's lack of international competitiveness.

Most of Porter's policy recommendations are sound, especially his call to reduce the budget deficit, upgrade worker and management skills and improve business-labor-government relations. Yet these policy recommendations are actually incompatible with his analysis.

**Business Quarterly* 57(3) (Winter 1992): 59–64.

This incompatibility arises because Porter insists on applying his home base diamond analysis to Canada, whereas a much more relevant concept for Canadian managers is that of a North American diamond. This approach, developed by Joe D'Cruz and myself in 1991,[3] suggests that to become globally competitive, Canadian managers need to design strategies across both the U.S. and Canadian diamonds. They need to benchmark decisions on a North American basis, not just a Canadian one. Yet Porter reflects this approach when he states that Canadian businesses can only 'tap into' the U.S. diamond but not develop competitive advantages from it.

Unfortunately, Porter's focus on the home base on which to build a successful business is consistent with an economic nationalist's call for national champions. The weak home country diamond analysis suggests that Canada needs another 20 Northern Telecoms. Porter's analysis might be misinterpreted by nationalists to mean the broken Canadian diamond should be fixed by an industrial policy.[4] Porter's view that multinationals can only succeed with a strong home country base may still be true for the U.S., but it is at least 30 years out of date for Canada.

Porter's old-fashioned, naïve and politically mischievous viewpoint is inconsistent with Canada's support of the free trade agreement, tax reform, constitutional renewal and other economic, social and political measures aimed at improving the climate for doing business in a Canadian economy that is interdependent with that of the United States. It is as if Porter/Monitor had never heard of, or participated in, the divisive free trade election in Canada in 1988. In this the forces of economic nationalism were narrowly defeated by the economic realism and sovereignty consideration underlying the free trade agreement.

Canadian managers should use a North American diamond

A better approach to Canada's public policy is that of the Rugman/ D'Cruz North American diamond framework. This approach says that a Canadian manager needs to consider the U.S. diamond as well as the Canadian and should design strategies across the two diamonds. This means that Canadians should view the U.S. market as a home market, not just as an export market. This does not preclude consideration of elements in the Canadian diamond; it does preclude excessive reliance on it alone.

In practice, Canadian businesses already use North American benchmarks in their search for global competitive advantage. Our research indicates that most Canadian managers of large firms already use this double diamond framework. The problem is that small businesses and people in services still think in terms of the Canadian diamond, not realizing that they are often indirectly involved across the North American diamond.

The rejection of the North American diamond concept by Porter is really quite stunning, implying that the Porter/Monitor group did not fully understand the nature and role of multinational enterprises in a small, open, trading economy like Canada's.

A multinational enterprise is defined as a corporation that operates across borders in the production and distribution of its goods and services. There are various types of management control exercised by modern multinationals, some being highly centralized, that is, Porter-type home based, others being much more decentralized, some even operating as networks of virtually autonomous firms. The actual choice of management structure depends upon the strategy being pursued by the multinational enterprise. To use Porter's terms, the multinational enterprise operates across diamonds.

Contrary to Porter's thinking, there is no particular reason why a multinational needs a home base. It just so happens that U.S.-based multinationals grow up in a large domestic market where new products can be rolled out across the U.S. regions. For the U.S. manager, Canada is just another region. But his is not the case for a Canadian manager.

A Canadian multinational needs to build competitive advantages based on a foreign diamond rather than on its home diamond alone. A multinational from a smaller economy will experience greater opportunities in a larger foreign diamond. This double diamond approach is relevant to over 95% of the world's nations, that is, all those that are not in the triad of the United States, Japan or Europe.

In practice, Canadian-owned multinationals such as Northern Telecom, Alcan, Bombardier, Inco and Seagram have competitive advantages derived from attributes of the U.S. or other foreign diamonds, rather than the Canadian diamond alone. A major characteristic of

Canadian-owned multinationals is that their ratio of foreign to domestic sales is often 79% to 90%, far higher than the average of U.S.-based multinationals at 25%.

Of course, this can raise the question of whether these Canadian-owned multinationals are really Canadian. Even to ask this question shows the basic error in the approach of Porter/Monitor. It does not matter to the strategy of the multinational if it is Canadian or North American. It does matter that a Canadian manager needs to think about more than the Canadian diamond to develop a successful global strategy.

Managers of Canadian businesses today cannot base their strategies on the Canadian home-country diamond alone and tap into the U.S. diamond as Porter recommends. To do so would be totally irresponsible and a recipe for disaster. Porter's strategy would have been suitable in the 1890s, but it is wrong for the 1990s. Instead, to become globally competitive a North American mindset is required for Canadian business decisions.

Porter's case studies fit the double diamond

The free trade agreement is the institutional device that recognizes the linkages of the Canadian and U.S. diamonds; it institutionalizes the double diamond for Canadian managers. The Monitor group, and Porter, overlooked the details of the free trade agreement. For example, the vital concept of national treatment and the five exempted service sectors are overlooked in the Porter/Monitor study.

Since Canadian managers already operate within the framework of the free trade agreement their investment decisions are already benchmarked at North American standards and not just those of the Canadian diamond. Consequently, managerial strategy is already North American; examining the Canadian diamond alone, as Porter does, is not good enough for any Canadian business or for any firms in a cluster.

Examples of the Porter/Monitor misunderstanding of the Rugman/ D'Cruz North American diamond abound in the study. The four detailed case studies are not fully explained, as alleged, by the Canadian diamond. They are better explained by the double diamond approach for the following reasons:

1. The success of Northern Telecom in the United States is as much due to the intangible marketing skills and insights of its former CEO, Mr. Walter Light, about the need to manage within the U.S. diamond as it is to observable R and D expenditures and protection for Bell Labs' research in Canada's home-country diamond. The whole organizational structure of Northern Telecom is designed around the North American diamond; it does not 'tap into' the U.S. market, but is totally integrated across the border.

2. The same analysis of the validity of the double diamond is also true for Seagram in the whiskey industry, rather than the Monitor single diamond approach. The success of Seagram was due largely to its understanding of demand conditions in the United States, and not just government taxes and regulations in Canada's diamond.

3. The Monitor case study of the newsprint industry is also quite banal; it appears that the Monitor team overlooked the fact that there are at least two newsprint clusters in Canada (west coast and eastern Canada), with different characteristics and strategies as they operate in the North American diamond.

4. The Monitor team took out their best examples of the Canadian diamond – hockey – perhaps because they had already used rugby football as their example for the New Zealand book.[5] Except for hockey, nearly everything else in Canada is better explained by the double diamond framework.

To summarize, the 'North American' diamond suggests that Canadian managers treat the U.S. market as their home market, not an export market, and that a Canadian manager needs to make strategic decisions based on as thorough an understanding of the U.S. diamond as of the Canadian diamond. Our field research has revealed that Canadian managers already do this. Why Porter wants to reject this current managerial reality is a puzzle.

Canada's resource industries are wrongly dismissed

Porter states that Canada's abundance of natural resources leads to resource-based industries that compete in commodity markets and lack the ability to achieve upgrading. He states that Canada is a resource-based economy that has not been able to move beyond his first Factor-Driven stage. (See box)

Porter's conclusion is the same as that reported in several throwaway lines in his book, that Canada (like Australia) is stuck at the Factor-Driven stage and lacks the ability to move on to the more desirable Innovation-Driven stage. Indeed, Porter implies that Canada may flip all the way to decline in the Wealth-Driven Stage, missing out the useful middle two stages of development. The argument here, and the superficial analysis of resource-based industries throughout the Monitor study, is questionable.

Many of Canada's resource-based firms have intangible firm-specific advantages in marketing and management skills.[6] In Porter's terms, these are often the source of their sustainable competitive advantages. Yet the Monitor group makes the mistake of only analyzing and measuring what they can see – output and exports of goods using the observable physical natural resources. But because you cannot measure something does not mean that the intangible firm-specific advantage is insignificant.

In short, Canada's resource-based industries already make attempts to add value through marketing and management skills; these are just as valuable as high-tech expenditures. Good case studies would reveal this; the superficial ones done by Monitor would miss it.

Ironically this point is confirmed later in the study when the monitor team makes the naïve argument that greater R and D expenditures and technological improvements will result in upgrading and productivity growth and benefits. If these intangible benefits exist for the production side of the business, why not for the marketing side?

Porter's four stages model is too simplistic and probably meaningless for Canadian policy makers. Specifically there is no valid reason why clusters of resource-based industries cannot be placed in Porter's Innovation-Driven stage, rather than the Factor-Driven stage. If there is value added in a resource-based industry due to marketing or management skills, it has just as much right to be in the Innovation-Driven stage as an R and D based business. The Monitor data themselves confirm that resource-based industries are Canada's most competitive industries, accounting for the largest share of world cluster exports.

Foreign ownership is not analyzed properly

In his discussion of foreign ownership in his 1990 book, Porter repeatedly states that 'inbound' foreign direct investment is not a source of competitive advantage for a nation; instead it brings the products of another country's diamond strength into the home base without adding any value. Consistent with this thinking, in the Monitor report, Porter states that a home base is superior to foreign ownership. This statement is just a simple repetition of the criticism of foreign investment built into Porter's 1990 book.

Porter states that local ownership and a local home base generate greater benefits than foreign ownership and a foreign home base. This is totally inaccurate and an insult to the Canadian managers and workers in foreign-owned firms operating in Canada in a socially useful manner. There is no serious literature in international business supporting such a nationalist bias.[7]

The 'home base' approach is also wrong since it does not specify the nature of benefit. Is this to be measured by wealth generation, by jobs, by R and D, by process technology, by regional benefits or by other criteria? The sorry experience of Canada's Foreign Investment Review Agency (FIRA) from 1974–1985, until it was abolished, is a testimony to the lack of validity of the concept calling for improvements in the net economic benefits of foreign investment. Porter's limited discussion of FIRA is totally inadequate, as it does not assess its impact on managerial behavior and strategy. FIRA was supposed to find the net benefit from foreign ownership; instead it made decisions based on political grounds. See the well known work by A.D. Safarian and my book, *Multinationals in Canada*.[8]

Porter's attempt to classify foreign direct investment into three alternatives (resource-based, market access-based and home-based) is not useful; indeed it is wrong. Multinationals exist to internalize (make proprietary) firm-specific advantages to conduct successful international business operations. In doing so managers evaluate sets of host-country factors, including availability of resources, tariffs and political risk, as well as home-country and international institutional factors, and consider these against various internal strategic factors to determine the location of their activities. Porter's three classifications are far too simplistic and are misleading.

Porter's logic is flawed

After Canadian managers have read Porter's study they should ask the following questions. First, does Canada need an industrial strategy to mend the broken Canadian diamond? Second, should Canada give up on its resource-based industries and replace them by innovation-driven industries? Third, does Canada need to keep out foreign-owned firms that do not develop product lines using Canada as a home base? The reason these questions are important is that Porter says that Canada's lack of international competitiveness is due to problems in these areas. Yet his analysis fails to provide logical support for his recommendations. Here is why.

First, Porter says that Canada's home country diamond is broken, but then says that he is not in favor of an industrial strategy to fix it. This is inconsistent, as shown above; the double diamond approach overcomes this inconsistency and is a much better method to develop a global strategy for Canadian firms.

Second, Porter says that Canada's most successful export industries are resource-based, but that Canadians rely on an 'old economic order' in which resources cannot be the basis for future success. He then says that more R and D is required for innovation-led growth to take place. This is neither necessary, nor feasible. Instead, the resource-based industries need to be properly evaluated and their value added recognized.[9]

Third, Porter says that most foreign-owned firms in Canada are not of use as they do not build upon a home base for their product lines. Porter says that R and D is lacking and that world product mandates are few. He invents a theory of foreign ownership to support this, which is not adequately explained in the September 1991 draft of his report, and is wrong in any case. The logical absurdities of Porter's one-way theory of multinationals were explored above. In practice, since there are two-way flows of trade and investments, a home-country model is useless for Canadian managers and policy makers.

Porter is out of date

Porter's book is 30 years out of date in its thinking about multinationals and in its analysis of Canadian management. Porter repeatedly states that Canada has lived well off an 'old economic order' and now a new vision is required – one where upgrading of skills is a priority. This is an agreeable recommendation but it is a pity that Porter, himself, could not follow his own advice and do some new thinking in a Canadian context. Porter has presented old economic wine in a new bottle, but few Canadians are likely to become intoxicated by his conceptually flawed analysis.

The application of Porter's irrelevant single diamond model to current Canadian conditions leads to misleading analysis, which is actually inconsistent with Porter's (correct) public policy recommendations. The recommendations are reasonable; in particular, upgrading of human resource skills is necessary. Yet the analysis itself is a mechanical application of Porter's single diamond formula. It was not worth the money. More relevant insights into Canadian strategic management and public policy issues come from the North American diamond framework. Porter's directions for the future of Canadian business are useless; he took a wrong turning when he crossed the border.

Porter's Stages of Competitive Development

Factor-Driven. The nation's companies draw their advantages almost solely from basic factors of production. They compete primarily on the basis of price in industries that require either little product or process technology or technology that is inexpensive and widely available.

Investment-Driven. National competitive advantage is based on the willingness and ability of a nation and its firms to invest aggressively. Foreign technology and methods are not just applied but improved upon.

Innovation-Driven. Consumer demand is sophisticated because of rising personal incomes, higher levels of education, increasing desire for convenience and the invigorating role of domestic rivalry. New competitive industries emerge out of related industries. Firms not

---

(Continued)

only appropriate and improve technology and methods from other nations but create them.

Wealth-Driven. The Wealth-driven stage ultimately leads to decline because the driving force in the economy is wealth that has already been achieved. Firms lose competitive advantage by ebbing rivalry and by influencing governments to insulate them from competitive pressures.

Notes

[1] Porter, Michael E. *The Competitive Advantage of Nations*. New York: Free Press; Toronto: Collier Macmillan, 1990.

[2] Rugman, Alan M., *Diamond in the Rough*, Business Quarterly 55(3) (Winter 1991): 61–64.

[3] Rugman, Alan M. and Joseph D'Cruz, *Fast Forward: Improving Canada's International Competitiveness*. Toronto: Kodak Canada, 1991. It should be noted that Porter does not cite this study correctly in Chapter 3 of his report; instead he cites the study referenced here as number 10.

[4] Crane, David, High Level of Foreign Ownership Hampers Our Ability to Compete. *The Toronto Star*, 19th October 1991.

[5] Crocombe, F.T., M.J. Enright and M.E. Porter, *Upgrading New Zealand's Competitive Advantage*. Auckland, NZ: Oxford University Press, 1991.

[6] Rugman, Alan M., and John McIlveen. Megafirms: *Strategies for Canada's Multinationals*. Toronto, Methuen, 1985.

[7] Porter actually cites Richard Caves' *Multinational Enterprises and Economic Analysis*, New York: Cambridge University Press, 1981 incorrectly, since there are no statements in the text to support such nonsense. Rather, there is a large literature finding the opposite of Porter, namely that the performance of capital is not determined by its ownership. This literature includes: Johnson, Harry G., *The Canadian Quandary: Economic Problems and Policies*, Toronto; New York: McGraw Hill, 1963; Safarian, A.E., *Foreign Ownership of Canadian Industry*, Toronto, New York: McGraw Hill-Ryerson, 1967; and Rugman, Alan M., *Multinationals in Canada: Theory, Performance and Economic Impact*, Boston: Martin Nijhoff/Kluwer, 1980.

[8] Safarian, A.E., *FIRA and FIRB: Canadian and Australian Policies on Foreign Direct Investment*. Toronto: Ontario Economics Council, 1985; and Rugman, Alan M., *Multinationals in Canada: Theory, Performance and Economic Impact*, Boston: Martin Nijhoff/Kluwer, 1980.

[9] Rugman, Alan M. and Joseph D'Cruz, *New Visions for Canadian Business: Strategies for Competing in the Global Economy*. Toronto: Kodak Canada, 1990.

The Innovative Society: Competitiveness in the 1990s

Bryne B. Purchase
Toronto: C.D. Howe Institute, 1991, 109 pp. *

Improving Canadian competitiveness is the theme of this year's annual policy review from the C.D. Howe Institute. The Institute acknowledges that Canada is in a recession, with job losses in services as well as in manufacturing, but it argues for a long-term perspective. Competitiveness needs to become the cornerstone of Canadian government policy; once it is, competitiveness becomes a form of economic security. To implement this, the institute develops nineteen recommendations, most of which are a familiar private sector wish list, but with a few new ones recommending improvements in the public sector.

The Institute states that 'competitiveness is measured by a high and continuously rising real standard of living; it is earned by constant improvements in labor productivity,' (p.6).

To become competitive Canada needs to be willing to accept change in its social and political structures as well as in its economic structure. 'Competitive activities do not just happen. They are part of a larger political and economic structure that encourages competition,' (p.10). It is also necessary for government to change and 'become more efficient in its choice of policy tools,' (p.12).

Chapter 2 argues that the package of proposals outlined in Mr. Wilson's 1984 economic agenda paper (the Free Trade Agreement and tax reform, including GST) 'represented a coherent and consistent framework for increasing Canadian competitiveness and productivity' (p.15). Chapter 3 demonstrates that it is now necessary to keep a perspective on the current recession and not destroy these vital structural and macroeconomic policies put in place by the federal government. These policies are the foundation for investment in the future competitiveness of Canada.

Canadian Public Policy 17(3) (Sept. 1991): 373–374.

Another theme running through these chapters is that it is necessary to 'think globally but act nationally'; i.e. economic policies are globally determined but social and political policies can be more decentralized: 'the compelling logic of centralization of economic policies in supranational institutions coexists with the natural drive towards decentralization of community and political attachments' (p.27).

Chapter 4 is a good synthesis of recent work on Canadian trade and investment policies, endorsing the FTA and its extension to include Mexico, and the projected GATT reforms. There is also keen awareness of the vital role played by the world's largest 600 multinational enterprises, which account for 20 per cent of the world's value added in manufacturing and agriculture (p.50).

The author does not support the Premier's Council of Ontario type of interventionist industrial policy, nor does he support strategic trade policy; 'Canada cannot win this game' (p.55). However, Canada should develop policies 'to become a favourable location for the more innovative sectors of the global economy' (p.55). The author also endorses the concept of increasing the value added of Canada's resource-based industries rather than opting for a simplistic high tech export strategy.

One minor caveat would be with regard to the author's view that research and development (R&D) is low due to the presence of foreign-owned firms in Canada (p.62). While foreign-owned firms do only about half as much R&D as their parents, their ratio of R&D to sales is approximately equal to that of Canadian-owned firms. Thus, it is not foreign-ownership that is the problem, but rather the nature of the Canadian economic space, where little R&D is undertaken by any of the players in Canada.

The most innovative thinking in the book comes in Chapter 5. This is one of the first studies to identify the government sector as a major problem, but also a potential solution, to the issue of Canadian competitiveness. 'Government inevitably must be a part of a competitiveness agenda in Canada' (p.89). This requires that all government institutions become more efficient and aware of competition. The Institute calls for 'establishing independent regulatory review agencies at both the federal and provincial levels of government' (p.86). These are required to assess the impact on competitiveness of all proposed government initiatives. This is an excellent idea. It alone is worth the price of the book.

Continental Accord: North American Economic Integration

Steven Globerman (ed.)

Vancouver, BC: The Fraser Institute, 1991, 174 pp.[*]

The negotiations for a North American Free Trade Agreement were concluded in principle on 10 August 1992, and a draft legal text was initialled by the trade ministers of Mexico, Canada and the United States in San Antonio in early October 1992. The NAFTA has still to be approved by each of the three federal governments, before it comes into effect, probably on 1st January 1994. Is NAFTA good or bad for international business? Several Asian nations in particular are concerned that NAFTA will reduce their market access. In fact, this turns out to be an unfounded fear. This book provides evidence that NAFTA was inevitable and that its impact will be trade creating and a stimulus for international business.

The book consists of five chapters and a useful statistical appendix on existing NAFTA trade and investment linkages. The first chapter is on a Mexican vision of NAFTA, by Rogelio Ramirez de la O. He explains that Mexico wishes to make up for the lost decade of the 1980s and make the switch from a protectionist and highly regulated economy towards trade and investment liberalization. He sees NAFTA as the institutional process by which Mexico can solve its foreign debt problems and provide an attractive location for foreign capital. The NAFTA is undoubtedly an important component of Mexico's agenda. The final NAFTA agreement should help in Mexico's transition from its present third world status to that of a wealthier society. The key to Mexico's world status will be the attraction of foreign direct investment after decades of restrictive policies that blocked it out. Here there is an important lesson for other third world countries – send out signals to attract foreign direct investment

---

[*]*Journal of International Business Studies* 24(1) (First Quarter 1993): 159–161.

and attempt to achieve secure access to a large triad market in order to develop globally competitive industries.

The second chapter is on a Canadian vision of NAFTA and is by Leonard Waverman of the University of Toronto. He articulates a positive vision of NAFTA. Using traditional economic methodology he demonstrates that the trade creation effects outweigh the trade distortion effects when tariffs are removed. He concludes that Canada has to be in NAFTA to enjoy the net trade creation effects. Indeed, the debate in Canada was how to avoid losing the benefits of the Canada-US Free Trade Agreement (FTA) and to incorporate it into NAFTA. The final text of NAFTA involves a complete rewriting of the FTA but it is as good a deal for Canada since the key provisions of the FTA are retained, especially in terms of market access to the United States and national treatment for investment.

A related paper (Chapter 4) by Richard Lipsey of Simon Fraser University develops the theory of why Canada needed to participate in NAFTA. He raises the spectre of the United States being at the centre of a 'hub-and-spoke' system if Canada were to decide not to participate in the negotiations and two separate trade agreements were to be concluded – one with Canada and a separate one with Mexico. Under these conditions the United States would be the hub, i.e. the one country to enjoy free access to the entire North American market while Mexico and Canada would be spokes with far fewer benefits. Fortunately, Canada did join the negotiations and NAFTA did become a true trilateral agreement, with three equal partners. Canada's participation has also laid the groundwork for Mexican-Canadian alliances in terms of future disputes over sensitive issues. The NAFTA has helped to construct a rules-based institutional system to offset the tremendous economic power of the United States relative to Canada and Mexico.

In Chapter 3 Clark Reynolds gives a US version of NAFTA. He states that the current US recession is due to a lack of international competitiveness in the United States and that NAFTA will help to foster beneficial business changes within the United States. Reynolds says that the United States needs NAFTA due to difficulties in the GATT and the reality of triad-based regional blocs. He argues that the economic development of Mexico will help political stability in the region and reduce the possibility of low wage jobs going to Mexico from the United

States (and Canada). To my mind the fear that NAFTA will cause a major shift of industries from the United States and Canada to Mexico due to its relatively lower wages is completely misguided. Labour costs are only one of several critical components in the cost of production. Others include: capital, managerial skills, tacit knowledge, infrastructure, etc. In these areas the United States and Canada retain tremendous advantages reflected in their greater productivity and wealth.

The fifth chapter by Rosemary Piper and Alan Reynolds looks at the EC experience and relates it to NAFTA. They demonstrate that the tremendous growth of ED intra-industry trade and investment will also occur in NAFTA. They argue that the steps taken to capture these economic benefits did not lead to a loss of political or cultural sovereignty. These latter issues are also addressed by others in the volume, particularly the Canadians, Lipsey and Waverman. The FTA has proved to be very unpopular in Canada, largely due to the country's poor economic performance, associated more with the recession than to the FTA itself. However, it is now quite clear that the FTA has not diminished Canadian sovereignty in any way. Since the FTA came into effect in 1989 Canada has managed to screw up its economic, social, cultural and political systems as much as before. Indeed, in late October 1992 Canadians rejected a referendum on renewed federalism without any American interference.

In terms of political reality, NAFTA conceivably provides the base for future steps toward North American political and economic integration, along the lines of the EC. The current NAFTA is unlike the EC in that there are no provisions for a powerful central bureaucracy, nor for any sort of common parliament. But these could be on the way, especially if more Latin American countries accede, thus making the day-to-day management of the agreement more demanding. Such institutional provisions would likely to be of benefit to Mexico and Canada in order to help enforce the rules-based regime of NAFTA as an offset to the previous U.S. power-based system. I believe that, ultimately, political sovereignty is highly correlated with economic prosperity. NAFTA is a positive step forward for all three member countries along both of these economic and political dimensions.

Finally, it is useful to take a broader perspective when evaluating the NAFTA. Does it foster triad power and hinder international business?

Here, my judgment is that the NAFTA is neutral. It is more a reaction by Canada and Mexico to U.S. protectionism than a deliberate attempt to form a fortress North America. Before the FTA, Canada and the United States were already highly integrated in terms of trade and investment. The same is now true for Mexico-U.S. economic relations. The FTA and NAFTA are sets of rules to govern the existing trilateral economic relationships, rather than to keep out other business partners. There are no provisions in the FTA or NAFTA that increase barriers against Asians, Europeans, or others. Indeed, NAFTA's investment provisions set a precedent by explicitly recognizing that investors from non-NAFTA countries are entitled to many of the rights accorded to investors from NAFTA countries. The rules of origin are written in such a way as to prevent Mexico from becoming an 'offshore' assembly platform. However, these provisions reflect current practices and should not be viewed as being more discriminatory towards 'outside' investors.

The NAFTA is like the EC; there are no new barriers being raised, but companies within these trade blocs should become more competitive. The lesson is: be an insider. Today a global strategy requires foreign direct investment across the triad, rather than exporting alone, in order to perform in the key global markets. While not perfect, NAFTA is a market-opening, GATT-consistent, forward-looking agreement.

Decision at Midnight: Inside the Canada-U.S. Free Trade Negotiations

Michael Hart (with Bill Dymond and Colin Robertson)
Vancouver: University of British Columbia Press, 1994, 472 pp.[*]

With each passing year it is becoming clearer that the single most important event in postwar Canadian history was the 1988 election on the issue of free trade and the implementation of the Canada-U.S. Free Trade Agreement (CUFTA) on January 1, 1989. The 1988 election saw the defeat of Canadian economic nationalism and the triumph of continentalism. The subsequent negotiation of the North American Free Trade Agreement (NAFTA) has built on the model of the CUFTA. In short, the CUFTA is a critical document, yet it is still one which is widely misunderstood, if not misrepresented. Hart's book is important as it explains the details of the CUFTA, and the negotiating process behind them. It is one of the most useful and insightful books on recent Canadian history, offering an unusual insider perspective on the process of bilateral trade negotiations and the ability of trade bureaucrats to set Canada's political and economic agenda when coupled with a government dedicated to the pursuit of free trade.

Michael Hart attempts to refute the Doern and Tomlin *Faith and Fear* (1991) thesis that the United States outnegotiated Canada. Their thesis is based on an evaluation of the 'wish list' that Canada had at the start of the negotiations and their interpretation of what was achieved; they see a gap, especially in terms of the process of the negotiations. But in his notes (p.414) Hart argues that Doern and Tomlin are wrong in their assessment that the United States outnegotiated Canada in terms of process and political strategy. Hart states that the positive outcome of the CUFTA outweighs the actual negotiating process. While he may well be correct here, my own feeling is that, overall, the Doern and Tomlin

Canadian Foreign Policy 2(3) (Winter 1994/1995): 124–128.

book is a much better study of CUFTA than Hart's, probably because it is more balanced in its use of sources and is more objective.

In any case, by his authoritative grasp of all of the details of the trade negotiations Hart makes a convincing case that Canada outnegotiated the United States on the details of the CUFTA. Canada had a focused team and a clear strategic objective. The objective of enhanced access to the U.S. market for Canadian business, secured by binding dispute settlement procedures, was achieved. The United States was disorganized, and its negotiator, Peter Murphy, had no clear vision or even a mandate other than to keep the Canadians busy while making as few concessions as possible until a final, political, deal was to be made.

Trade agreements are complicated; the details matter. Michael Hart is a details man and he knows the CUFTA inside out. He has told me that he literally wrote the CUFTA by entering agreed upon changes in the single, master text on his Macintosh. In this, he had the blessing of Canadian chief negotiator Simon Reisman and the other senior members of the Trade Negotiations Office (TNO): Gordon Ritchie, Charles Stedman and Alan Nymark. So is Michael Hart just a secretary or is he a player? The answer (according to Hart) tends more to the latter since control of the text and mastery of the details in the trade agreement and backroom work have more long-term effect than the public posturing and political spin of the ministers and lead negotiators. In other words, the trade bureaucracy actually makes trade policy, since process is what matters. Insiders own the show. In the case of the CUFTA the chief negotiator had a clear mandate from the Prime Minister and Cabinet to deliver a trade agreement, so control of the process of negotiations brought complete power to the insider trade bureaucracy erected by Reisman in the TNO. There was consultation with business groups and with ministers and a final political fix but, in the end, the trade team wrote the CUFTA.

Such is the impression created by Hart's book. It is an honest and persuasive account of several years of preparatory work followed by two years of intense, technical, detailed negotiations. Yet it is a flawed account. It is too self-centered and self-serving. At critical stages the Canadian trade bureaucracy was stopped cold in its tracks by overarching political issues which were only solved by the total commitment to free trade of the Prime Minister. Examples are the problems in securing 'fast track' approval for the CUFTA in the Senate in April 1985; the frequent lack of engagement by Murphy, which required the Prime Minister to go one on one with President Reagan; and the need for Reisman to suspend negotiations in September 1987 in order to have the politicians cut a deal. Indeed, the hero is Brian Mulroney, not Michael Hart or Simon Reisman. The latter were agents of the Prime Minister. There was a strong congruence of their agendas but the CUFTA owes as much to the political courage of Mulroney as the brilliant technical work of Reisman's team.

The main theme of Hart's book is that Canada did its homework and was well prepared for the free trade negotiations. Hart paints a convincing picture that the government, trade bureaucracy and leading negotiators were all converted to the need for market access to the United States and that this grouping was strong enough to marginalize the economic nationalists opposed to free trade. Of particular interest is Hart's discussion (p.398) of the displacement of old style External Affairs trade veterans opposed to free trade (John Holmes, John Halstead, George Ignatieff, Ken Wardroper and Michel Dupuy) with the young turks (Derek Burney, Don Campbell, Gerry Shannon, Michael Hart, etc.) in favor of free trade.

In contrast to the careful preparation of the Canadians, the U.S. side is portrayed as ill prepared for trade negotiations, being quite ignorant of Canada and lacking in any 'big vision.' In particular, U.S. chief negotiator Peter Murphy comes off as a cartoon figure, a technical trade engineer with red hair but with no real mandate and no clout with Congress (he apparently dealt with Congress only through Senator Lloyd Bentsen's finance committee counsel). Yet Hart and company appear to have underestimated Murphy and they took too long to realize that their 'big deal' vision of the CUFTA would not fly with Murphy. The reality was that a trade deal with Murphy and the U.S. Congress would be a technical war of attrition. That they persisted with the technical details is a tribute to the professional expertise of the TNO, but it made most of the fifteen months of negotiations in the 1986/1987 period frustrating and semi-redundant.

The twenty-two plenary negotiating sessions, according to Hart, were an exercise in frustration with Murphy being unable to engage in serious discussions. Instead he kept to a narrow U.S. technical agenda of 'irritants' and failed to deliver a big, comprehensive agreement.

There was no substantive movement on the 'deal breaker' of dispute settlement, disappointing U.S. proposals on trade in services and on government procurement, and an unacceptable proposal on investment, which Reisman refused to consider. This raises the question of the value of Reisman sticking to the negotiations with Murphy when it became clear that Murphy had no clout with Congress, or even with the Administration. Murphy was a technical American trade official, apparently with about as much political clout in Washington as someone like Michael Hart would have in Ottawa.

Hart reveals that Reisman made the nearly fatal mistake of agreeing that Murphy alone would deal with Congress. When it became known that Murphy did not have access to more than one member of Congress, Reisman should have adopted a proactive lobbying strategy with the key trade committee members in the Senate and House. As it was Canadian Ambassador Allan Gotlieb helped to save the day, by conducting a useful insider lobbying campaign which provided vital intelligence for the final political push when Derek Burney (acting for the Prime Minister) cut a last minute deal with Howard Baker (acting for the President).

From this it emerges that the negotiations both started too soon and ended too soon. Canada did its homework but was overprepared. The United States never did its homework, failed to engage in the negotiations, and was only saved in the end by intervention of the President's top political team. When I say the negotiation ended too soon I also mean that the TNO was abolished too soon. The TNO was not on guard in 1988, after the signing of the CUFTA but before its approval by Congress. The enabling legislation of the CUFTA in Congress contained many subtle changes (e.g. on investment related issues, research and development, dispute settlement, etc.) that should have been caught by a Canadian side aware of the critical importance of the details. But only Alan Nymark was left from the original TNO team to watch over the Congress. Reisman, Ritchie, Stedman and all the others in the TNO had either left the government or had been reassigned.

The organization of this book is flawed. It is written as a diary, using a chronological ordering. Yet Hart digresses into long technical discussions of negotiating issues, usually the first time they came up at a plenary (and then often does not return to these issues). For example, we are suddenly treated to long discussions of trade in services, government procurement, investment, dispute settlement procedures, agriculture and other issues without these topics being properly identified; more and better subheadings would have been helpful.

Hart is also too dismissive of the value of consultations with both the provinces and the private sector. He sees these as groups to be managed and fed information in briefing sessions, but whose views made no impact on the negotiations. This is a pretty unflattering assessment of the excellent work done by Alan Nymark with the premiers and Gordon Ritchie with the private sector's International Trade Advisory Committee (ITAC) and SAGITs. My own experience on ITAC was that there was a useful two-way exchange of information with Reisman, Ritchie, the Trade Minister and the Prime Minister on both strategic and technical issues and that the private sector's role was critical at two stages: first, in lobbying for 'fast-track approval,' which was partly achieved by ITAC members calling senior U.S. business contacts to influence critical Senators; second, in 'selling' the CUFTA, which was done mainly through the Canadian Alliance for Trade and Job Opportunity founded as a result of an ITAC discussion, a point not reported by Hart on p. 244. The CUFTA exists today because it was 'sold' through the personal belief and commitment of business leaders to the entire country in the 1988 election, reflecting their participation and stake in it. If Hart were to write a second (and potentially more interesting) book about the 1988 election and the fight for the CUFTA then the important role of ITAC, the SAGITs and political leaders would require much greater recognition. Examples of Hart's inflated view of the role of the TNO abound, for example:

1. Hart's view of the first ministers' quarterly meetings is that the premiers 'proved good students and the prime minister and his team good teachers' (p. 266). This is not too smart an insight to put on paper.
2. Hart's view is that the communications strategy required that the TNO write speeches for Ministers; indeed on page 231 he states that after the March 16, 1987 debate 'Ministers now had speeches with which they were comfortable and which they could use time and again across the country'. This is an arrogant view that ministers and their staffs are too dumb to articulate Canada's trade

strategy without TNO briefs – a view at odds with the passionate and informed speeches of many ministers (and other Tory politicians) in the 1988 election.

3. On p. 439 Hart dismisses the role of Toronto's 'Annex intellectuals' as major (nationalist) players in the free trade story. As a resident of the Annex (albeit not at the time of the CUFTA) I find it necessary to state that there is a balance of views and the Annex is not 100 percent nationalist. Others of Hart's comments are great, e.g. on page 438 that Linda McQuaig's book on free trade is 'muddled' and a 'work of fiction', as is Lawrence Martin's book.

Hart's footnotes (25 pages), chronology (6 pages) and further reading (7 pages) are all valuable components of the book, but Hart is not always precise on the technical details. For examples on p. 161 his discussion of the U.S. Shakes and Shingles tariff of 35 percent imposed in May 1986 fails to disclose that this was a purely technical track decision of a section 201 case and was probably completely de-linked from the trade negotiations. Hart sees it as a political negotiating ploy. In *Administered Protection in America* (1987), Andrew Anderson and I have demonstrated that this technical track remedy was misunderstood by Canadian politicians and the Canadian trade team.

Hart's book was delayed for six years before being cleared for publication by the Department of External Affairs. Why? There is little in the book that is new; the details of the CUFTA are well known and the principals have been extensively interviewed and several other 'insider' accounts published. After reading Hart's book carefully I can only conclude that there remains a perception at External Affairs (now Foreign Affairs) that Reisman's tactics and strategy do not stand up well to outside analysis. Reisman appears as a Shakespearean tragic hero with a fatal flaw flailing anyway in a Lear-like fashion against his younger intellectual inferior, Murphy, and never being able to engage the real U.S. power brokers. According to Hart, trade minister Pat Carney and finance Minister Michael Wilson were very much second violins in Burney's final orchestration of the deal. In other words, while Hart's book does not reveal any dark secrets it does wash a lot of dirty laundry, often in an unintentional manner, due to the one dimensional view of the principal author.

The Post-NAFTA Political Economy: Mexico and the Western Hemisphere

Carol Wise (ed.)
University Park, PA: Pennsylvania State University Press, 1998, 382 pp.[*]

The nine essays in this book, prepared in early 1998, focus on the impact of NAFTA on Mexico and attempt to draw implications of this experience for a Free Trade Area of the Americas (FTAA). In a valuable introduction Carol Wise states that the four essays evaluating the economic and political impact of NAFTA and Mexico 'confirm the success of NAFTA in producing many of the benefits suggested by integration theory' (p. 6). However, she says that there are unresolved social adjustment problems. Two of these macroeconomic policy essays involve Manuel Pastor, Jr. the impact of NAFTA is also assessed by Jonathan Heath, Peter Andreas and Denise Dresser. Wise also states that the remaining two essays, on the implications of NAFTA for the FTAA, suggest that the FTAA process is still on track, but in a watered down format to that proposed at the 1994 Miami summit. There is no research on Canada's role within FTAA, which is a pity as scholarship in that area is more established and is of a higher standard than is in evidence in this book. For example, the Maxfield and Shapiro chapter on assessing whether Mexico's 'wins' (p. 84) (on automobile rules, energy, agriculture and bi-national panels for dispute settlement) were first made by Canada in the Canada-U.S. Free Trade Agreement (FTA).

Two chapters illustrate the diversity of scholarship on NAFTA. In the last essay Stephan Haggard rigorously synthesizes a wide literature on regionalism and applies it to an FTAA. He reviews the existing subnational agreements with insight and balance. In contrast, Ngaire Woods reviews the role of the IMF and U.S. government in the 1995 Mexican bailout after the peso crisis. The author does not refer to any investment-related NAFTA literature or to the document itself. Yet, even a casual reading of the investment provisions of NAFTA would have

[*]*International Affairs* 75(3) (July 1999): 675–676.

led Woods away from the secondary impact of NAFTA on portfolio investment towards a study of foreign direct investment, which is the key to NAFTA adjustment. There are no provisions in NAFTA for the integrated regional monetary mechanisms favored by Woods. The reason lies in Canada's preference for economic integration with, but political independence from, the United States, a model agreed to in the Canada-U.S. FTA of 1989, which Mexico adopted five years later. As Haggard states, the FTA 'provided a template for NAFTA' (p. 302).

Linking Trade, Environment and Social Cohesion: NAFTA Expansion, Global Challenges

By John J. Kirton and Virginia W. Maclaren
*Aldershot: Ashgate, 2000, 404 pp.**

In response to the civil society criticism of globalization, some new research is being released which demonstrates the continuing importance and relevance of regional economic blocks such as the European Union and the North American Free Trade Agreement. Indeed, this reviewer has calculated that 57% of all the exports of the NAFTA members are now intra-regional, while it is 62% in the European Union (E.U.). It is also unlikely that these regional groupings are stepping stones to globalization, as intra-regional trade and investment are growing faster than inter-regional. So what is really going on in NAFTA? This book provides clues and offers new analytical insights into the world's most important regional trade and investment agreement, other than the E.U.

This edited collection of conference papers from a 2001 conference at the University of Toronto, covers the exceptionally interesting topic of the influence of the civil society on environmental and labor standards on trade agreements. These are considered within the institutional framework of NAFTA. There is incisive original research, especially on the new Chapter 11 investor-state cases (by Soloway, Gaines, and Kirton) and on the use of citizen's Articles 14 and 15 of NAFTA (by Kirton, Tollefson, Alanis, Wilson). The labor chapters are also of interest, as are the two outstanding introductory and overview chapters by Pierre Marc Johnson and William Dymond. And, as usual, John Kirton has a comprehensive introduction, as well as two good chapters. I now turn to an assessment of the more interesting chapters.

The book opens with an excellent introduction by the editors and is followed in Chapter 2 with an authoritative and balanced essay by former Quebec premier, Pierre Marc Johnson. He states that the Seattle defeat of the WTO is 'the end of globalization', a theme also developed

Business Horizons 46(1) (January/February 2003): 69–71.

by this reviewer. Johnson is sympathetic to the agenda of the civil society for greater 'transparency, accountability, and participation, as well as substantive (progress on) social, environmental and human rights issues' (p. 28). Johnson states that the MAI was 'blocked by an unprecedented international mobilization of civil society' (p. 30) by activist NGOs. He argues that one of the main concerns of the civil society is environmental reform. Finally, he examines the NAFTA commission on environmental co-operation and its work. This is viewed favorably, especially the Articles 14 and 15 which permit citizen group participation in environmental issues at NAFTA. He is less enthusiastic about Chapter 11 but does not discuss any cases.

The tension in Johnson's essay between trade and investment rule making (as advanced through NAFTA and the WTO) and the concerns of the civil society (about transparency, participation, reform of global governance and the paramouncy of environmental issues over economic/trade ones) is reflected in subsequent chapters in the book. In general, the majority of the papers look at the evidence on globalization and find much more to cheer than the NGOs would jeer.

In Chapter 3, former senior Canadian trade negotiator, Bill Dymond, states that the agenda of the civil society, as reflected in Ralph Nader's U.S. presidential campaign in 2000 only secured 3% of the vote. In Canada, public support is even lower. Both the U.S. and Canadian governments are pursuing strategies of trade and investment liberal-ization. The defeat of the MAI and the Seattle failure of the WTO reflected more a lack of consensus among major governments rather than 'civil society agitation' (p. 38). The future agenda of the WTO is to further 'positive rule making' across the new agenda issues of environment, labor, competition policy and standards. These rules are reinforced by dispute settlement procedures at the WTO and in NAFTA. They are a new form of global governance, but are viewed by Dymond as essentially technical, whereas most NGOs are concerned with the perceived political power of firms. For example, Dymond is rightly dismissive of the more absurd concerns about the NAFTA Chapter 11 cases, stating that both Ethyl and Myers were caused by mistakes in Canadian government policy making; in Ethyl: 'the action taken by Canada on environmental grounds...could not be sustained' (p. 41).

This analysis of NAFTA Chapter 11 cases is confirmed in later chapters by trade lawyers Sanford Gaines and Julie Soloway. In particular, Soloway, in a brilliant and incisive essay in Chapter 7, demonstrates that in the first three key Chapter 11 cases (Metalclad, Pope and Talbot and S.D. Myers) the tribunals gave deference to the environmental policies of host governments and did not approve the expropriation claims of foreign investors. Before making any more arguments that NAFTA restricts the sovereignty of nations to take environmental measures, critics of NAFTA should read this chapter as it demonstrates the opposite.

Chapter 8 is by noted environmentalist Konrad von Moltke. As an advocate of sustainable development, he argues that business will need to make major investments to change its behavior in accord with sounder environmental principles. Therefore he states that the lesson of the defeat of the MAI is being misunderstood. Environmentalists should not oppose an investment agreement, as progress towards sustainable development is not possible without structural change by business and this requires investment. Indeed, he states that environmental agreements, like Kyoto, which produce public goods, are really investment agreements (p. 150). Von Moltke analyzes the type of future MAI required with considerable insight and balance. He states that FDI gives a firm a type of 'economic citizenship' with rights in the host economy. The institutional structure of different economies is what is being co-coordinated in an MAI. He ends by advocating sectoral agreements, adding investment protocols to Kyoto, for example. The WTO is not the forum for such types of MAIs.

There is a minor factual error on p. 145. The UNCTNC was not 'shut down' for failing to deliver a code of conduct for TNCs. Instead, it moved from New York to the Geneva office of UNCTAD, where it produces the *World Investment Report* each year. Thus is has not been 'terminated' but it has evolved into a more technical and scientific body but no less of a policy one, as it advocated the MAI and provided research for it (as the OECD had no FDI researchers there, only trade economists).

The NAFTA Chapter 14 citizen submission procedures are discussed by Chris Tollefson in Chapter 9 in a well researched and careful piece of research. There have been 28 such cases i.e. there were twice as many of these 'civil society' cases as of the 'business' Chapter 11 cases in the first seven years of NAFTA. Tollefson discusses these 28 cases in detail.

A Mexican law professor, Gustavo Alanis Ortega, then discusses just one Chapter 14 case, the initial Cozumel case where NAFTA's environmental commission determined in a factual record that Mexico's environmental authorities has misapplied its own regulations when approving the construction of a pier in Cozumel.

In another short commentary, American consultant Serena Wilson also discusses Articles 14 and 15. She states that only two submissions have been successful and 18 were terminated. Also the time taken to review submissions is too long.

Overall the book reads well, there is a nice introduction, careful and detailed research, and reasonable public policy conclusions. The book should have an impact on future public policy and firm-level strategy as NAFTA becomes recognized as a model trade and investment agreement. It is to be expanded to the Free Trade Agreement of the Americas in 2005, and it will probably become the model for an Asian free trade agreement later. This book will be of interest to trade experts, lawyers, managers and students. Its principal audience will be researchers in international business, international economics, international relations, and strategic management.

79 It's the Crude, Dude: War; Big Oil and the Fight for the Planet

Linda McQuaig
Scarborough, ON: Doubleday Canada, 2004, 346 pp.[*]

The main theme of Linda McQuaig's new book is the argument that the U.S. invasion of Iraq was to secure access to and maintain long term control of its 'massive' oil reserves, supposedly 'at least 10% of the world's oil.' Indeed, McQuaig thinks that Iraq's oil wealth is potentially second only to Saudi Arabia, which has 25% of the world's oil reserves. A second theme is that the world should try to rely less on oil in the future as its price is going up as it becomes scarcer. The world should switch to alternative sources of energy. As McQuaig puts it, 'there's not enough oil to meet the world's growing consumption, but that growing consumption is itself threatening to ruin the world.' The last phrase takes us to her third theme; that global warming is mainly caused by gasoline emissions, and that drivers of SUVs and the producers of oil are both engaged in immoral activities. As Americans are the principal drivers of SUVs, and ExxonMobil is a U.S. company, Americans are especially immoral. (This last argument is phrased somewhat more eloquently but is nevertheless the accusation.)

The book's first two chapters related to the rather silly title of the book. They appear to have been positioned there to 'sex up' the book with a focus on the war in Iraq and McQuaig's restatement of the theory that President Bush started the war to capture Iraq's oil. McQuaig summarizes media stories of the last two years about the Iraq war. She re-discovers that President Bush is an oil man. She alleges that he is now an agent for the U.S. corporate big oil lobby, which is portrayed as being self-centered, rich, immoral, greedy and anti-competitive. Yet most of the book is not about the Iraq war. Seven of the remaining eight chapters consist of a rather well written and insightful history of the economics

[*]*Literary Review of Canada* 12(10) (December 2004): 8–9.

of the United States and world oil industry. As this is turf usually covered by dry academic historians and even more boring economists, Linda McQuaig at least makes the history and economics come alive with chapter-opening vignettes of the nineteenth century investors and American capitalists who started up the U.S. oil industry and the mainly Arab nationalists who created OPEC and the state-owned oil business.

McQuaig starts her main argument with a somewhat tacky criticism of the influence of Dick Cheney on U.S. energy policy, first as CEO of Halliburton, then as vice-president heading up a review of U.S. energy policy. After proving to her own satisfaction that big oil is now running the U.S. government, she asserts that Cheney and Bush are agents of the U.S. oil lobby. She then relates an interesting story on how President Hugo Chávez of Venezuela reconstituted the OPEC oil cartel and got it working again in September 2000. So after a decade of low oil prices, up they went again. McQuaig paints Chávez as a hero. After all, higher oil prices may even help stop global warming. Yet she goes on to report that the reason for the rapid growth in market share by SUVs during the last 20 years is entirely due to the role of Congress rather than to the impact of lower oil prices. All of the factors leading to the success of SUVs predate Bush, including the protective tariffs on Japanese light trucks and the exemption of SUVs from fuel emissions standards. As for Bush's refusal to sign the Kyoto Protocol, Al Gore's 'crucial role' in the success of the Kyoto Summit of 1997 (he must have done this after inventing the Internet!) may be just as good a reason for Bush to block it as is McQuaig's preference for the big oil conspiracy.

McQuaig reprises the lessons of the anti-competitive cartel created by John D. Rockefeller's Standard Oil, then discusses the nationalization of oil in Libya and the creation of OPEC. Most of this history and economics are better presented here than in textbooks on the topic. Yet McQuaig is not consistent in her analysis. She does not recognize the economic logic of the inefficiency of the OPEC cartel as she did in the case of Rockefeller cartel. The reason is, apparently that she sympathizes with anti-globalization thinking: 'What defines this movement is not an opposition to global connectedness but an opposition to corporate control'. I see this as her key idea: corporate cartels are bad, but nation state cartels like OPEC are good. This generalizes to McQuaig's rather simplistic anti-globalization creed that corporations (especially the oil business) are evil, so government control and regulation of the oil sector are required.

McQuaig takes great pleasure in reporting at length the media coverage and speculation about the failure to find weapons of mass destruction in Iraq after the U.S. invasion. She argues that the true reason for the U.S. invasion of Iraq was to obtain control of its oil. While there appears to be no actual evidence of this, and so far the United States does not seem to have increased its imports of oil from Iraq, McQuaig lays out a set of factors that, in a trial, might be the described as circumstantial evidence. Here Vice President Cheney is seen by McQuaig as having left his fingerprints all over the Iraq invasion, with help from U.S. oil multinationals and conservative Washington D.C. think tanks. With guilt by association as her analytical method throughout the book we have as cardboard villains the likes of Bush, Cheney, all corporate oil executives and managers and the American drivers of SUVs. The last category consists, to a large extent, of suburban soccer moms – an unlikely target for McQuaig to label as immoral.

McQuaig argues that the United States has always wanted control over Iraq's oil, not to just have access to it. She sees the first Gulf War of 1991 and the Iraq invasion of 2003 as examples of the use of U.S. military power to achieve an oil objective foisted on the U.S. government by the big oil lobby. Saddam Hussein is portrayed by the United States, says McQuaig, as 'king of the vandals' and the world's foremost villain. Yet McQuaig knows better. It is just a big oil agenda that is being followed by President Bush in Iraq.

The most objectionable chapter is McQuaig's last, in which she finally gets around to September 11th. (Surely any book that is serious about analyzing American foreign policy would start with September 11th, rather than tacking it on as an afterthought.) Her main point is that Americans now suffer a 'willful blindness' in fighting terrorism; they should try a little harder to understand Arabs and be a little more sympathetic to them. Coming from a Canadian nationalist like McQuaig, this will come over as somewhat patronizing at best and close to superficial thinking at worst. I would advise McQuaig to talk to more Americans; in reality there is little difference between the suburbs of Indianapolis and Mississauga.

I do not agree with McQuaig's sympathetic portrayal of Islamic fundamentalist activities which she says 'only turned to terrorism after 1991'. McQuaig states that 'tempting as it is simply to dismiss Osama bin Laden as a crazed madman, his grievances are fairly straightforward, even if his methods are barbaric.' She says his grievances are justified. She argues that the foreign policy of the United States in the Middle East has been to control its oil and that this explains the resulting Arab resentment of foreign domination on which terrorism builds. It is muddled thinking like this which makes it difficult for Canadian nationalists like McQuaig to be taken seriously. Her anti-Americanism has spilled over into far too sympathetic a portrait of Osama bin Laden. It is not helpful to U.S.-Canadian relations to have such political intellectual rubbish in print. It is irresponsible to peddle such an agenda when Canada is an ally of the United States in the war on terrorism. I would expect that many readers of McQuaig will find similar problems with this part of her book.

If we were to accept McQuaig's more interesting economic arguments, what could be done to fix the trio of interlinked problems of the U.S. desire for control of Iraq's oil, its coming scarcity and higher prices, and oil's contribution to global warming? I would suggest that the first one is rather easy to fix and is driven by the second. The Alberta tar sands could be fully developed with a world price of oil at over $20 per barrel over the long term. Western Canadian oil could thereby replace all U.S. oil imports from Iraq. But McQuaig does not like this. As a Canadian nationalist, she does not want Americans to have secure access to Canadian oil. Here the Canada-U.S Free Trade Agreement and NAFTA energy provisions are, again, misinterpreted by her. All they require is that existing business contracts be carried out; a federal Canadian government can still tax and regulate the western Canadian oil industry but not by overnight changes in policy as occurred with Trudean's national oil policy of 1980. If there are to be massive investments to develop the Alberta tar sands fully, then it is perfectly reasonable for inventors to be able to recover this outlay without it being stolen by a nationalist Canadian government. With the FTA and NAFTA, Canada enjoys the economic benefits of access to the U.S. market. The days of economic nationalism are over, and Canada can play a very useful role as an energy supplier to the United States.

Canada's role as a partner for the United States in terms of oil supply can be seen from recent data on U.S. oil consumption. The United States produces 41 percent of all the oil it consumes. Its largest single outside suppliers are Canada with 10% of all U.S. oil consumption, Mexico with 8 percent and Venezuela with 8 percent. In other words, the NAFTA partners as a group supply 59 percent of all the oil the United States consumes. Only 11.5 percent of all the oil that is consumed by the United States comes from all the countries in the Persian Gulf, including Iraq, Saudi Arabia, the United Arab Emirates, Kuwait, Qatar, and Iran. There are trade data that indicate that Canada could attempt to pick up the 11.5 percent of the entire Persian Gulf's imports to the United States and let North America remove itself from the politics of the Middle East oil situation. Canada's oil reserves in the Athabasca tar sands need a stable world oil price of over $20 a barrel. If McQuaig's book is taken seriously as a criticism of Bush and the Iraq war, then the oil question could be solved by Canada. McQuaig should move to Alberta and encourage more exports of Canadian oil to the United States if she really believed her own logic. But she does not, and she wants to keep the United States as a villain whatever the evidence.

It is not clear why readers need to buy McQuaig's book to re-read what they are fed on a daily basis in *The Toronto Star* and CBC. It shows an untimely lack of insight into American values and beliefs in that McQuaig still does not recognize the true significance of September 11th. She does not understand the new American foreign policy which emerged after September 11th: namely that the U.S. government will fight terrorism offshore and take action against any government that supports terrorism. The latter point is the reason used by President Bush for the invasion of Iraq – that it had links to extremist Islamic terrorists who attacked Americans on September 11th. Current events in Iraq certainly reveal the ongoing presence of Islamic militants, and the United States prefers to fight them in Iraq rather than in New York. This reason for the Iraq war plays well in the U.S. Midwest and South, and to ignore it risks a basic misunderstanding of why many Americans are proud to enroll in the military and fight in Iraq. When I talk to U.S. soldiers in airplanes during their leaves they all say they are fighting the war on terrorism; none of them are fighting for Iraq's oil. So, while Canada could actually supply the oil that the United States wants, this would not end the war in Iraq.

Part V

Regulation of Multinationals: Civil Society and Development

Introduction to Part V

The focus of readings in Part V is the important topic of economic development. There is a rich history of literature in this area as scholars in international business and related cognate areas of economics and international political economy have been working on this topic for the last 50 years. In this part, Reviews 80 to 89 are reprinted reviews of books written in the 1970s. At that time MNEs were seen as vehicles for transferring technology to developing countries, thereby helping to upgrade their potential for economic development. Most of my comments on these books argue for the free entry of MNEs and the application of 'national treatment' such that foreign MNEs are treated by governments in the same way as domestic firms in the application of host country laws and regulations.

Reviews 91 to 100 deal with the literature since 1999. This latter set of literature has been complicated by the entry into the agenda for economic development of civil society and non-governmental organisation (NGOs). I criticise the role of activist (non civil!) NGOs in my reviews of books dealing with trade negotiations (Reviews 95 and 97). I also discuss the way in which NGOs have sometimes hindered the use of environmental regulations to change corporate strategy (Reviews 93 and 99). Overall, the books reviewed here provide fascinating insights into the complex relationships between MNEs, governments, and civil society. In addition, the reviews deal with issues in stakeholder theory, ethics, and corporate social responsibility.

In order to model these complex interactions between firms, governments, and other actors I have developed the model shown in Figure 8. This is based upon the flagship/five partners analysis of Rugman and D'Cruz (2000). As can be seen in Figure 8 the flagship firm is an MNE, which has four partners: key suppliers, key customers, competitors joining in joint ventures, and the non business infrastructure.

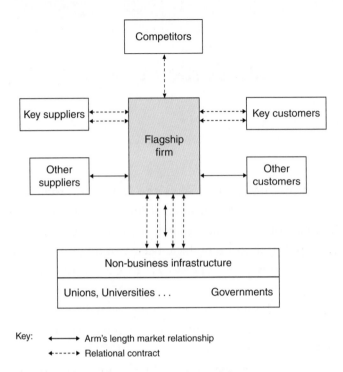

Key: ⟵——⟶ Arm's length market relationship
       ⟵-----▶ Relational contract

Figure 8 **The Five Partners Business Networks Model**
Source: Adapted from Alan M. Rugman and Joseph R. D'Cruz, *Multinationals as Flagship Firms*: Oxford University Press, 2000, p. 26.

Essentially the model captures the main elements of what has become known as the stakeholder model of public policy. This asserts that a large business has responsibilities beyond operating efficiently and thereby making profits for its financial shareholders. These extra responsibilities include the necessity to operate fairly with regards to its employees; the geographic regimes in which it is based (which raises sometimes conflicting issues for MNEs operating across national borders); and members of society at large, whose interests are often represented by self appointed NGOs. In this modern era of corporate social responsibility and stakeholder theory, the MNE faces complex competing pressures. These arise because the interests of the shareholders of the firm (the desire to earn profits) may well conflict with the interests of NGOs and governments (who are more concerned about what economists would call 'equity' issues in the sense of equal treatment for all groups).

This conflict between efficiency and equity is a recurrent theme throughout the books reviewed in this part. It is the major theme developed in the Reviews 80 to 89, written in the 1970s. These reviews deal with books in the broad area of economic development. They deal with issues in the transfer of technology to less developed countries by MNEs. Some of the authors of these books, written and reviewed in the 1970s, feel that it is the role of government to act as an agency for economic development. I criticise this thinking since government is not a business; instead, governments need to facilitate the economic and business activities of MNEs as these are the vehicles for technology transfer and knowledge generation. I argue that MNEs need to retain propriety control of the knowledge which they have generated in a world of market imperfections. Thus internalisation theory was being introduced into the book review literature even in the 1970s. In an interesting parallel, Review 99, published in 2003, repeats this internalisation theory argument in the context of regulation of the natural environment, since much environmental law and policy still fails to recognise the external benefits brought by the knowledge generation of MNEs.

Overall, the books reviewed in Part V reflect a consistent pattern of criticism of books which advocate government intervention, protectionism, and other forms of regulation of the MNE. Reviews 80 to 89, written in the 1970s, can be compared with the later set of Reviews, 91 to 100, all written some 20 years later. In the intervening period I did not focus my research on issues of economic development. However, I was involved in research dealing with free trade agreements (especially NAFTA) and the role of government in facilitating international competitiveness (the topic of Part IV in this book).

Both the early set of book reviews and the more recent ones draw out the economic efficiency versus equity theme. Praise is given to writers who advance thinking in this area. For example, the work of Amartya Sen is praised as being 'a compelling and visionary track for our times' (Review 94). In contrast, scholars who fail to understand the business and efficiency aspects of free trade agreements, such as Susan Aaronson, are criticised for paying too much attention to the 'crackpot ideas of the NGOs' (Review 97). However, even when books like this are criticised I recognise the need for analysis of the new actors on the stage of international business, such as NGOs. I also recognise and highlight the complexities of free trade agreements. These are really investment agreements, as they now contain national treatment provisions for FDI, such that MNEs are not subject to discriminatory regulation by host country governments. I refer to the inclusion of FDI as the 'deepening' of trade agreements. The days of shallow integration by the negotiated removal of tariffs is now being complemented by the increased facilitation of MNE activity across national borders through adoption of the legal principle of national treatment. The only surprising aspect of this deepening of trade agreements is the NGO opposition to the proposed multilateral agreement on investment (MAI), which is brilliantly analysed by the late Monte Graham (Review 95).

In conclusion, the reviews of these books on economic development and the regulations of MNEs reflect my concern with what I regard as superficial thinking which ignores the benefits that MNEs bring to the increase in world economic welfare. An excessive degree of protection and regulation of MNEs will kill the goose which lays the golden egg of economic development. The MNE has been shown to be the key institution operating at the centre of localised clusters which provide external benefits to partner firms and to other institutions in the non-government infrastructure.

Looking again at Figure 8 it can be seen that MNEs are best regarded as flagship firms. Their partnerships with key suppliers and key customers are business-to-business relationships. These are built upon long-term relational contracts in which trust and other intangible aspects of business become important. These relational contracts are now well established in business. Yet, long term relational contracts do not exist between MNEs and non-business groups, such as NGOs, and some host country governments. Until such relational contracts develop and deepen, such that trust exists, there is unlikely to be any solution to the underlying conflicts which remain today based on the efficiency objectives of MNEs versus the distributional objectives of governments and NGOs.

Importing Technology into Africa: Foreign Investment and the Supply of Technological Innovations

D. Babatunde Thomas

(Praeger Special Studies in International Economics and Development). New York: Praeger, 1976, 202 pp.*

The transfer of technology from advanced to less developed nations raises many interesting questions for economic analysis, some of which are explored in this volume. The basic premise of the chapters written by Thomas is that the transfer of technology is embodied in the multinational enterprise (MNE) and that it is the duty of the MNE to ensure that it operates as a satisfactory engine for the development of host nations. Unfortunately, but not surprisingly, it is found that the MNE has devoted more effort towards profit maximization than to the promotion of world economic development. For example, the MNE in Africa has tended to use capital intensive instead of labour intensive techniques of production, and has often installed obsolete equipment. In addition the MNE uses expatriate management and research skills instead of promoting the establishment of indigenous educational centers which would improve the volume of human capital in the host nation. To solve these problems it is recommended that the government of a host nation engage in bargaining with the MNE in order to arrange contractual codes of operation whereby direct foreign investment (DFI) by the MNE will have greater spillover benefits for the host nation's development objectives.

There are several problems with this argument. First it is not at all clear that it is the duty of a MNE to promote development, or to transfer technology by itself. These are the planning goals of the host nation and are the responsibility of the local government, which logically may proceed to tax away any monopoly profits of the MNE but cannot expect it to operate as a development agency. Second, the volume ignores the modern theory of DFI, which finds that the MNE expands abroad to extend the market for a monopoly advantage it has achieved in an area of knowledge,

---

Kyklos 30(2) (1977): 325–326.

research, technology or management. The market imperfections approach assumes that the MNE responds to an externality in one of these areas, and that the monopoly advantage is firm specific. In this case no transfer of technology is to be expected since it is in the interest of the MNE to protect its advantage. However, there is a solution to this problem, which is that the government of a host nation should provide a direct subsidy to local industry in order to overcome the original imperfection in the market. Similarly the government should subsidize education and training services in the hope of realizing external benefits, rather than prompting the MNE to help this sector in an indirect manner. Third, it is necessary to distinguish between efficiency and distributional objectives. As just shown the MNE cannot be as efficient as a host government in technology transfer, since it is a second best vehicle. While the MNE can be taxed on distributional grounds (with the funds being used for the subsidies just suggested), it is incorrect to expect the MNE to transfer technology, and inappropriate to criticize it for failing to do something which it has never attempted in the first place.

The patchwork construction of the book is disappointing. The editor contributes three chapters on the theory of technological transfer and one on the Nigerian oil industry. There is an historical essay by Mira Wilkins on the diffusion of technology by the MNE in Africa. There are two studies of East Africa, one by Chudson on the need for public policy to control the operations of the MNE, and one by Schilie on the link between scientific research and its application to technology in the context of an examination of the lack of cooperation between national and regional institutions. The narrow focus of these case studies suggests that the title is misleading. The content of much of the book also suggests an inappropriate and superficial approach to the problems of technology transfer by the MNE.

The Multinational Corporation and Social Change

D.E. Apter and L.W. Goodman (eds)

New York: Praeger, distributed by Martin Robertson, 1976, xiii, 234 pp.*

It is fitting that this collection of papers, delivered at a conference in May 1974 at Yale University's Institute for Social and Policy Studies, should be dedicated to the late Stephen Hymer. His seminal work on the multinational corporation (MNC) takes the broad perspective of political economy rather than the narrower viewpoint of analytical economics. These essays follow in this tradition and focus upon political questions of distribution, power, and control of the MNC instead of the economic issue of its efficiency as an agency for international development. Contributions by Apter, W. Goldstein, Goodman, Magdoff, and Muller examine the social and political aspects of the MNC, while those by Ranis, Tsurumi, and Vernon use a little economic theory. One of the themes in an otherwise heterogeneous volume is that the MNC is not sufficiently accountable to nation states and that it often serves as an instrument for capitalism, or even imperialism. To solve these problems it is advocated by several writers that governments be more rigorous in their use of countervailing power. Also recommended are greater use of planning, socialism, codes of conduct for the MNC, third world orders, and other fashionable panaceas. While many readers trained in economic theory will find much to dispute in this book, it cannot be denied that many relevant questions are raised and that to answer them a broad perspective many be helpful.

**The Economic Journal* 87 (346) (June 1977): 403–404.

National Control of Foreign Business Entry: A Survey of Fifteen Countries

R.D. Robinson

New York: Praeger, Distributed by Martin Robertson & Co. 1976, xxxii, 508 pp.[*]

Government regulations which restrict the free entry of foreign direct investment (FDI) are surveyed in this volume. There are fifteen case studies of 'entry control systems' for nations ranging from Latin America to Southeast Asia, but also including Sweden and Japan. The types of official regulations vary enormously, from taxes, tariffs, royalties, and other objective policy variables to perceptual and subjective influence of equity ownership, distribution of profits, market shares, and management operations. The appendices take 150 pages to list relevant government forms and regulations affecting FDI. Out of this chaos Robinson erects a taxonomy of thirty types of control, but the overall impression remains one of red tape and conflicting policy objectives. The host nations wish to cream off any monopoly profits earned by multinational firms, yet it is not clear if, at the margin, administrative barriers redistribute income or merely discourage new FDI. If the latter occurs then most of the nations discussed here will eventually forfeit the economic benefits of transfer of technology, research, knowledge, and management skills in return for the goals of reduced foreign ownership of local industry and greater political independence. Although the book is basically a research report for the U.S. Bureau of Labor, Robinson (who is a professor of international business at MIT) is able to draw together the diverse country studies to conclude that 'national sovereignty is not at bay ... but is as lusty as ever. And its impact on corporations with global reach is such as to restrict significantly their options'.

The Economic Journal, 87(346) (June 1977), p. 410.

83 Economics and the Environment

A.V. Kneese

Harmondsworth, UK: Penguin Books, 1977, 286 pp.

This well-written book succeeds admirably in its objective of integrating economic theory with environmental problems. Professor Kneese manages to teach quite a bit of relevant economics as he outlines the appropriate method for modeling various issues in environmental production and consumption. His background as an economist with Resources for the Future has undoubtedly helped to develop both his ability to explain complex ideas in a constructive fashion and his perspective of the interdependencies of wide environmental issues.

The economics used is standard neoclassical micro theory, adjusted for the concept of externalities. Kneese takes a liberal viewpoint of the usefulness of micro theory with its emphasis on Pareto optimality, and is able to draw the (correct) distinction between efficiency and distributional objectives. Only the former are satisfied by economic theory, and Kneese is aware that many environmental problems have as much to do with concepts of equity and justice, as with efficiency only.

The major modification to economic theory which is stressed is the need to incorporate environmental 'residuals' as external costs of production and/or consumption. A good example of the powerful nature of economic analysis is given in Chapter three where a Leontief input-output model is successfully modified to incorporate residual elements in the matrix, and is then applied to estimate the impact of population growth on the US economy. This type of model appears to give a more optimistic result on future growth than that of the Club of Rome's 'Limits to Growth.'

In the subsequent chapter Kneese is very critical of the latter model (as most economists would be) for its 'false precision' and 'highly premature' world modeling. He does not foresee the inevitable collapse of the world

Environment and Planning A 9(10) (October 1977): 1204.

economy through exponential increases in pollution and population, but only linear growth of energy, food, and other resources. He is concerned that the rate of technological innovation cannot match the demands of high population growth, but does believe that a solution may be possible through the price system.

Kneese's main reservation about the future is the Faustian bargain involved in nuclear fission energy development. Here the problems of waste disposal of plutonium are immense and on such a long-term scale that conventional cost-benefit analysis cannot handle the ethical problems involved.

Kneese is cynical about the ability of governments to overcome long-range environmental problems and in his more pessimistic sections, foresees either a breakdown of world order into war, famine, and anarchy, or the development of a more rigid social order in which individual freedom is sacrificed for overall control and planning. Kneese mainly sees this as a longer-run problem, but it is of obvious concern to present policy.

84 The International Taxation of Multinational Enterprises

J.D.R. Adams and John Whalley
London: Associated Business Programmes, 1977, viii, 178 pp.[*]

A good book on the economic and legal aspects of international taxation of the multinational enterprise (MNE) is sorely needed. This book goes only a fraction of the way towards meeting this need. It is a superficial review of national tax laws, with a heavy bias towards the British system, and lacks a sustained analysis of international tax agreements. The major problem with the book is that the authors have very little to say about what most economists would regard as the central aspect of taxation of the MNE, namely transfer pricing. There are only a few scattered references to transfer pricing in the text and only the very last chapter has a discussion of a concept which should have been worked into the heart of the book. Consequently, the book is of little value to academic specialists working on the MNE and it will not appeal much to students or financial managers of the MNE. Another annoying feature of the book is that chapters 1,3, 6, 12, 14, and 15, which are apparently written by a good economist, Whalley, are too short and few in number to compensate for the purely descriptive legal chapters. The latter convey relatively little information, following a pedantic framework of legal statement and worked arithmetic examples but with no analysis. The result is a catalogue of issues, such as double taxation, the overspill problem, tax harmonization, and so on. Unfortunately, there are no research results, either theoretical or empirical, to report, so that book remains a rather bland overview of the MNE and international tax policy.

---

[*]*The Economic Journal* 88(352) (December 1978): 905.

The Multinational Corporation, the Nation State and the Trade Unions: A European Perspective

Gunnar Hedlund and Lars Otterbeck
Kent, Ohio: Kent State University Press, 1977, ix, 168 pp.[*]

Using Sweden as a case study the authors of this monograph report on the attitudes of influential decision makers towards the multinational corporation (MNC). Three groups of people were interviewed; business executives, trade-union leaders, and politicians from the major Swedish parties. The interviews were conducted between 1972 and 1974, with a total of 108 persons being consulted. Each interview lasted several hours since the authors chose to probe for responses to alternative scenarios governing the future role of the MNC in Swedish society. One of the mildly surprising results was that none of the groups perceived the MNC as an immediate or potential threat to Sweden and consequently no strong feelings were expressed in favor of regulation of the MNC. There was general acceptance of the economic benefits of 'internationalization' and a rejection of ethnocentric restrictions. To some extent these findings interact with the perceptions of the authors themselves, both of whom teach international business at the Stockholm School of Economics. The enlightened liberalism of the authors' viewpoint towards the MNC must have some impact on the content, style, and interpretation of interviews. Presumably a Marxist interviewer would come to different conclusions by asking slightly different questions but still using the same techniques. It is for this reason that the subjective and qualitative nature of studies, such as this one, which report on attitudes towards the MNC must gradually give way to more abstract and analytical work.

---

[*] *The Economic Journal* Book notes, 88(352) (December 1978): 906.

86 Reducing Global Inequalities

W. Howard Wriggins and Gunnar Adler-Karlsson
New York: McGraw Hill, 1978, xiv, 193 pp.*

Rich Nations and Poor Nations in the World Economy

Albert Fishlow,
Carlos F. Díaz-Alejandro, Richard R. Fagan,
and Roger D. Hansen
New York: McGraw Hill, 1978, xii, 264 pp.*

Commissioned by the 1980s project of the Council on Foreign Relations, these two volumes of essays are the first of several dozen books to be published by the project, which focuses on North-South relationships. The major essay in these two volumes, judged by its prior circulation and influence on thinking in academic and public policy circles, is that by Carlos Díaz-Alejandro on delinking North and South. His criticisms of laissez-faire as a false strategy in a world full of market imperfections and second best solutions are well made. Perhaps surprising to some of his readers, however, will be his rejection of the polar opposite case, namely, pure delinking. He believes that such a policy of national self-sufficiency is as impossible in today's interdependent world as is the laissez-faire policy of development by free trade. In practice we have both economic linkages between nations and political constraints (in the form of regulations, tariffs, and taxes) on a pure market solution to development problems. Thus, in recommending selective delinking for the South, Díaz-Alejandro steers a middle course. This policy will bring in some of the benefits of Northern technology and production skills while allowing the South to avoid some of the costs of the existing world economic order, such as commodity price fluctuations, deteriorating terms of trade, and other

**Journal of Developing Areas* 13(3) (April 1979): 347–348.

foreign exchange problems. However, he does not support a Prebisch-type policy of self-reliant industrialization to replace trade, even for large nations, since the South cannot escape completely the worldwide influence of Northern capital and technology.

The rejection by Diaz-Alejandro of the strong form of the delinking hypothesis leads to the same general conclusion as those reached by Albert Fishlow in a more conventional economic theory approach. Fishlow argues that the world economic order can be reformed satisfactorily by removal of tariff barriers and by increased financials flows (in the form of private direct investment) to less developed countries (LDCs). Both economists, therefore, end up advocating development within the frame-work of a reformed international economy rather than by turning to self-reliant industrialization. These conclusions differ sharply from those of political scientists, such as Fagen, Wriggens, and Adler-Karlsson, who do not appear to understand the efficiency considerations of concern to economists. Focusing instead upon socioeconomic and political arguments that decry the dependency of LDCs on the North, they tend to advocate more radical changes in the world economic order, such as that of Adler-Karlsson for self-reliance and political decentralization to the village level. It is to be hoped that the laudable concern with world equity does not destroy the world economy by adoption of inefficient policies of self-reliance, policies which are especially inappropriate for the smaller LDCs.

The underlying assumption in the essays in these books is that the South has not been receiving an equitable share of the world's wealth and power. Several of the authors use this assumption to argue for policies that will either reform the present system or radically change it. In doing so they examine the perceived inefficiencies of the world system which have led to the inequitable distribution of income between North and South. Yet as any well-trained economist knows, equity and efficiency are different animals and they cannot be easily reconciled. Therefore, it is worth making a very simple point, namely that if an inequitable world income distribution is being assumed, the correct method to change it is by a worldwide system of taxes and subsidies. Ultimately world income can only be redistributed through taxation of the richer nations and subsidies to the poorer ones. Since such redistributional policies are ineffective within nation states, even when they have strong governments, we should not be surprised at the failures of such policies on an international level where there exists no strong central authority. The unsavory conclusion is that achievement of an equitable distribution of the world's wealth requires a genuine policy of international distribution of income, but such a policy is likely to be, in practice, an impossible dream.

87 American Multinationals and American Interests

C. Fred Bergsten, Thomas Horst, and Theodore H. Moran
*Washington, DC: The Brookings Institution, 1978, 547 pp.**

In this ambitious book the authors face the difficult task of integrating the economic and political aspects of American multinational activities as they affect US public policy. They examine the contribution of multinationals to the home economy in chapters on the balance of payments, labour, resources, taxation, competition and antitrust policy, trade and exports, and the international monetary system. Political issues of multinationals are discussed in the context of American foreign policy towards developing and industrialized countries. Their approach is to summarize the major theoretical and empirical contributions to the recent literature on multinationals, a task which is achieved in a reasonably balanced manner, and to report some of the new empirical work on the profitability and other economic characteristics of US multinationals. A key finding is that US tax policy towards multinationals is close to neutrality and that 'as a general rule multinationals do not escape taxation by investing overseas' (p.210). Another is that exports and foreign direct investment seem to be complementary. Yet another is that there is little statistical support for the notion 'that the surge in foreign direct investment over the last decades significantly affected income shares' (p. 109) to the detriment of labour. More surprising are the results on page 241 which show that the earnings (on assets) for groups of US multinationals are greater than for groups of domestic firms. Previous work has found that earnings (on equity) are about the same for multinational and uninational firms. Here the authors use their new (industry-level) data on the profitability of multinationals to conclude that the oligopolistic structure of these firms needs to be modified. They advocate increased antitrust activity and even the divestment of some foreign subsidiaries to reduce the market power of US multinationals. This work on profitability is

---

The Economic Journal 89(356): 1029–1030.

somewhat controversial and should be interpreted with caution. It will be interesting to see if the 'Brookings view' of the world leads to greater US regulation of multinationals. If so, we may expect to witness the demise of many American multinationals since they will then be subject to major economic controls in their home nation in addition to the severe barriers being erected by the governments of many host nations. The concern for equity, manifest in this book, may well compromise the efficiency of multinational firms.

Distortion or Development? Contending Perspectives on the Multinational Corporations

Thomas J. Biersteker
*Cambridge, MA: MIT Press, 1978, 199 pp.**

The objective of this book is to compare and evaluate two contending paradigms of the effects of multinationals enterprises (MNEs) on development. These alternative theoretical perspectives are identified as the 'critical perspective' of dependency theory and the 'neoconventional perspective' of economists such as Ray Vernon and his colleagues who have participated in the Harvard Business School's MNE project. Biersteker gives a thorough taxonomic account of these perspectives, in Chapters 1 and 2 respectively, and then points up their major areas of agreement and disagreement in Chapter 3. Here he makes a useful distinction between matched arguments, where contending propositions can be contrasted, and mismatched arguments, 'in which the two approaches direct their arguments past each other' (p. 49). In the remaining half of the book the author applies his theoretical analysis to a case study of multinational investment in Nigeria.

The findings of the theoretical section are neatly summarized in a series of seven tables. In each of the first two chapters are listed the main points made by proponents of each perspective, with, in Chapter 3, the author's interpretation of matched and mismatched arguments about the impact of the MNE on development. The seven topics are: balance of payments effects; displacement of indigenous production; extent of technology transfer; appropriateness of the technology; patterns of consumption; local social structures; and income distribution effects. Given the emotional nature of much of the criticism of the MNE, the author is to be congratulated on his excellent analytical statement of the critical perspective and his balanced assessment of it and the contending neoconventional perspective. On methodological grounds some economists might quibble with this approach, since not all

*Political Science Quarterly 94(4) (Winter 1979–1980): 722–724.

the contending propositions can be tested. Yet it is a useful contribution to have the nonaddressed arguments and mismatched propositions of the two paradigms expressed explicitly. It may help the two camps understand each other's work, instead of persisting in the common practice of ignoring it.

The empirical work of Chapters 4 through 8 is based on an interesting case study of Nigeria that uses an elaborate data base (described in an appendix) with information on sixty economic and financial variables for a sample of foreign and domestic firms in the industry groups of textiles, cement, sawmilling, and sugar refining. Data for the 1963–1972 period are collected for sixty firms, giving a total of 293 cases after allowing for missing or unreliable data. There may be more of the latter than the author believes since some of the financial information on capital sourcing, remitted profits, dividends, and transfer pricing came from interviews with firm accountants and managers. The information from such interviews will probably incorporate many subjective biases and is less reliable than the data from the Central Bank and Industrial Survey Division of the government statistics office. Fortunately most data come from these official sources.

Biersteker does not find all that much evidence from his field work on Nigeria to support the critical perspective of the MNE. For example, in Chapter 5 he reports that local financing predominates (as it does elsewhere), exporting is substantial, transfer pricing does not exist, and the remission of profits is not a problem. Although there is a net outflow of capital from MNEs in manufacturing, this outflow is trivial relative to Nigeria's oil revenues. Due to the abundant foreign-exchange reserves, there has been less tension in Nigeria between the MNE and nation-state than in other developing nations. Indeed, dependency theory seems less applicable to Africa, in general, than to Latin America.

I have two comments on this chapter. First, when testing the linkages hypothesis (p. 90), I think that the imports percentage should be treated as an independent variable rather than as a dependent variable, since in the present form only a couple of dummy variables are significant and size is not – a surprising result. Second, the author argues that when Biafra was blockaded during the civil war the region was able to develop indigenous production, even in the relatively sophisticated technology of petroleum refining. He says that 'the Biafran case suggests that feasible alternatives to the multinational corporation exist in Nigeria' (p. 100). Yet this historical situation seems more an example of response to war conditions than a scientific experiment in alternative technology. Further, the author ignores the basic question of costs and fails to ask if such indigenous production is efficient. But perhaps such comments are too 'neoconventional'?

Multinationals from Small Countries

Tamir Agmon and Charles P. Kindleberger (eds)
Cambridge, MA: MIT Press, 1977, xv, 224 pp.[*]

If there is a theory of economic development, it is subject to constant change. Indeed the field is probably too large to produce a satisfactory theory which can integrate all of the areas studied by development economists (and noneconomists). The volume under review fits only loosely into the development field and will be of equal interest to those specializing in international economics and international business. However, this book cannot be ignored by development economists as it focuses on the role and activity of a principal agent in developing nations – the multinational enterprise (MNE). Given the fashionable nature of work on the MNE in recent literature, the editors of this book have been clever enough to carve out a new niche for themselves, one which is certainly worthy of our attention and which should be incorporated into the theory of development.

Agmon and Kindleberger have identified a gap in the literature on the MNE. They invited seven authors to write papers dealing with the foreign investment undertaken by MNEs based in 'small' nations. Many of us are used to thinking of the MNEs as originating in the United States, Western Europe, or, perhaps, Japan, This book does not study such MNEs. Instead, the writers consider MNEs in the 'small' nations of Latin America, France, Sweden, Switzerland, and Australia. Canada is, unfortunately, not examined although it has proportionately more inward and outward foreign direct investment (FDI) than any other country and, in the terminology of the book, is a small nation par excellence.

The papers of greatest interest to readers of this journal will probably be those of Carlos Díaz-Alejandro of Yale and Louis Wells of the Harvard Business School. These authors deal with FDI in Latin America

Economic Development and Cultural Change 28(4) (July 1980): 871–875.

and 'developing countries,' respectively. The main points of these papers are discussed below. The book also features papers by Niehans on Switzerland, Carlson on Sweden, Bertin on France, and Hughes on technology transfer in Australia. These papers are of uneven quality and are not always directed toward the central issue of small country MNEs.

Rather than give a summary of each paper, I shall, instead, concentrate on three central themes which emerge from the book. These are: first, the extent to which a common theory of direct foreign investment (DFI) is recognized by the authors of the more theoretical papers; second, the argument raised by several writers that small scale MNEs are efficient in small nations and can assist in the development process; third, the roles of the public sector and political factors in an analysis of the MNE.

The modern theory of DFI is recognized explicitly by the majority of the authors. This theory is attributed to the seminal work by Hymer[1] in 1960 in which he hypothesized that the MNE would exploit abroad an advantage acquired in one or more of the many segments of the product and factor markets. The ability of the MNE to create an internal market to substitute for the missing external market for knowledge, information, research, and technological skills has been recognized in more recent work by Buckley and Casson.[2] The latter refinement of Hymer's market imperfections hypothesis is not developed by economists writing in this volume, nor does an explicit statement of it appear anywhere. This is unfortunate since the concept of internalization advanced by Buckley and Casson is a potential unifying theory of DFI, and until it becomes accepted as a general theory much of the writing on the MNE will continue to be unstructured.

The most stimulating and provocative paper in the book is that by Agmon and Lessard. In their essay they concentrate on the capital market imperfections faced by the MNEs operating abroad. They list as many as 13 imperfections in financial markets that can affect MNEs based in small nations. These include: foreign exchange controls; different national tax rates; restrictions on foreign investment; information and transactions costs; constraints on the domain of contracts; government regulations affecting interest rates, credit allocations, and securities; and the small size or thinness of many overseas financial markets. The authors argue that 'some of these effects can be offset by the existence of conglomerate business groups that internalize many capital market functions' (p.213).

As far as I can recall this is the only explicit mention of internalization in the whole book, but even there the authors do not take up the point and instead choose to emphasize the related concept of international diversification.

In a world of capital market imperfections, it is impossible for an individual investor, especially one based in a small nation, to purchase shares in the corporations of various nations. Therefore the benefits of risk reduction through international diversification can only be achieved in an indirect manner – by the purchase of shares in an MNE which has a stable stream of earnings over time due to its production and sales in nations whose factor and goods markets are not perfectly correlated with that of the investor.[3]

Agmon and Lessard accept the point that the MNE is a surrogate vehicle for international diversification only in passing and do not make enough of it. In my opinion it is of central importance to their study, yet their thinking is apparently still dominated by vestiges of capital market theory which are relevant only in a world of integrated capital markets (as they would readily agree). Thus, that paper is not as precise as it could be and does not develop its very stimulating arguments with sufficient clarity or in enough detail. Despite this I suggest that it be read first by those with a more theoretical inclination, since it sets the stage for the excellent essay by Jürg Niehans.

Niehans probably has one of the best analytical minds in the profession, and his incursion into the realm of political economy in this paper on small MNEs in Switzerland is full of good theoretical insights. He examines the intermediate product flows to these MNEs and works in both the market imperfections and international diversification aspects of the theory of DFI to help explain the flows. Next he twists the theory of DFI to help explain the key characteristic of the MNE, as he sees it, which is the scale advantage resulting from the vertical integration of production. His major hypothesis is derived from two counterfactual exercises in which the contribution of five large MNEs to the Swiss economy is evaluated by assuming them away and examining the economy in their absence. In the first exercise protection is assumed away which leads, naturally, to more foreign trade and welfare gains. There is a relative contraction of MNEs due to the fact that the incentive for their formation (in the form of a tariff) has been removed. In the second exercise other types of market imperfections (which lead to the emergence of the MNE) are assumed away, with a smaller gain in efficiency, since technology transfer is reduced.

Niehans concludes that the MNE is a second best method for small nations such as Switzerland to achieve vital economies of scale. In a perfect world with no barriers to trade the MNE is unnecessary. However, in the real world characterized by government imposed regulations, tariffs, and other market imperfections it is an agency which 'helps to equalize the economic opportunities between firms of small and large countries' (p.37). The comment by Michael Adler on this paper raises some further issues which cannot be discussed here, although they are of interest. Instead, I now take up the point about economies of scale since this is the second major theme identified in the book.

Two authors argue that MNEs in small nations can be efficient at adapting technology to the requirements of these nations. Helen Hughes uses Australia as a case study of transfer of technology both to a small nation (itself) and also from it to developing nations in Southeast Asia and its neighbor Papua New Guinea. She thinks that, in general, it is necessary to 'scale down' technology for the Australian market. Once MNEs have done this they can then act as technological intermediaries in the servicing of markets in developing nations. In practice there is insufficient latitude given to the subsidiaries of major MNEs by their parent firms, with the result that there is a lack of adaptation of technology to the needs of low income nations. Hughes believes that Australia could be a much better intermediary in the transfer of technology than it has been so far. She is also a good enough economist to place part of the blame on the inward looking policies of the Australian governments. Protection has encouraged inward DFI but it has not fostered outward DFI.

I do not find this as surprising as Hughes since the tariff will encourage an inefficient manufacturing sector to develop. A protected industry is unlikely to be characterized by innovation, research, or adaptation of technology. Instead, as shown by Sune Carlson in his essay on the internationalization process, a nation (such as Sweden) which is committed more to free trade than to protection will be more successful in both the absorption and re-export of technology. To an extent, Carlson's thesis is derived from consideration of marketing factors rather than purely production ones. Yet he does demonstrate that an outward looking small nation can have successful MNEs of its own.

The second writer to advocate the adaptation of technology as the major role for MNEs from small nations is Louis Wells. He believes in this as a possible model for developing nations, that is, that large-scale technology can be adapted to the smaller markets of such nations. He finds that 'some entrepreneurs have found a niche for small-scale technology' (p.140) and that they need not be overwhelmed by the MNEs based in large industrialized nations. This is a good hypothesis which cries out for some empirical verification (like many other statements in the book). In fact the main shortcoming of the book is the lack of empirical work reported, a factor which is perhaps not too surprising given the new ground covered by most of the authors.

The third theme running through several of the essays is the role of the government in fostering outward DFI and in the more familiar area of regulating inward flows of DFI. Díaz-Alejandro places most emphasis on the large public sector, common to Latin American nations, and draws the interesting implications that this has for state-owned MNEs. He also identifies the 'symbiotic relation between state and large private or public enterprises' (p.181) which raises the interesting implication that the MNE of a small nation will take on the political hue of its government. The MNE is not always a vehicle for capitalism but may be a result of state socialism. Either type of MNE can contribute to development. Díaz-Alejandro does not argue this point directly, but it appears to be implicit in his paper. One point he does make which may surprise some readers is that Latin American MNEs 'can be a positive force in the region's development, if encouraged in a selective and rational fashion' (p.191).

In a comment on Wells's paper, Steve Kobrin also dwells on the vital importance of political factors in explaining DFI. He gives a good summary of the literature on political economy of the MNE with its emphasis on dependency, control, and power. He states, correctly, that MNEs are 'significant transnational political actors in their own right' (p.161) and draws the implication that they have not used their power to foster a redistribution of world income. On a brighter note, Kobrin advances the argument that MNEs based in small (and especially developing) nations may face fewer political problems than traditional

MNEs. Unfortunately the MNEs from small nations are unlikely to be as efficient as those from major industrialized nations.

In conclusion, we are again confronted with the familiar trade-off between equity and efficiency. This trade-off is, of course, at the heart of economic theory so we cannot expect a book on the MNE to solve it. The contribution of this volume is its primary focus on issues of economies and efficiency, with a detailed evaluation of the role of MNEs based in small nations. While the MNE cannot be expected to serve as a development agency (for this is the job of the government), it has been shown that the MNE is an efficient institution which responds to exogenous market imperfections. The MNE can be adapted to serve as an intermediary in the transfer of technology and can help to equalize the economic opportunities between poor and rich nations. In this way the MNE serves to promote the growth and development of all nations.

Notes

[1] Stephen H. Hymer. *The International Operations of National Firms: A Study of Direct Foreign Investment* (Cambridge, MA: M.I.T. Press, 1976).

[2] Peter Buckley and Mark Casson. *The Future of the Multinational Enterprise* (London: Macmillan, 1976).

[3] For a more detailed explanation of international diversification, along with bibliographic sources, see Alan M. Rugman, *International Diversification and the Multinational Enterprise* (Lexington, MA: D.C. Heath & Co., Lexington Books, 1979).

North-South Technology Transfer: A Case Study of Petrochemicals in Latin America

Mariluz Cortes and Peter Bocock
Baltimore and London: The Johns Hopkins University Press, 1984, 176 pp.[*]

Do we really need yet another tiresome study of technology transfer based on the premise that the developing countries somehow have a birthright to the know-how of developed nations? This is the implicit assumption running through the four chapters of this short book. The first chapter is a background review of the theory of technology transfer, the second analyzes its 'supply' in the petrochemical industry, the third its 'demand' in the seven Latin American nations, and the fourth draws some lessons. The basic weakness of research such as this is that technology transfer is only analyzed from a government policy perspective. Yet, since technology usually resides with in the multinational enterprise (for very good business reasons) it is also necessary to focus upon the issue from the viewpoint of the firm.

[*]*Journal of Policy Analysis and Management* 4(3) (Spring 1985): 465–466.

International Trade Policy and the Pacific Rim: Proceedings of the IEA Conference held in Sydney Australia

John Piggott and Alan Woodland (eds)

Basingstoke, UK: Macmillan in association with IEA, 1999, 440 pp. *

This book represents the proceedings of a conference organized at the request of the International Economic Association in Sydney, Australia in July 1996. There are 17 papers plus an introduction and two conference summaries. Twelve of the papers have comments giving a total of 32 contributions. These are arranged in 4 parts: Part 1 deals with the trade policy and economic growth in the Asia Pacific region; Part 2 addresses aspects of the 'new regionalism' compared with multilateralism; Part 3 has three views on the Asia Pacific Economic Cooperation forum (APEC); Part 4 consists of three papers on trade and growth theory.

In part 1 the lead paper is by David Greenaway, followed by three papers on trade policy in China (by Barry Naughton), on Australia-New Zealand (by Peter J. Lloyd), and on Malaysia. A final paper asks if East Asia countries are more 'open' than NAFTA or the EC.

In part 2 papers by Wilfred Ethier and by Kyle Bagwell and Robert Staiger, use a game theoretic approach to regionalism and multilateralism in trade policy. Richard Harris and Nicolas Schmitt model export incentives and protection. James Anderson addresses some welfare aspects of trade reform with a government budget constraint. Finally, Wolfgang Mayer develops a model of the political economy of administered protection.

In part 3 there are three largely descriptive papers on APEC, two of them from the perspective of the two main member economies, Japan and the United States.

In part 4, Scott Taylor develops a model of trade policy in endogenous growth models, followed by papers on technology transfer and foreign

---

The Economic Journal, book note: 16/09/99: http://www.reg.org.uk/ecojbknotes/row.asp?id=16389.

direct investment. The last paper, by Motoshige Itoh, is a case study of Sony and its subsidiaries in Southeast Asia.

This conference was conceived in 1992 by the IEA, at a time when the Asian economic miracle was an unchallenged assumption for the participants. While the Asian economic collapse of 1997/8 has badly tarnished the performance of such divergent economies as Japan, Korea, Malaysia, Thailand, and Hong Kong, much of the analysis of the primarily theoretical and empirical papers in this book remains valid. I found the papers by Ethier, Harris and Schmitt, Mayer and Itoh to be particularly interesting and robust.

Some of the policy papers travel less well, especially the largely speculative papers on APEC which has no permanent organizing secretariat or structure and is subject to the political whims of the annual host nation. In Vancouver in 1997 the Canadians kept it moving whereas in Malaysia in 1998 APEC went off the tracks.

Leaving recent economic reality aside, the conference was poorly served in a purely analytical sense by the prejudice against papers on multinational enterprises and foreign direct investment (FDI). With the exception of the case study of FDI by Itoh, none of the other papers engages with the substantive issue of 'deep' integration through FDI in the Asia Pacific Region, rather than the 'shallow' integration to be achieved by tariff cuts and the conventional agenda of trade policy. Given the empirical evidence on the importance of FDI in the region, this is a rather sad omission which gives the reader of this book pause in recommending it. Ignoring the strategies of multinational enterprises as they affect the trade and economic development of the Asia Pacific is rather like leaving the Prince of Denmark out of Hamlet. Not that it is a bad book, just one which is now out of date in policy terms and was never up to date in using the emerging analytical framework of deep integration.

The World Trade Organization: Constitution and Jurisprudence

John H. Jackson
London: The Royal Institute of International Affairs, 1998, 208 pp.*

The focus of this book is upon the 'institutional and jurispruden-tial aspects of the World Trade Organization' (p. 10), rather than its economic and political dimensions. In a narrative of exceptional insight and clarity, Professor Jackson provides a definitive analysis of the work-ings of the WTO. In Chapter 1 there is a brief review of the antecedents to the WTO in the work of the General Agreement on Tariffs and Trade (GATT), formed in 1947. In Chapter 2 the activities of GATT are reviewed, including the eight rounds of tariff cuts, concluding with the Uruguay Round of 1986–1994. The nature of GATT as a rule-oriented system rather than a negotiation/power-oriented system is made clear. Chapter 3 examines the legal basis of the WTO, its institutional structure and its role in international law. This work is carried on in Chapter 4 which reports on the WTO's new dispute settlement mech-anisms (DSMs). The procedure and rules of the appellate system are especially well done. Although the focus of the book is on the institu-tional structure of the WTO and DSMs, there is good insight shown into the rules of the system, which are reproduced in several appendices. The depth of scholarship is revealed in the 25 pages of careful footnotes which follow the 100 pages of text.

A successful institution such as the WTO has many parents. In the forward Benn Steil makes the claim that Jackson's earlier 1990 book 'laid the foundation for the proposed "World Trade Organization."' Jackson is more accurate on pages 27 and 29 reporting, correctly, that it was a proposal by the Canadian government in early 1990 that was the first to call publicly for the establishment of the WTO. In turn, this proposal was strongly influenced by my former colleague, Dr. Sylvia Ostry, Chair

---

**International Affairs* 75(2) (April 1999): 400–401

of the Centre for International Studies at the University of Toronto. The Canadian proposal built on the work of Jackson and others at an informal meeting in Geneva in 1989 and this proposal was then incorporated into the 'Dunkel Text' of 1991 which eventually became the final text of the Uruguay Round adopted in Marrakesh in April 1994. In approving the Uruguay Round on its 'fast track' system, the United States insisted on the name WTO, rather than the European Community preference for a 'Multinational Trade Organization' (MTO). So the Canadian proposal literally gave the WTO its name.

93 Trade, Investment and the Environment

Halina Ward and Duncan Brack (eds)
London: Earthscan/Royal Institute of International Affairs, 2000, 298 pp.[*]

This is an excellent book, in the finest traditions of a Chatham House trade policy publication. It is timely, balanced and informative. Based on a conference in October 1998, its focus on the new agenda of the World Trade Organization (WTO), in terms of how environmental and investment issues link to multilateral trade policy, is still highly relevant today. In anticipation of the November 1999 Seattle fiasco, the editors invited contributions from NGOs as well as from trade experts and business-oriented groups. This has produced a balanced set of viewpoints, with some subtle guidance from the editors towards pushing ahead at the WTO to incorporate these new issues into its rules-based system. Their overall assessment of globalization, in a fine introductory synthesis, is positive and supportive of new institutional, process-based improvements in the current system of global governance.

It is impossible to summarize the 26 papers in the book but a few themes are developed throughout. There is a good material in at least five of the chapters on the shrimp/turtle dispute and the failed WTO appeal that upset environmentalists who did not understand the technical nature of the WTO appellate system. This is representative of the first key theme of how environmental issues are handled by the WTO and how this might need to be reformed in light of the political pressure brought by NGOs. Duncan Brack is representative in calling for changes in WTO rules to reconcile them with multilateral environmental agreements. A second theme concerns the capture of environmental regulations by wealthy 'triad' countries (North America, European Union and Japan) to be used as entry barriers against each other's exports, and also to impose process and production methods (PPMs) and higher standards on poorer,

[*]*International Affairs* 76(2) (April 2000): 365–366.

developing countries. This argument for PPMs is often used by NGOs at the same time as they state that developing countries are pollution havens. Yet in a recent study on environmental regulations and corporate strategy in North America I found no evidence for pollution havens or any type of eco-colonialism.

A major strength of the book is its focus on foreign direct investment, as well as on trade, and the problems that this raises for 'deep integration' at the WTO. There are four interesting viewpoints on the failed Multilateral Agreement on Investment (MAI) including an insider negotiating essay by Jan Huner, which reveals how much the proposed MAI was based on the successful investment provisions of NAFTA. These include three items. First, acceptance of the principle of national treatment but with reservations for key service sectors such as culture, health, social services, education and transportation. Second, acceptance of investor-state dispute settlement. Third, the use of NAFTA Article 1114 which states that environmental and social standards should not be lowered to attract investment. The logic of this type of contribution is that we still need an MAI.

94 Development as Freedom

By Amartya Sen
Oxford: Oxford University Press, 1999, 381 pp.[*]

The, by now, well known theme of Nobel Prize Winner Sen's latest book is that development increases human freedom. Development occurs when a series of 'unfreedoms' is removed. These include: poverty, tyranny, lack of public infrastructure, slavery, lack of educational and health opportunities, no social rights, gender discrimination, etc. In other words a set of 'public goods' is required to foster development and individual choice. Development as freedom is much broader than economic growth, technology transfer, or raising standards of living. These are instruments to facilitate development and freedom.

Leading the way in fostering development is the market. 'It is very hard indeed to see how any reasonable critic can be against the market mechanism as such' and any market imperfections 'have to be dealt with not by suppressing the markets but by allowing them to function better and with greater fairness...' (p. 142). Using this logic I could interpret Sen to be in favor of free trade, the World Trade Organization, the World Bank, foreign direct investment and the efficiency aspects of multinational enterprises. Unfortunately, he has almost no discussion of those aspects of globalization as they relate to development. But readers can take comfort in that his broad principle of development as freedom is amenable to the current debate. Indeed, the opponents of global capitalism need to read Sen to understand that globalization and development can be complements.

One minor criticism I have is that the publisher really misses the boat with 51 pages of footnotes totally divorced from the text. It is virtually impossible to read Sen in depth without recourse to the endnotes, and

[*]*International Affairs* 77(2) (April 2001): 435–436.

yet this is made difficult. A scholarly publisher should be more scholarly and treat a Nobel Prize Winner better than this.

I was also struck by a paradox in reading this book. What an extraordinary life of privilege is led by both the writer and reviewer of this book. As tenured professors of economics and management respectively, we seem to be the limiting case of perfect freedom. We are the opposite of indentured workers and slaves. We have satisfactory (if not extravagant) incomes, lives of privilege and, above all, the time and means to explore ideas and philosophy. What a contrast to the half of the world of such concern to Sen which lacks all of these attributes, living in poverty, illiteracy, oppression and backwardness. And what an achievement of Sen's to still identify with this world in such an insightful manner. He brings a lifetime of work on the economics of equity to build a compelling and visionary tract for our times.

Fighting the Wrong Enemy: Antiglobal Activists and Multinational Enterprises

Edward M. Graham
Washington, DC: Institute for International Economics, 2000, 234 pp.[*]

Graham explodes the myth that antiglobal activists defeated the Multi-national Agreement on Investment (MAI). Using careful analysis and 'insider' information as a closely involved and well-informed expert on U.S. foreign direct investment policy-making, Graham concludes that the draft MAI was a very weak document. In fact, the investment liberal-ization being negotiated in the MAI was so weak that the U.S. business community stopped supporting it long before antiglobal activists started to protest against it in Paris. There was also a lack of leadership by the U.S. government, as well as tepid support in the E.U. and eventually hostility to the MAI by the French government of Lionel Jospin as he was dependent upon left wing 'green' support in his political coalition.

One of the most useful contributions of Graham's book is his objective discussion of environmental issues in trade and investment agreements. He has useful insights on the environmental provisions of NAFTA, espe-cially the important initial chapter 11 investor-state case on MMT (a gasoline additive). The Canadian Minister of the Environment, Sheila Copps, banned trade and interprovincial trade in MMT, citing it as an environmental and health hazard. The producer of MMT, a U.S. company called Ethyl, used the chapter 11 provisions to win a settlement from the Canadian government for denial of its business. The Canadian antiglobal activists claimed that this case demonstrated that multina-tional enterprises (MNEs) could overturn the environmental decisions of host country governments. The draft text of the MAI had a similar provision to NAFTA chapter 11, so the antiglobal activists claimed that the MAI was a charter of rights for MNEs to overturn the sovereign

---

[*]*International Affairs* 77(4) (October 2001): 994–995.

domain of governments. They claimed that the MAI was a 'NAFTA on steroids'.

I think that Graham gives far too much attention to this case which was a purely technical application of chapter 11 incited by trade lawyers hungry for business, and it has no long term policy relevance. The Canadian Minister apparently ignored the advice of her bureaucrats in banning the trade in MMT. As soon as trade-related measures are introduced then NAFTA applies. Instead, Copps should have banned the production of MMT, as an environmental hazard, an internal matter subject to Canadian laws. Several subsequent NAFTA chapter 11 cases have been resolved on technical grounds with no loss of sovereignty to host nations in their environmental policies.

Perhaps what this case really illustrates is the dialogue of the deaf taking place between trade experts and activists. The latter used the MMT case in a general assault on the MAI, and subsequent international trade and investment liberalization initiatives at the WTO and G7 summits. Graham argues that, as a consequence, the environmental NGOs especially have missed the boat. He states that trade negotiators were open and willing to incorporate environmental concerns into the MAI but that violent opposition to it has now closed the window for co-operation between NGOs and governments. Indeed, any more Genoas will probably permanently alienate the general public from the anti-capitalist agenda of the more extreme antiglobal activists. A small and over-publicized section of the NGO movement is apparently opposed to any reforms of the global governance mechanisms; they continue to protest violently against the MNEs. Eventually the more serious NGOs must disassociate themselves from these violent activists in order to push forward a more sensible co-operative reformist agenda for the civil society.

Guiding Global Order: G8 Governance in the Twenty-First Century

John J. Kirton, Joseph P. Daniels and Andreas Freytag (eds)
Aldershot, UK: Ashgate, 2001, xxiii, 268 pp.[*]

This is the fifth in an excellent series of international public policy books produced by the G8 research group at the University of Toronto. The G8 research group is a network of professors, students and public policy officials who provide academic analysis and informed commentary on the annual G8 summit issues. The current volume examines global governance and the role and function of international financial institutions, a recurring topic at G8 meetings and a high priority at the Cologne Summit of 1999 and the Okinawa Summit of 2000.

The most interesting scholarly feature of this volume is the blending of topical essays by mainly North American and European scholars. North Americans such as George von Furstenburg and Don Brean examine international financial and corporate governance issues respectively. The former analyzes the increasing importance of regional currencies such as the euro and the dollar. He finds that 'dollarization' is inferior to the multinational monetary union of Europe. The latter argues that the G8 may emerge as a forum for corporate governance but with an 'outsider model' of a market-oriented system rather than an insider model of institutional regulation.

German scholars from the University of Cologne, such as Juergen Donges, Andreas Freytag and Martin Theuringer, examine macroeconomic stabilization policies in an international context. Klemens Fischer examines the similar agendas of the E.U. and G8. British scholar Razeem Sally advances a powerful philosophical case against the civil society agenda of misinformed non-governmental organizations. 'Most arguments for global governance are in fact bad economics and even worse political economy' (p. 55). Sally also argues that the importance of

---

[*]*International Affairs* 77(4) (October 2001): 995–996.

national governments has not diminished relative to global governance since, rather paradoxically, most of the international policy co-ordination over the last 50 years has actually increased the political power and discretionary spending of national governments.

There is also a timely paper by Barbara Dluhosch on debt rescheduling through the highly indebted poor countries (HIPC) initiative. This reviews one of the most urgent aspects of the agenda of the civil society. In another quite brilliant paper former Quebec premier, Pierre Marc Johnson, examines another – environmental regulations and sustainable development. Overall, there are 16 original essays, including comprehensive introductory and concluding pieces by the G8 project director, John Kirton and his co-authors for this volume. One important conclusion is that in the final communiqué of the Cologne summit, the G8 leaders accept the need for 'socially sustainable globalization.' Kirton et al. argue that Cologne represents a threshold whereby the leaders of the richest capitalist countries started to move to accept major parts of the agenda of civil society. In particular, 'social progress and environmental protection were assigned equal value to the prosperity which had dominated' previous summits (p. 295). I highly recommend this book and others in the G8 and global governance series.

Taking Trade to the Streets: The Lost History of Public Efforts to Shape Globalization

Susan Ariel Aaronson

*Ann Arbor, MI: The University of Michigan Press, 2001, 264 pp.**

The author has produced a book which digs into the attitudes of anti-globalization activists, especially their criticisms of the World Trade Organization (WTO), the North American Free Trade Agreement (NAFTA) and the philosophy of free trade. Several different types of trade critics are identified, ranging from left-wing activist groups like Greenpeace and Ralph Nader's organization to right wingers like Pat Buchanan and Ross Perot, with unions, economic nationalists and protectionists along for the ride.

Chapters 2, 3, and 4 (of seven) are scholarly and reasonably accurate descriptions of the history of U.S. trade policy. Chapter 2 deals with U.S. protectionism starting with the Boston Tea Party and ending with the Smoot–Hawley tariff. It then goes on to outline the period of trade liberalization that occurred in the 1930s, followed by post-war institutions like the General Agreement on Tariffs and Trade (GATT). Chapter 3 discusses GATT issues and the business-led agenda of tariff cuts and deregulation. Chapter 4 covers strategic trade policy, competitiveness and the new U.S. protectionism as it evolved in the 1980s. Each of these three chapters offers a standard neo-liberal perspective on trade liberalization although obvious gaps in economic insight become apparent, as, for example in the discussion of strategic trade policy that omits the special limiting conditions of this insufficient and misconceived protectionist public policy.

The remaining four chapters describe the agendas of non-governmental organizations (NGOs) in the trade arena. Chapter 5 discusses the Canadian and U.S. NGOs' opposition to NAFTA and Chapter 6 the food safety, environmental and labor standards disputes at the WTO.

Business History Review 76(4) (Winter 2002): 883–885.

Chapters 1 offers an introduction and Chapter 7 a conclusion to the theme that NGOs are important new actors that have prodded U.S. trade policy to move toward protectionism, although Aaronson notes that not all NGOs favor protection. This group of chapters appears to have been tacked on to the previous mainly scholarly study to 'tart up' the book and add spice to the pedestrian discussion of U.S. trade policy that constitutes the core of the book.

The author has worked hard to give the NGO chapters a scholarly appearance. There are well over 100 footnotes per chapter, although the majority is from NGO and journalistic sources rather than from the academic, government and policy sources that document carefully written chapters. Unfortunately, serious readers will quickly see that the reporting of the NGO case amounts to an unbalanced attack on free trade, globalization, multinationals and capitalism. One-sided statements by NGOs about globalization and trade policy are reported uncritically in these four chapters. The author reports only one side of the current debates and does not present alternative viewpoints and countervailing evidence. As an example, consider Chapter 5. The first half is about the Canadian left-wing, economic-nationalist, NGO-led opposition to the Canada-U.S. Free Trade Agreements of 1989 and the subsequent passage of NAFTA. The author reports in detail on the musings of Maude Barlow, Chair of the Council of Canadians, a nationalist group that organized a coalition of radical NGOs and unions to run against NAFTA in the 1993 federal election in Canada, in which they won less than 3% of the popular vote. It could be said that this anti-capitalist coalition is of marginal interest, and that it had a trivial impact on mainstream economic policy in Canada. The second half of the chapter describes the subsequent opposition to NAFTA in the United States, without once considering any of the undoubted economic and political advantages of the agreement that led to its adoption by the U.S. Congress in 1993. As only criticisms of NAFTA are documented, the result is an irrelevant caricature of the agreement.

Moreover, Aaronson displays an outdated American-centric attitude, as evidenced by her claim that 'globalization can be defined as the growing social, political and economic integration of the United States with other nations of the world' (p. xiv). This will not go down well in Europe or Asia, since the United States is home to only 185 of the world's top 500 multinationals. Further, she offers no informed insight about the often eccentric ideas of the NGOs she reviews in such detail, nor does she provide an analytical framework to make sense of them. What purports to be a book about business history offers little about business, although it does present a history of the marginalized NGOs who command a trivial percentage of the popular vote in Canadian and U.S. elections. The author needs to broaden her horizons and examine business and government as closely as she has the anti-globalization NGOs.

98 Globalization and National Economic Welfare

M. Panić
Basingstoke: Palgrave Macmillan, 2003, 302 pp.*

The focus of this book is the need for more effective economic policy by nation-states in a world of increasing economic interdependence. Although the author refers to globalization in the title of the book and writes about it in Chapter 1, most of the book is about what economists would call international economic integration and development policy. Indeed, globalization appears in the title of two of the 11 chapters; and only one of them is about multinational enterprises, although the author admits that these are the major drivers of globalization.

The key themes of the volume are developed in Chapter 1, a long 50-page economic analysis of globalization. This is strong on the economic virtues of capitalism and the role of multilateral enterprises as agents of international economic interdependence. Efficient capitalism requires effective property rights, appropriate institutions and the means to create productive wealth. But there are relatively ineffective multilateral organizations and institutions to deal with the power of multinational enterprises. One result is an increase in world income inequality: the benefits of globalization are not spread evenly; they go mainly to the owners of capital. The author argues for more effective nation-state intervention, regulations and control over multinationals in order to promote growth and reduce income inequality.

The end result of this process is ineffective bargaining between multinationals and nation-states as the dynamics of capitalism simultaneously lead to its unsustainability owing to widening income inequalities. While the author would prefer an effective form of global governance, he laments the lack of appropriate international institutions. This is an out-of–date

**International Affairs* 79(4) (July 2003): 905–906.

analysis of international business. It totally neglects research from business school economists such as myself who find that most multinationals are from the 'triad' of Europe, Asia and North America. Their activities are almost entirely intra-regional, not global, and there is such effective competition across the triad regions that few multinationals can sustain excess profits.

The book is disjointed as well as out of date. All but two of the 11 chapters have been published previously, most as book chapters. All are rather dated: Chapter 7 goes back to 1976 and Chapter 2 to 1988. Altogether, five of the chapters were first published ten or more years ago and another four, five or more years ago. The book is hardly on the cutting edge of new scholarship on globalization. It is a very old-fashioned economics book which should have been called something like: *International Economic Growth and National Policy*, as this better reflects its content. The use of the word 'globalization' in the title appears to be purely opportunistic. On the other hand, the author, a Cambridge University economist, shows insight into international economics and development issues, and he assembles some relevant, if again out-of-date, data to support his points about increasing international interdependence. He is also probably quite correct in arguing that the perceived adverse effects of economic integration need to be regulated by national (or regional?) governments. There are no great success stories of global governance and multilateral organizations, and so the author makes a case for the state to regulate the firm. Although this is not a new idea in the realm of international political economy, it is good to know that economists still believe it.

99 The Economic Dynamics of Environmental Law

David M. Driesen (ed.)
*Cambridge, MA: MIT Press, 2003, 291 pp.**

In this book environmental lawyer David Driesen mounts a criticism of the use of economic efficiency analysis in public policy and law affecting the natural environment. By efficiency he has in mind the idealized form of neoclassical economics where free markets exist. He points out, correctly, that free markets face market imperfections and regulations. Then he argues that cost-benefit analysis and other economic tools are being misapplied in environmental law and that an alternative is required.

Driesen's key argument is that economic efficiency is static, and so it is therefore an unsuitable standard for environmental regulations, in comparison to economic dynamics, which is alleged to be a more effective regulatory tool. This thinking is very muddled. While the basic neoclassical economics model is typically first developed in static terms, its free market principles are easy to extend dynamically. Thus it is a trivial criticism of economic efficiency to state that it is static and that dynamics are better; in fact the dynamics just need a bit more math. Second, virtually all principles allegedly better covered by economic dynamics can also be developed by a process of comparative statics, e.g. by the development of a set of contingent statements in the form of a model. I have developed analysis for environmental regulators and managers of firms using 2×2 matrixes which are completely adequate comparative static theories.

What makes Driesen's criticisms of economic efficiency even more misleading is his apparent lack of understanding of transaction cost economics. Since Ronald Coase in 1937, economists have recognized that when market imperfections (transaction costs) exist there is an alternative

Environmental Science & Policy 6(6) (December 2003): 547.

method of organization, namely within a firm (or hierarchy). The logic of firms being an efficient alternative to imperfect markets is completely lost on Driesen. Yet, in its extreme form it would demonstrate that business organizations can substitute for markets such that additional environmental regulation of the type presented here is not required. This argument has even been applied to multinational firms, by this reviewer and other international business scholars. It was shown a quarter century ago that multinational firms can internalize transaction costs (such as knowledge as a public good) in an efficient manner and thereby replace markets. Ronald Coase won the Nobel Prize in economics for this original insight, taken on board by economists and international business scholars, but not apparently by environmental lawyers.

It is argued in Part II that economic efficiency ignores technology and innovation, and that the design of environmental regulation needs to stimulate the latter. This is another piece of nonsense. Where will the innovation come from? It has to be through investment by business. Therefore, to achieve innovation requires that firms be encouraged to invest in sustainable development and build the environment into their planning decisions. Then they can develop firm-specific green 'capabilities' (a strategic advantage concept developed in business schools) based on innovation embedded in the firms. This business school thinking would also throw more light on the analysis of economic dynamic reform of Part III, which is a promising section of the book. Here there is some interesting work on the need to privatize environmental law, i.e. have firms do more innovation and encourage them to develop their own standard setting.

Overall, this is a disappointing book offering only a superficial review of economics as it applies to the environment. Driesen needs to incorporate transaction cost economics and business strategy models into his framework in order to make this analysis relevant for the manager who must actually invest to improve the environment. The thinking in the book is more suitable for policy makers and regulators, rather than managers. Further, there are no data and no empirical tests of the theories advanced; neither are there case studies. Instead, there is a repetitive but uninformed criticism of market-based economic theory. In particular, there is no attempt to link into abundant parallel work which examines case studies of how firms actually develop strategies to manage environmental issues and regulations. Yet this firm-state interaction is clearly the most relevant and interesting set of issues for those concerned with sustainable development. The innovation, technology and environmentally sensitive advances need to be made by firms and the environmental law regime needs research which bridges the firm-state divide rather than broadening it.

Trading Blocs: States, Firms, and Regions in the World Economy

Kerry A. Chase

Ann Arbor, MI: The University Michigan Press, 2005, 322 pp.[*]

The focus of this book by Prof. Kerry Chase is that the process of international trade liberalization has resulted in the development of three major regional economic blocs: the European Union, the North American Free Trade Agreement, and a partial regional agreement in Asia largely driven by Japan. These three economics blocs are known in business schools as the 'triad' of Europe, North America, and Asia. In *The Regional Multinationals* (2005), I have shown that the majority of international trade and investment takes place within these triad blocs rather than between them, and that even the world's largest 500 firms average over 72% of their sales within their home region. Basically, the analysis by Chase is fully consistent with such findings.

Chapters 2 and 8 develop an analysis of the political economy of trade in a regional context. Chapter 2 develops a model where the key independent variables explaining trade policies are aspects of scale economies and data on intraregional trade. There are two key elements to this theory. First, the triad regional trade agreements have been developed due to lobbying pressures by firms seeking economies of scale. Second, the regional agreements have also been driven, especially in more recent years, by firms seeking rules to guarantee access to production-sharing networks that cross national borders. It is the interplay between these two factors that explains the rapid economic growth of the EU and NAFTA, in particular, and which should lead to an eventual regional trade agreement in Asia.

Chapter 3 and 4 are case studies that test the theoretical model in the interwar period. Chapter 3 applies it to Britain, Japan, and Germany.

---

[*]*Perspectives on Politics* 4(4) (December 2006): 803–804.

It is found that British firms achieved scale economies in manufacturing through the use of Imperial Preferences. These effectively locked in the British Commonwealth market for sales, but also tied in the resources and other value chain inputs required to develop a successful production network. In contrast, Japan and Germany lacked an effective economic empire which Chase argues, which was one incentive for Japanese economic imperialism in Southeast Asia and for German expansion, leading to their military adventures in the Second World War.

Chapters 5, 6, and 7 test the basic model across the core triad regions of the EU (Chapter 5), NAFTA (Chapter 6), and Japan (Chapter 7). These chapters are fascinating in that Chase is able to develop convincing evidence that the dual aspects of the theory are required for successful regional integration. Significant coefficients leap out for scale and intraregional trade variables, and these are interpreted by Chase in a novel manner. For example, scale economies and production networks were not fully developed in the EU until the 1992 measures were introduced. Similarly, although the Canada/US Autopac was in effect, full scale economies and production network efficiencies were not realized in NAFTA until the Canada/U.S. Free Trade Agreement (CUFTA) of 1988 came into effect. Both in Europe and North America, production-sharing networks had been developing, but it was not until 1992 and 1988, respectively, that multinational enterprises (MNEs) were able to fully develop these networks in clusters spanning the national borders of each region. Chase shows, correctly, that outsourcing and offshoring are the mirror images of production-sharing networks. Thus, the concerns of trade unions about job losses are largely misplaced since home-based MNEs need to outsource within regional clusters in order to achieve efficient manufacturing production. Although he does not discuss this, the same logic for outsourcing and offshoring now applies to the service sector.

Another theme runs throughout the book. This is that multilateralism, in particular the successful rounds of trade liberalization at the GATT and World Trade Organization, is fully consistent with the new regionalism. Chase states that 'extant trading blocs do not pose a threat to the multilateral trading system' (p. 261). The reasoning here is that the creation of the large trading blocs in the EU and NAFTA has been driven by firms working in accord with states. In simple terms, this means that regional trade agreements are efficiency driven. In fact, they often represent a set of rules being put in place to recognize the reality of existing regional economic integration, often driven by MNEs seeking production-sharing networks across borders. The author develops an interesting sub-theme to the effect that while the EU discriminates against 'outsiders,' the result is simply to speed up the substitution of foreign direct investment (FDI) for exports. This is efficiency enhancing; for example, FDI in the EU by U.S. MNEs turns the U.S. firms into 'insiders.' Similarly, NAFTA's legal instruments to exclude outsiders, such as the rules of origin, also lead to Japanese MNEs increasing their FDI in the United States at the expense of exports. Thus, both in the EU and NAFTA, the deepening of the regional trade agreements has led to increased inward FDI and cross investments by MNEs. The result is a greater degree of international integration by MNEs operating across the broad triad regions.

The analysis in this book by a political scientist is more consistent with the thinking in business schools by scholars of international business. Indeed, many of the theories and cases in *Trading Blocs* were anticipated by international business scholars in work published by some ten to twenty years ago. In contrast, the work by Chase would raise tensions with traditional trade economists, such as Jagdish Bhagwati since they are still influenced by fairly static concepts of comparative advantage. Chase has positioned his theory as a dynamic one that cleverly integrates increasing returns to scale with the more recent development of production-sharing networks, where the latter is difficult for economists to model. Economists traditionally ignore the strategic dimension of MNEs and the alliances and joint ventures that are often required to develop successful and efficient production-sharing networks across borders. My conclusion is that this book will be more favorably received in business schools than in economics departments. Its reception in political science departments will depend partly on the legacy of vested interests. Chase himself states that 'these findings challenge work in the field that explains trading blocs in terms of alliances and power politics, transaction costs in multilateral negotiations, and intergovernmental bargains among nations' (p. 257). However my reading of the book is that his focus on economic efficiency and the role of MNEs in developing economies of scale and production-sharing networks across national borders is fairly consistent with these related explanations of multilateral trade liberalization. In other words, the new regionalism created by MNEs is the driver behind globalization in terms of the increased international economic integration we all observe in the data on trade and FDI.

Conclusion

The 100 book reviews republished in this book offer a unique insight into the development of the field of international business. As an author I have been fortunate to participate actively in the development of some of the key literature in this field. In my own research publications I have always attempted to build upon the work of others. This set of book reviews starting in 1973 serves as a base for much of my reading and understanding about the development of the field of international business. As discussed in the introductory chapter these reviews should be of interest to other readers for the following four reasons.

First, the book reviews incorporate the perspective of the Reading School. Some of the earlier reviews were written in the academic year 1976/77 when I was a visiting professor at the University of Reading. At that time Mark Casson (in association with Peter Buckley) was developing the theory of internalization and engaging in related analytical work on the role of the MNE as the central institution in the field of international business. At the same time John Dunning was bringing together his thinking on what would become known as the eclectic paradigm of international business. As discussed in the introduction to Chapter 1, today's theory of the MNE combines the insights from internalization theory and the eclectic paradigm into the firm and country matrix outlined in my introduction to Chapter 1. The Reading School brought insights from economics to analyze the MNE, and this thinking is also relevant to the books reviewed in Chapter 2. However, in that chapter I used the economic integration and national responsiveness framework to illustrate that most of the books by economists tended to focus upon country factors, rather than on the integration of firm and country factors. Again, in Chapter 3 on globalization, I have demonstrated that there is an excessive focus upon worldwide economic integration in much of the literature. In particular, the popular thinking demonstrated by Thomas Friedman tends to ignore the empirical reality under which integration by MNEs is occurring on an intra-regional basis. Again, in Chapter 4 we see that much of the literature on free trade and the need to reduce regulation to improve international competitiveness is also based primarily on economic concepts of efficiency and integration. In Chapter 4, I used the Porter single diamond and my double diamond frameworks to add insights into the books reviewed. Only in Chapter 5, which deals with business networks and clusters in terms of my five partners/flagship model, do some of the non-economic issues of economic development, poverty, and the role of NGOs assume centre stage.

Second, while the focus of the Reading School upon economics is an essential driver in the development of thinking about international business over the last forty years, there have been valuable inputs from other disciplines. For example, in Chapters 2, 3, 4, and 5 many of the books discuss issues in regulation and public policy. These issues of international political economy are also a component of the Reading School. Indeed, the work of John Dunning, in particular, seeks to embed the role of the government along with the role of the firm as the twin drivers of the field. In short, Dunning seeks to make government policy endogenous in the analysis of international business. I do not disagree with this approach, but I have often found it necessary in analysis of the MNE and its strategy to model government policy as exogenous, before relaxing this assumption. The reader of the book reviews will notice this tension in the literature. Again, the firm and country matrix is a useful way to bridge the two streams of thinking about the role of government. In cell 1 of Figure 1 government policy is an exogenous CSA. In cell 3 of Figure 1, it becomes endogenous to the extent that a firm can develop an FSA in aspects of business government relations. A modern example of cell 3 is the takeover of the IBM personal computer division by the Chinese firm, Lenovo. To the extent that this takeover of a high-tech U.S. industry was not contested by protectionists in the U.S. Congress, Lenovo clearly demonstrated a strong FSA in business government relations. In contrast, other attempts by Chinese firms to make acquisitions in the U.S. energy sector (a cell 1 strategy) are unlikely to be approved by U.S. policy makers on national security grounds.

Third, in Chapter 2 and in Chapter 4 many of the book reviews deal with Canada. The reader may question the relevance of this material. Yet, the Canadian experience in international business is a more useful model for most countries than is the experience of the United States and Japan. These are the only two large economies which have developed internal Porter 'diamond' characteristics to enhance their international competitiveness. All other countries need to follow a double diamond approach to succeed in international business. As a double diamond framework was invented in a Canadian context, this experience is relevant for Asian economies today, including China and India. As mentioned in the introduction to Chapter 4, the double diamond framework has already been shown to be relevant for the development of MNEs from countries like Korea, the UK, New Zealand, Austria, Ireland, etc. If the MNEs from the emerging markets of Brazil, Russia, India, China, and South Africa (BRICS) wish to move from cell 1 of Figure 1 to cell 3, then they will need to adopt double diamond strategies in order to acquire FSAs relevant in host economies as well as at home. Put more simply Chinese firms can continue to enjoy the economies of scale based upon cheap labour (a cell 1 attribute), and they can take this overseas. But if they wish to develop long-run FSAs in managerial knowledge and systems integration (a cell 3 position in Figure 1) then they will need to understand the markets of their customers as well as their home market.

Fourth, this book has practical relevance. While the majority of books reviewed are of academic monographs and related research materials, a large number of books were also written for managers and the general reader. Many of the core ideas in these books have entered the mindsets of managers. These include: Vernon's product life cycle; the integration and responsiveness framework of Bartlett and Ghoshal; Hymer's concept of knowledge-based firm-specific advantages; the efficiency nature of free trade; the costs of protection and unnecessary regulation; the role of NGOs and the stakeholder model; and the nature of economic integration and globalization. Many of these concepts have been developed through rigorous academic research and debate. Academics have sought to popularize their research. This book is unique in that it reviews not only pure academic research but also the popular literature. Commonalities across these two approaches have been exposed and discussed. Thus the reader will be able to conclude this book by observing the close connection between academic research and good public thinking about the basic issues of international business.

Acknowledgments

I wish to express by thanks to all the people who made this volume possible. The authors of the books I have reviewed in this volume have been essential in the evolution of the field of international business. Palgrave Macmillan editor, Ursula Gavin, heartily endorsed the idea of this volume and Mark Cooper provided editorial assistance. The task of archival searching, bibliographic verification, and keying in reviews was performed by Anne Hasiuk, with the assistance of Mildred Harris. Proofreading was undertaken by Helen Rugman.

I am grateful to the following for permission to reproduce the following reviews:

Academy of Management

The Quest for Global Dominance, Vijay Govindarajan and Anil K. Gupta, San Francisco: Jossey-Bass, 2001, in *Academy of Management Executive* 16(3) (Aug. 2002): 157–159.

Academy of Political Science

Distortion or Development? Contending Perspectives on the Multinational Corporation, Thomas J. Biersteker, Cambridge, MA: MIT Press, 1978, in *Political Science Quarterly* 94(4) (Winter 1979–1980): 722–724.

Cambridge University Press

Nationalism, Technology and the Future of Canada, Wallace Gagne (ed.), Toronto: Macmillan of Canada, 1976, in *Journal of Economic History* 38(2) (June 1978): 539–540; *Weathering the Storm: Canadian–U.S. Relations, 1980–83* , David Leyton–Brown, Toronto: C.D. Howe Institute and National Planning Association, 1985, in *Canadian Journal of Political Science* 18(4) (December 1985): 796–797; *Trading Blocs: States, Firms, and Regions in the World Economy*, Kerry A. Chase, Ann Arbor, MI: The University Michigan Press, 2005, in *Perspectives on Politics* 4(4) (December 2006): 803–804.

Canadian Foreign Policy/La politique étrangère du Canada (Carleton University)

Decision at Midnight: Inside the Canada–U.S. Free Trade Negotiations , Michael Hart (with Bill Dymond and Colin Robertson), Vancouver: University of British Columbia Press, 1994, in *Canadian Foreign Policy* 2(3) (Winter 1994/1995): 124–128.

Canadian Journal of Economics/Revue canadienne d'économique; Canadian Public Policy/Analyse de politiques; Canadian Economics Association/Association canadienne d'économique

Multinational Enterprises and Economic Analysis, Richard E. Caves, Cambridge and New York: Cambridge University Press, 1982, in *Canadian Journal of Economics* 16(4) (November 1983): 742–744; *The Floating Canadian Dollar: Exchange Flexibility and Monetary Independence*, Paul Wonnacott, Washington, DC: American Enterprise Institute for Public Policy Research, 1972, in *Canadian Journal of Economics* 6(1) (February 1973): 140–141; *The Impact of Free Trade in Canada*, Roma Dauphin, Ottawa, Economic Council of Canada, Supply and Services Canada, 1978, in *Canadian Public Policy* 4(4) (Autumn 1978): 576–577; *Canada – United States Free Trade and Canadian Independence*, Peyton V. Lyon. Ottawa: Economic Council of Canada, 1975, in *Canadian Public Policy/Analyse de politiques*, 2(1) (Winter 1976): 124–125; *Canadian Multinationals*, Jorge Niosi, Toronto: Between the Lines, 1985, in *Canadian Public Policy* 12(1) (March 1986): 273–274; *The Innovative Society: Competitiveness in the 1990s*, Bryne B. Purchase, Toronto: C.D. Howe Institute, 1991, in *Canadian Public Policy* 17(3) (Sept. 1991): 373–374.

Elsevier

Transfer Pricing in Multinational Firms: A Heuristic Programming Approach and a Case Study, Lars Nieckels, Stockholm: Almqvist and Wiksell International; New York: John Wiley, 1976, in *The Journal of International Economics* 7(2) (May 1977): 217–219; *Ruling the Waves: Cycles of Discovery Chaos and Wealth from the Compass to the Internet*, Debora L. Spar, New York: Harcourt, 2001, in *Business Horizons* 45(2) (March–April 2002): 84–85; *Globalization and its Discontents*, Joseph Stiglitz, New York: Norton, 2002, in *Long Range Planning* 35(6) (2002): 654–656; *Linking Trade, Environment and Social Cohesion: NAFTA Expansion, Global Challenges*, John J. Kirton, and Virginia W. Maclaren, Aldershot: Ashgate, 2000, in *Business Horizons* 46(1) (Jan/Feb 2003): 69–71; *The Economic Dynamics of Environmental Law*, David M. Driesen, Cambridge, MA: MIT Press, 2003, in *Environmental Science & Policy* 6(6) (December 2003): 547.

Harvard Business School

Between Dependency and Autonomy: India's Experience with the International Computer Industry, Joseph M. Grieco, Berkeley: University of California Press, 1984, in *Business History Review* 59(3) (Autumn 1985): 533–535; *Taking Trade to the Streets: The Lost History of Public Efforts to Shape Globalization*, Susan Ariel Aaronson, Ann Arbor, MI: The University of Michigan Press, 2001, in *Business History Review* 76(4) (Winter 2002): 883–885.

Institute for Research on Public Policy (Montreal)

US Competitiveness in the World Economy, Bruce R. Scott and George C. Lodge (eds), Boston: Harvard Business School Press, 1985, in *Policy Options politiques* 6(4) (April/avril 1985): 15–16.

International Research Center for Energy and Economic Development

Energy from the Arctic: Facts and Issues, Judith Maxwell, Montreal: Canadian–American Committee, 1973, in *Journal of Energy and Development* 1(2) (1976): 352–354; *The Effects of Energy Price Changes on Commodity Prices, Interprovincial Trade and Employment*, J.R. Melvin, Toronto and Buffalo: University of Toronto Press, 1976, in *Journal of Energy and Development* 2(2) (Spring 1977): 346–349; *Coal and Canada–U.S. Energy Relations* , Richard L. Gordon. Montreal: Canadian–American Committee, 1976, in *Journal of Energy and Development* 3(2) (Spring 1978): 439–441.

Ivey Publishing

The Competitive Advantage of Nations, Michael E. Porter. New York: Free Press; Toronto: Collier Macmillan, 1990, in *Business Quarterly* 55(3) (Winter 1990): 61–64; *Canada at the Crossroads: The Reality of a New Competitive Environment*. Michael Porter, Ottawa: Business Council on National Issues and Minister of Supply and Services, October 1991, in *Business Quarterly* 57(3) (Winter 1992): 59–64.

Journal of Developing Areas (Tennessee State University)

Reducing Global Inequalities, W. Howard Wriggins and Gunnar Adler-Karlsson, New York: McGraw Hill, 1978, and *Rich Nations and Poor Nations in the World Economy*, Albert Fishlow, Carlos F. Díaz-Alejandro, Richard R. Fagan and Roger D. Hansen, New York: McGraw Hill, 1978, in *Journal of Developing Areas* 13(3) (April 1979): 347–348.

PalgraveMacmillan

Oligopolistic Reaction and Multinational Enterprise, Frederick T. Knickerbocker, Boston: Division of Research, Graduate School of Business Administration, Harvard University, 1973, in *Eastern Economic Journal* 1(1) (Jan. 74): 86–87; *The International Operations of National Firms: A Study of Direct Foreign Investment*, Stephen H. Hymer, Cambridge, MA: MIT Press, 1976, in *Journal of International Business Studies* 9(2) (Fall 1978): 103–104; *Multinational Management*, David Rutenberg, Boston, MA: Little, Brown and Company, 1982, in *Journal of International Business Studies* 14(2) (Fall 1983): 160–162; *Licensing in International Strategy*, Farok Contractor, Westport, CT: Quorum Books, 1985, in *Journal of International Business Studies* 18(1) (Spring 1987): 99–101; *Politics and International Investment*, Witold Henisz, Cheltenham: E. Elgar, 2002, in *Journal of International Business Studies* 34(2) (March 2003): 223–225; *Redefining Global Strategy: Crossing Borders in a World Where Differences Still Matter*, Pankaj Ghemawat, Boston, MA: Harvard Business School, 2007, in *Journal of International Business Studies*, (2008) forthcoming; *Continental Accord: North American Economic Integration*, Steven Globerman (ed.), Vancouver, BC: The Fraser Institute, 1991, in *Journal of International Business Studies* 24(1) (First Quarter 1993): 159–161; *It's the Crude, Dude: War, Big Oil and the Fight for the Planet*, Linda McQuaig, Doubleday Canada: Random House, in *Literary Review of Canada* 12(10) (December 2004): 8–9.

Pion Press

Economics and the Environment, A.V. Kneese. Harmondsworth, UK: Penguin Books, 1977, in *Environment and Planning A* 9(10) (1977): 1204.

Southern Economic Association

The Future of the Multinational Enterprise, Peter J. Buckley and Mark Casson, London: Macmillan UK; New York: Holmes and Meyer, 1976, in *The Southern Economic Journal* 44(2) (October 1977): 410–411; *A Framework of International Banking*, Stephen F. Frowen (ed.), Guildford, UK: Guildford Educational Press/Philip Thorn Associates, 1979, in *The Southern Economic Journal* 46(3) (January 1980): 990–991.

United Nations Commission on Trade and Development

Global Capitalism at Bay? John H. Dunning, London, New York: Routledge, 2001, in *Transnational Corporations* 11(1) (April 2002): 113–116;

Wiley/Blackwell

The Multinational Enterprise, John H. Dunning (ed.), New York: Praeger, 1972, in *The Economic Journal* 40(1) (July 1973): 156–157; *The Multinational Corporation and the Resource Cost of International Technology Transfer*, D.J. Teece, Cambridge,

MA: Ballinger, 1977; distributed by J. Wiley & Sons, in *The Economic Journal* 87(347) (September 1977): 666; *A Bibliography of International Business*, M.Z. Brooke, M. Black and P. Neville, London: Macmillan, 1977, in *The Economic Journal* 87(348) (December 1977): 829–860; *Political Risks in International Business: Investment Behavior of Multinational Corporations*, Lars H. Thunell, New York: Praeger, 1977, distributed by Martin Robertson, in *The Economic Journal* 88(349) (March 1978): 200; *Storm over the Multinationals: The Real Issues*, Raymond Vernon, London: Macmillan, 1977, in *The Economic Journal* 88(350) (June 1978): 404; *Research and Development Abroad U.S. Multinationals*, Robert Ronstadt, New York; London: Praeger, 1977, in *The Economic Journal* 88(351) (September 1978): 640; *European Research in International Business*, Michel Ghertman and James Leontiades, Amsterdam: North Holland Publishing Co., 1978, in *The Economic Journal* 89(353) (March 1979): 219–220; *The Multinational Corporation: A Radical Approach*, Stephen H. Hymer, Cambridge: Cambridge University Press, 1979, in *The Economic Journal* 90(360) (December 1980): 985; *Technology Licensing and Multinational Enterprises*, Piero Telesio, New York: Praeger, 1979, in *The Economic Journal* 90(360) (December 1980): 986–987; *The World Directory of Multinational Enterprises*, John M. Stopford, John H. Dunning, and Klaus O. Haberich (eds), London: Macmillan, 1980, in *The Economic Journal* 91(364) (December 1981): 1112–1113; *The Multinational Corporation*, Sanjaya Lall, London: Macmillan, 1980, in *The Economic Journal* 92(365) (March 1982): 196–198; *Multinational Corporations in the 1980s*, Charles P. Kindleberger and David B. Audretsch (eds), Cambridge, MA and London: MIT Press, 1983, in *The World Economy* (Sept. 1983): 356; *Multinational Excursions*, Charles P. Kindleberger, Cambridge, MA/ London: MIT Press, 1984, in Book notes, *The Economic Journal* 95(379) (September 1985): 865; *International Monetary Policy: Bretton Woods and After*, W.M. Scammell, London: Macmillan, 1975, in *Kyklos* 29(1) (1976): 180–181; *Financial Policies for the Multinational Company: The Management of Foreign Exchange*, R. Aggarwal, New York: Praeger, 1976; distributed by Martin Robertson & Co., in *The Economic Journal* 87(347) (June 1977): 403; *International Capital Markets*, Edwin J. Elton and Martin J. Gruber (eds), Amsterdam; New York: North-Holland/American Elsevier, 1975, in *Journal of Finance* 32(4) (September 1977): 1382–1384; *The Failure of World Monetary Reform, 1971–74*, John Williamson, Thomas Nelson & Sons, 1977, and *The Evolution of the International Monetary System, 1945–77*, Brian Tew, London: Hutchinson, 1977, in *Economica* 45(18) (November 1978): 421–422; *New Means of Financing International Needs*, Eleanor Steinberg and Joseph Yager, with Gerard Brannon, Washington, DC: The Brookings Institution, 1978, in *Kyklos* 31(4) (1978): 738–739; *Mad Money: When Markets Outgrow Governments*, Susan Strange, Manchester, UK: Manchester University Press, 1998, in *International Affairs* 75(2) (April 1999): 414; *Price Elasticities in International Trade: An Annotated Bibliography*, Robert M. Stern, Jonathan Francis, and Bruce Schumacher, London: Macmillan for the Trade Policy Research Center, 1976, with Lars Lundgren, in *Kyklos* 30(3) (August 1977): 570–571; *Fiscal Transfer Pricing in Multinational Corporations*, G.F. Mathewson and G.D. Quirin, Toronto: University of Toronto Press, 1979, in *The Economic Journal* 90(358) (June

1980): 460; *Transfer Pricing and Multinational Corporations: An Overview of Concepts, Mechanisms and Regulations*, Sylvain Plasschaert, Farnborough: Saxon House, 1979, in *The Economic Journal* 90(358) (June 1980): 460–461; *Measurement of Nontariff Barriers*, Alan V. Deardorff and Robert M. Stern, Ann Arbor, MI: University of Michigan Press, 1998, in *The Economic Journal* Book notes web page http://www.res.org.uk/ecojbknotes/default.asp; *Rags and Riches: Implementing Apparel Quotas under the Multi-Fibre Arrangements*, Kala Marathe Krishna and Ling Hui Tan, Ann Arbor, MI: University of Michigan Press, 1998, in *The Economic Journal* 111, Book notes: http://www.res.org.uk/ecojbknotes/default.asp; *Trade Rules in the Making: Challenges in Regional and Multilateral Negotiations*, Miguel Rodriguez Mendoza, Patrick Low, and Barbara Kotschwar (eds), Washington, DC: Brookings Institution Press/OAS, 1999, in *The Economic Journal* 111(469) (February 2001): F162–F163; *Globalisation and International Trade Liberalisation: Continuity and Change*, Martin Richardson (ed.), Cheltenham, UK: Edward Elgar, 2000, in *Business Strategy Review* 12(2) (Summer 2001): 74; *Free Trade under Fire*, Douglas A. Irwin, Princeton, NJ and Woodstock, UK: Princeton University Press, 2002, in *International Affairs* 78(4) (October 2002): 909–910; *Transnational Monopoly Capitalism*, K. Cowling, and R. Sugden, Brighton, UK: Wheatsheaf Books, 1987, in *The Economic Record* 68(190) (Sept 1989): 314–315; *Runaway World: How Globalization Is Reshaping our Lives*, Anthony Giddens, London: Profile, 1999, in *Business Strategy Review* 12(2) (Summer 2001): 69–76; *Globalization and Culture*, John Tomlinson, Oxford: Polity, 1999, in *International Affairs* 75(4) (October 1999): 837; *Future Positive: International Co-operation in the 21st Century*, Michael Edwards, London: Earthscan, 1999, in *International Affairs* 76(1) (Jan. 2000): 151–152; *Globalism and the New Regionalism*, Bjorn Hettne, András Inotai and Osvaldo Sunkel (eds), Basingstoke: Macmillan, 1999, in *International Affairs* 76(1) (January 2000): 146; *Globalisation and the Asia-Pacific: Contested Territories*, Kris Olds, Peter Dicken, Philip F. Kelly, Lily Kong and Henry Wei-Chung Yeung (eds), London and New York: Routledge, 1999, in *International Affairs* 76(4) (October 2000): 904; *Globalization and Its Critics: Perspectives from Political Economy*, Randall D. Germain (ed.), Basingstoke, UK: Macmillan, 2000, in *International Affairs* 76(4) (Oct. 2000): 868; *The Challenge of Global Capitalism: The World Economy in the 21st Century*, Robert Gilpin, Princeton, NJ: Princeton University Press, 2000, in *International Affairs* 77(1) (Jan. 2001): 200; *The Political Economy of Globalization*, Ngaire Woods (ed.), London: Macmillan, 2000, in *International Affairs* 77(1) (January 2001): 200–201; *Global Transformations: Politics, Economics and Culture*, David Held, Anthony McGrew, David Goldblatt, and Jonathan Perraton, Cambridge, UK: Polity Press, 1999, in *International Affairs* 77(2) (April 2001): 434; *The Invisible Continent: Four Strategic Imperatives of the New Economy*, Kenichi Ohmae, London: Nicholas Brealey, 2000, in *International Affairs* 77(3) (July 2001): 715–716; *Governing Globalization: Power, Authority and Global Governance*, David Held and Anthony McGrew (ed.), Cambridge, UK: Polity Press, 2002, in *International Affairs* 80(1) (January 2004): 139; *Tariff and Science Policies: Applications of a Model of Nationalism*, D.J. Daly, and S. Globerman, Toronto and Buffalo: University of Toronto Press for the Ontario Economic Council, 1976, in *Canadian Journal of Economics* 11(3) (August 1978): 632–634; *Foreign and Domestic*

Firms in Canada: A Comparative Study of Financial Structure and Performance, Daniel Shapiro, Toronto: Butterworths, 1980, in *Canadian Journal of Economics* 14(4) (November 1981): 739–741; *The Post-NAFTA Political Economy: Mexico and the Western Hemisphere*, Carol Wise (ed.), University Park, PA: Pennsylvania State University Press, 1998, in *International Affairs* 75(3) (July1999): 675–676; *Importing Technology into Africa: Foreign Investment and the Supply of Technological Innovations*, D. Babatunde Thomas, (Praeger Special Studies in International Economics and Development), New York: Praeger, 1976, in *Kyklos* 30(2) (1977): 325–326; *The Multinational Corporation and Social Change*, D.E. Apter and L.W. Goodman (ed.), New York: Praeger; Distributed by Martin Robertson, 1976, in *The Economic Journal* 87 (346) (June 1977): 403–404; *National Control of Foreign Business Entry: A Survey of Fifteen Countries*, R.D. Robinson, New York: Praeger, 1976, distributed by Martin Robertson & Co., in *The Economic Journal* 87(346) (June 1977): 410; *The International Taxation of Multinational Enterprises*, J.D.R. Adams, and John Whalley, London: Associated Business Programmes, 1977, in Book notes, *The Economic Journal* 88(352) (December 1978): 905; *The Multinational Corporation, the Nation State and the Trade Unions: A European Perspective*, Gunnar Hedlund and Lars Otterbeck, Kent, OH: Kent State University Press, 1977, in *The Economic Journal* 88(352) (December 1978): 906; *American Multinationals and American Interests*, C. Fred Bergsten, Thomas Horst and Theodore H. Moran, Washington, DC: The Brookings Institution, 1978, in *The Economic Journal* 89(356): 1029–1030; *North-South Technology Transfer: A Case Study of Petrochemicals in Latin America*, Mariluz Cortez and Peter Bocock, Baltimore and London: The Johns Hopkins University Press, 1984, in *Journal of Policy Analysis and Management* 4(3) (Spring 1985): 465–466; *International Trade Policy and the Pacific Rim: Proceedings of the IEA Conference* held in Sydney Australia, John Piggott and Alan Woodland (eds), Basingstoke: Macmillan in association with IEA, 1999, in *The Economic Journal*, http://www.reg.org.uk/ecojbknotes/row.asp?id=16389; *The World Trade Organization: Constitution and Jurisprudence*, John H. Jackson, London: The Royal Institute of International Affairs. 1998, in *International Affairs* 75(2) (April 1999): 400–401; *Trade, Investment and the Environment*, Halina Ward and Duncan Brack (eds), London: Earthscan/Royal Institute of International Affairs, 2000, in *International Affairs* 76(2) (April 2000): 365–366; *Development as Freedom*, Amartya Sen, Oxford: Oxford University Press, 1999, *International Affairs* 77(2) (April 2001): 435–436; *Fighting the Wrong Enemy: Antiglobal Activists and Multinational Enterprises*, Edward M. Graham. Washington, DC: Institute for International Economics, 2000, in *International Affairs* 77(4) (October 2001): 994–995; *Guiding Global Order: G8 Governance in the Twenty-First Century*, John J. Kirton, Joseph P. Daniels, and Andreas Freytag (eds), Aldershot: Ashgate, 2001, in *International Affairs* 77(4) (October 2001): 995–996; *Globalization and National Economic Welfare*, M. Panic, Basingstoke, UK: Palgrave Macmillan, 2003, in *International Affairs* 79(4) (July 2003): 905–906.

In some instances I have been unable to trace the owners of the copyright and I would appreciate any information that would enable me to do so. These are: *Managing Across Borders*, Christopher Bartlett and Sumantra Ghoshal, Boston:

Harvard, 1989, in *The Globe & Mail* (Toronto, Canada) (October 9, 1989): B2; *Third World Multinationals: The Rise of Foreign Direct Investment from Developing Countries*, Louis T. Wells, Jr. London: MIT Press, 1983, in *Third World Affairs* (1986): 444–445; *Juggernaut: The German Way of Business*, Philip Glouchevitch, Simon & Schuster, 1992, in *Financial Times of Canada* (December 12, 1992): 23; *Managing the Multinational Enterprise*, John M. Stopford and Louis T. Wells, New York: Basic Books, 1972, unpublished, written 1973; *The Great Canadian Stampede: The Rush to Economic Nationalism*, Alan Heisey, Toronto: Griffin House, 1973, in *The Canadian Forum* 54(644) (Sept. 1974): 47; *Multinationals from Small Countries*, Tamir Agmon and Charles P. Kindleberger (eds), Cambridge, MA: MIT Press, 1977, in *Economic Development and Cultural Change* 28: 4 (July 1980): 871–875.

Index

University of Toronto, 241
University of Warwick (UK), 140

Venezuela, 58, 126, 246
Vernon, Raymond, xxviii, 4, 6, 32, 126, 259
  product life cycle model, 4, 47

Wal-Mart, 123, 155, 163, 306
Ward, Halina, 284–5
Wardroper, Ken, 235
Wells, Louis T., Jr., 19–21, 56–9, 277
Wetter, Theresa, 110
Whalley, John, 263
Williamson, John, 92–3
Williams, Phil, 159
Wilson, Michael, 238
Wise, Carol, 239–40

Wonnacott, Paul, 84–5
Woodland, Alan, 280–81
Woods, Ngaire, 145, 159, 240
World Bank, 107, 124, 156, 157, 158, 159, 286
World Investment Report (WIR), 243
World Trade Organization (WTO), xxvi, 109,
  110, 112, 114, 130, 159, 241, 243, 282–3, 284,
  286, 289, 292, 301
World's Largest Corporations (*Fortune* 500 annual
  statistical table), 58, 121, 134, 154, 165
Wriggins, W. Howard, 265–7

Yager, Joseph, 94–6
Yahoo!, 153
Yeung, Henry Wei-chung, 140–1
YPF (Argentina), 58